TWAYNE'S WORLD AUTHORS SERIES

A Survey of the World's Literature

Sylvia E. Bowman, Indiana University

GENERAL EDITOR

AUSTRALIA

Joseph Jones, University of Texas at Austin

EDITOR

Price Warung

TWAS 383

Price Warung

PRICE WARUNG
(WILLIAM ASTLEY)

By BARRY ANDREWS

University of New South Wales

TWAYNE PUBLISHERS

A DIVISION OF G. K. HALL & CO., BOSTON

Library of Congress Cataloging in Publication Data

Andrews, B G
  Price Warung (William Astley)

  (Twayne's world authors series; TWAS 383: Australia)
  Bibliography: p. 181–89.
  Includes index.
  1.   Astley, William, 1855–1911.   I.   Title.
PR9619.3.A76Z57   823   75-29305
ISBN 0-8057-6225-6

FOR NAOMI AND LUKE

Contents

About the Author

Barry Andrews is Lecturer in English in the Faculty of Military Studies, University of New South Wales at Duntroon, Australia. Born in Sydney in 1943, he was educated at the University of New South Wales (MA Hons) and Sydney (Dip. Ed.). Before taking up his present position in 1970 he was Junior Lecturer in English at Sydney Teachers' College, a University of New South Wales Post-Graduate Research Scholar, and a teacher with the New South Wales Department of Education. His edition of a selection of William Astley's stories, *Tales of the Convict System*, was published by the University of Queensland Press in 1975. He has contributed articles to the *Australian Dictionary of Biography, Australian Literary Studies, Labour History,* and other journals. Mr. Andrews is at present co-editing a bibliography of Australian Literature in the Nineteenth Century. He is married with two children and lives in Canberra.

Preface

William Astley, "Price Warung" as he was known, is not a major Australian writer. A prolific contributor to the *Bulletin* during its most illustrious decade, the last before Federation, his work was as well-known then as that of contemporaries like Henry Lawson and "Banjo" Paterson. But whereas Lawson and Paterson were to become favorite sons of Australian literature, Astley soon slipped into obscurity. At his death in 1911 he was already being spoken of as a writer from a generation gone by, and since then there has been only passing reference to him. He is usually cataloged in the *Bulletin* school of writers along with the Beckes, the Favencs, and the Dysons. His work is represented once in most of the standard anthologies of Australian short stories, and his name is modestly commemorated by a *cul-de-sac* on the upper slopes of Garran, a suburb of Canberra where the streets are named after Australian writers. (As a fervent nationalist Astley would have enjoyed the tribute; as an equally fervent socialist, at least for a time, he would have preferred the area not to be one of the most exclusive in the national capital.)

It is not the purpose of this study to suggest that Astley's work deserves a higher status in Australian fiction—indeed, it is partly my intention to affirm that Astley possessed a minor talent, narrowly based, his achievement such that although he wrote over a hundred short stories not many of them can survive serious criticism. But I also believe that Astley is an important historical figure, in that he reflects the attitudes, the aspirations, and the achievements of many Australian writers at the turn of the century. An active political journalist and commentator as well as a short story writer, he subscribed to most of the radical theology of the *Bulletin*. He shared its prejudices and its hopes and he proclaimed his faith in the aggressive tones so characteristic of the magazine. Because in these ways he sums up much of the legend of the 1890's, it is worthwhile trying, as Vance Palmer suggested[1], to penetrate the fog that hangs around his memory—and also, it must be added, around his work.

In telling Astley's story, however, it is important to stress that his limitations as a writer are no less significant than his achievements. So clearly was he a product of his times that if we can see in his work some of the directions which Australian literature was taking, we can also see how far it had to go. What is important about Astley is that he was a victim as well as a product of the search for a national identity which preoccupied many Australian writers and some Australian publishers during the period when the nation came into being. The effect on the writers was such that, encouraged by magazines like the *Bulletin* to liberate themselves from the chains of cultural subservience, to exploit the resources of indigenous material, and to write in a distinctive, no-nonsense way, they became enmeshed in the cult of the stockwhip; or as John Barnes has put it, they exchanged one form of provincialism for another.[2] Astley's liberation, however, did not proceed even that far. So concerned was he to establish a sense of national identity through his journalism and his fiction that he never had time to find his own identity as an artist. He remained a self-conscious and imitative writer who preferred to be informed by what he had read rather than by what he had experienced or imagined, and this meant that although he espoused the kind of values which attracted the attention of Archibald of the *Bulletin*, he was never completely cast in the magazine's distinctive mold. In the long run Astley's work confirms the belief of recent critics that to see the literature of the 1880's and 1890's in the narrow terms of the legend is an oversimplification, and that even then, at the most self-consciously "Australian" stage of its evolution, Australian literature was still an extension of European culture.

Such is the scope of this study, the first of Astley's work yet to appear. Its organization has been largely determined by three considerations. First, not many readers will be familiar either with the details of Astley's life (he was a mysterious figure even at the height of his popularity) or with his work. Much of his journalism lies hidden in the files of old newspapers, the several collections of stories which he had published from 1892 to 1898 have long been out of print, and even the selection published in 1960 under the title of *Convict Days* has become a collector's item. As a result, there is more exposition, documentation, and quotation than is perhaps normal with volumes in this series. There are chapters on Astley's life, his political journalism, and his literary ideas, but, in addition, I have thought it desirable to survey the convict stories and to give some idea of the way they were written as part of my discussion of them. Secondly, I believe that the historical element looms so large in the convict stories that they should be looked at both as history and as fiction, which in turn has meant looking at them as legend and as polemics, and also meant that their failings have received as much attention as their merits. Finally, although it is normal in this series to treat consecutively the several works of an author, the similarities in subject-matter, theme, and technique among Astley's convict stories have led me to group them together for the purposes of analysis and discussion. With the exception of "Tales of the Riverine," little attempt has been made to treat each series (or individual stories) in any self-contained way.

BARRY ANDREWS

University of New South Wales,
Royal Military College,
Duntroon, Australia

Acknowledgments

I should like to record my debt of gratitude to the many people who have assisted this work in its preparation. I am grateful, first, to the trustees of the Library of New South Wales, the State Libraries of Victoria and Tasmania, and the National Library of Australia for permission to quote from manuscript and printed material in their collections, and to the staffs of those libraries for their grace and competence. For assistance outside the libraries I am grateful to Mrs. J. N. Rutherford, Mr. Theo Barker and the late Mr. R. Dow of Bathurst, Mr. and Mrs. F. Gidley, Mr. Ken Levis, and the staffs of the Lidcombe State Hospital, the Nhill Shire Office, and the Commonwealth Literary Fund. Secondly, I must thank the many people who showed interest in this work, in particular my former teachers Professor Harold Oliver and Professor Harry Heseltine; my present colleagues Professor Grahame Johnston, Mr. Bill Wilde, Dr. Roger Thompson, Dr. John McCarthy, and Mr. Neil Gow; and Professor Joseph Jones, Mr. John Anderson, Professor A. T. Yarwood, Mr. John Ryan and, most importantly, my wife Robyn. I am indebted to Miss Pam Capsticks and Miss Gail Sheridan for their help in typing the manuscript.

It was inevitable in writing this study that I made use of the material about Astley which I have previously had published. For permission to do so I am grateful to the editors of *Australian Literary Studies*, *Labour History* and the *Australian Dictionary of Biography*, and to the proprietors of the University of Queensland Press.

Chronology

1855   William Astley born August 13 in Liverpool, England.

1859   Arrives with family in Melbourne.

1868   Family settled in Richmond. Astley attends St. Stephen's Church School, Richmond, and later the Model School in Carlton.

1875   Begins career as journalist.

1884   Marries Louisa Frances Cape, Launceston, September 22.

1890   "Tales of the System" serialized in *Bulletin*.

1891   "Tales of the Old Regime," "Tales of Old Sydney" serialized in *Bulletin*.

1892   "Tales of the Early Days" serialized in *Bulletin*, *Tales of the Convict System* published.

1893   Editor *Australian Workman*.

1894   *Tales of the Early Days* published.

1896   Organizes People's Federal Convention, Bathurst.

1897   "Tales of the Isle of Death" serialized in *Truth*, *Tales of the Old Regime and The Bullet of the Fated Ten* published.

1898   *Tales of the Isle of Death (Norfolk Island)* and *Half-Crown Bob and Tales of the Riverine* published.

1908   Awarded Commonwealth Literary Fund pension.

1911   Astley dies October 5 at Rookwood Benevolent Asylum; buried at Waverley Cemetery.

CHAPTER 1

The Man

"YOU have asked me about Price Warung. What I know or have heard of him is somewhat vague and 'Tittle-Tatlish'." So wrote N. G. Rankin in 1931 to an exasperated Nettie Palmer, who was experiencing the frustrations shared by all who have tried to piece together an outline of William Astley's life.[1] The difficulty stems partly from Astley's nomadic movements during his working life, partly from the ill-health which was to make him a recluse as well as an invalid during his last years, and partly from an aloofness of temperament which meant that he was never easily accessible. Even at the height of his popularity, in the 1890's, he was never one of the Bohemian circle of authors and artists that the *Bulletin* gathered about itself. To that gay coterie which had "more fun than work," as Randolph Bedford nostalgically recalled,[2] Astley was an anonymous figure, of ordinary proportions, hiding behind a black beard, *pince-nez*, and a pseudonym, a man to whom Frank Fox confessed in 1893, "though in common with all other readers of Australian Literature I know 'Price Warung,' I am quite ignorant as to whether that is a mere pen name or is your true title."[3]

There were some people,[4] nonetheless, who years later were able to remember him. They recalled that he had a precise, alert manner, that he was a natty though unobtrusive dresser, that he was erratic in his financial dealings but sensitive on the point, that he was a good talker when he did unwind, and that he had an air of mystery about him. "He gave you the impression," said F. J. Broomfield, "that he was the confidential agent of a mysterious and hidden personality of consummate Power and resource—the Keeper of dark and deadly secrets it would be death to reveal." This was the effect on Broomfield, a rare *Bulletin* friend; to a casual acquaintance like Thorold Waters he was a "sinister-looking type" who wrote "darkling short stories."[5] Undoubtedly the somber tone of his writing contributed to his reputation for solitariness, but other rumors have clustered about his name: drug-addiction, imprisonment for "embezzlement" and "forgery," a propensity to quaint nineteenth-century illnesses like "nervous debility" and "brain fever."[6]

Some of those rumors have a basis in truth, but there is more to Astley than they allow. For one thing, he was not a friendless man, nor was he an eccentric living on the edge of his society. He was involved in it, he tried to reform it, he flourished as a writer, for a time, because of it. And although there are still large gaps in the record, enough evidence survives for it to be possible to separate some of the fact from the fiction and chronicle the major events in his life. The evidence is strongest for the period from 1890 to 1893, when he was a regular contributor to the *Bulletin* and active as a political journalist: those years can be documented pretty fully from his private papers. For the other phases of his life, from 1855 to 1890 and from 1894 to 1911, we are forced to rely much more heavily on the scrappy accounts left by several of the people who were able to get to know or to keep track of him, and on the newspapers with which he was associated.

I *Early Years*

William Astley was born in Liverpool, England, on August 13, 1855, the second son of Thomas Astley and his wife Mary Elizabeth, whose maiden name of Price gave William the first part of his pen name. (The second comes from an aboriginal word for part of Sydney.)[7] Four years later the family emigrated to Australia, probably in search of gold, for Astley remembered his parents as "adventurous souls who made up that glorious inrush into Victoria of the Fifties and Sixties,"[8] but by 1868 Thomas had returned to his former occupation as a watchmaker and had settled his family in the Melbourne suburb of Richmond. Next door to the family home was St. Stephen's Anglican Church, and it was there that William received most of his formal education, which in 1868 began with the preaching of a sermon at ten past nine, and continued with lessons in reading, writing, arithmetic, and natural history until two in the afternoon, when those pupils who could afford the extra payment of a shilling a week stayed behind to receive tuition from visiting masters in classics, European languages, singing, and drawing.[9] It is not clear just how much schooling Astley received but already his literary inclinations had been noticed by his teachers.[10] Probably it was they who encouraged him to commence employment in the bookselling trade (one of his employers, William Robertson, was linked with the firm which later published his books)[11] and to continue his education through membership in the local young men's mutual improvement society, where he helped organize spelling bees and elocution evenings, took part in parliamentary debates and readings of Shakespeare, and listened to lectures on "The Use and Abuse of Poetry" and "The Influence of the Press."[12]

II *Itinerant Journalist*

By 1875 Astley was ready to begin his career as a journalist. That year he helped found the *Richmond Guardian* and while his partner set the type, Astley scouted for news and advertisements, practised the shorthand he had by now acquired,[13] and wrote the editorials.[14] The partners sold out in 1876, leaving Astley free to move to a job as reporter with the *Riverine Herald* at Echuca, on the Murray River. Although his two years there seem to have been uneventful, they provided him with the background material for his riverboat stories, and they may also have aroused his interest in Federation. (Living in a border town, the citizens of Echuca often saw themselves as victims of the fiscal rivalry between the colonies of New South Wales and Victoria.) A nervous illness forced him to return to Melbourne in 1878 and incapacitated him until 1880; when he was fit to resume it was to become a "scribbling globe-trotter,"[15] as he put it, travelling over the southeastern corner of Australia on such a succession of assignments that his precise movements in the next decade are difficult to trace. It seems that he was first at Casterton, then at Melbourne as the correspondent for a number of interstate and Victorian provincial newspapers, and then at Sydney, where for a short time he edited the *Australian Graphic*. When it folded early in 1884 he went to Tasmania, acquired a wife, (Louisa Frances Cape)[16] and took her immediately to the mainland, where he worked as a reporter for the *Warrnambool Standard*. Then followed assignments with the Sydney *Globe*, the *Bathurst Times*, the *Tumut Independent*, the Sydney *Storekeeper*, and the *Nhill Free Press*. The Federal Convention held in March 1891 enticed him back to Sydney, and it was only then, almost a year after he had begun to write for the *Bulletin*, that he decided to make Sydney his base—at least for a time.

III *Introduction to the Convicts*

So ended the first phase of Astley's life, one which was significant not merely for the valuable experience he gained as a journalist. It was perhaps. the happiest period of his life, certainly the most sociable: he swam and played cricket, he went to balls and dinner parties, he took part in community affairs. Even more important for his literary career, he became immersed in a study of the system of transportation which had led to the founding of the Australian colonies and brought over 150,000 convicts to the eastern part of the continent between 1788 and 1853.[17] Astley's introduction to the "System" was a dramatic one, and if we may believe the only published version of the events, the first pages of the well-known story "The *Henry Porcher* Bolter," it came as a result of his visits as a boy of fifteen to an old lag in Richmond. He was a recluse, Astley recalls, and his collection of books and his life story fired the boy's imagination:

How the writer came to know him need not here be related. Suffice it that between us there was an intimacy of a kind. He tolerated the school-boy, and the schoolboy regarded him with something of respect and more of fear. For he was not a lovable character.

Two services did the ex-convict do to the schoolboy. He introduced him to the System and the Régime—a service which was of very questionable value. And he made him free of a marvellous collection of books. As to which privilege also the writer has his doubts. If he had not had permission to ramble at will through the bolter's books, he might have developed into a portly and wealthy banker, instead of a hard-up journalist.

This last remark is not altogether by the way. Had it not been for the "bolter" and his books probably these "Tales of the Régime" would never have been written.

Astley's suggestion that as an impressionable schoolboy he had his appetite whetted and his taste sharpened by these meetings with an old convict, has some circumstantial support: he was fifteen and living in Richmond in 1870, and when "The *Henry Porcher* Bolter" appeared in the *Bulletin* in 1891, another former resident of Richmond testified to the existence of a recluse in the district twenty years before.[18] *Astley's* recluse, however, is an invention, for it is revealed that he is the William Shovey listed as a runaway in the

Sydney Gazette notice reproduced in the story. Although the document is an accurate copy of a list of absconders published in the *Sydney Gazette* in May 1827, "Shovey's" original, William Storey, did not thereafter avoid capture and die a recluse in 1870, leaving instructions to Astley not to publicize his existence for another twenty years. He was recaptured in less than a week, convicted of burglary six weeks later, and afterwards sent to Norfolk Island, where he was killed in 1838.[19]

It might seem, then, that Broomfield was right when he doubted that "there was any old Convict" to tell Astley tales: "I knew the man's methods, if I did not know his inner self. 'Price Warung' was a *documentist*. A scrap of paper with an old-time date sent him into the past in true clairvoyant fashion." Yet even if "The *Henry Porcher* Bolter" is a piece of autobiographical fiction inspired by a scrap of paper, in this case part of the *Sydney Gazette*, Astley *was* introduced to convict history by a survivor of the early days, and his invention of the old Richmond lag is a characteristic attempt to conceal the identity of an informant. In 1892, writing privately of his introduction to the convicts, he again stated that as a "boy of fifteen I was fascinated by certain convict narratives, which were," he continued, "told to me by a prominent old-Time 'Official'."[20] The identity of the "official" remained obscure for several more years, but in 1898 Astley stated[21] that he was a doctor, and a year later he was more specific. Writing in a copy of *Tales of the Isle of Death*,[22] which he presented to the famous Australian book-collector, David Scott Mitchell, he revealed the man in question to be a Dr. Henry Graham, who had appeared in disguise not only as a convict in "The *Henry Porcher* Bolter" but also as a lieutenant of marines in one of the Norfolk Island stories.[23]

IV *Graham's Influence on Astley*

Beyond Astley's statement to Mitchell that he knew Graham "in boyhood and to early manhood" there is little evidence to indicate the origin and the length of their association, but its importance can hardly be overestimated. What Graham had to tell Astley was based solidly on his extensive knowledge of the darker side of the convict system. Educated in England, Graham arrived in New South Wales in the late 1830's, and from 1839 to 1850 he served as a medical officer at several penal stations in the eastern colonies, including successive terms at Port Macquarie, Norfolk Island, and Port Arthur.[24] This means Graham was a government official during a decade when the transportation system was rigorously administered; most of his time during that decade was spent at the secondary punishment centers, where the system operated at its harshest; and most of his dealings were with the more incorrigible convicts. He was able to judge, therefore, the efficacy of extreme forms of punishment, for his Tasmanian experience alone brought him into contact with silent prisons, human tramways "powered" by convicts, underground coal mines with little air and no light, and chain gangs. His Norfolk Island service, moreover, meant that he was able to compare differing styles of penal administration, for during the six years he spent there from 1841 to 1846 he worked under its three most famous commandants, the pioneering liberal Alexander Maconochie, the weak but brutal Joseph Childs, and the celebrated autocrat John Price.

The effect of this experience cannot be disputed. Astley acknowledged that most of his information on what he called[25] "the 'inside' official life" at Norfolk Island was derived from Graham, which makes him the main source for all the tales involving Maconochie, Childs (christened "Scragge" by Astley),[26] and Price. The tales number two dozen in all, roughly a quarter of the total output, and if it is accepted that Graham had stories to tell of his Tasmanian experiences, then he becomes a potential source of information for another third. It would be wrong, though, to see him merely as a fascinating *raconteur* whose stories can be linked with some of Astley's. His influence was more comprehensive in the sense that he must have played a significant part in forming Astley's attitudes toward the transportation system and ultimately toward history and politics. Though sometimes stern and a firm believer in punishment as an ultimate deterrent (as was Maconochie), Graham was a humane man, "kind-hearted" as the convict memoirist John Mortlock put it,[27] and appalled by the excesses that were too often perpetrated at the penal stations, particularly the cruelty and treachery which marked the regimes of Childs and Price and prevented the reclamation of so many convicts. He imbued in Astley a deep sense of sympathy for the convicts, a feeling that they were more victims than villains, or at least that part of their villainy stemmed from their victimization. The real villains, the true agents of evil, were not the convicts but the penal administrators and those in power in England whose decisions had led to transportation in the first place. Astley believed so strongly in this paradox that he was preoccupied in all his writing with the way people in authority could be corrupted by power.

V *Astley's Research*

We will probably never know if Henry Graham, like the *Henry Porcher* convict, had a library through which Astley was able to roam, but Astley resolved after their meetings to "collect at first hand such material as I could relating to the convict days."[28] Later he was to make extravagant claims about the amount of data he gathered during the next twenty years. "My collection of documents . . . has cost me over £2000," he maintained on one occasion; on another, "I have over 50,000p Foolscap of notes"; on a third, "my historical material embraces 1800 . . . [books and] . . . 1200 pamphlets."[29] Nor had he lost control over such a collection. "As a slight indication of the labours I have expended," he wrote, when applying in 1892 for the editorship of the *Historical Records of New South Wales*, "I may mention I have personally indexed 1300 works on Australasia, over 1000 pamphlets, a complete series of newspapers from 1803 to the present day, and many hundreds of State papers [i.e. British parliamentary papers], copying many thousand pages of notes, diaries etc kept by other persons. . . . My index," he concluded, "comprises 340 volumes and 320,000 distinct Entries."[30]

There can be little doubt that these statistics were exaggerated, chiefly because they were designed to impress prospective employers, publishers, or critics who had questioned Astley's authority. But there is likewise little doubt that Astley made a careful study of the convict system during the two decades which were to elapse before the publication in the *Bulletin* of his first story. Although most of the evidence relating to the kind of material he studied and the way in which he organized his research dates from the period *after* he began writing,[31] he was obviously a more eclectic student than either Marcus Clarke or William Gosse Hay, the two writers of convict fiction who were most nearly his contemporaries. Clarke, even though he documented his research, seems merely to have dipped into transportation records as a prelude to *For the Term of his Natural Life*. Hay, abhorring "vulgar inaccuracy," was more painstaking and conscientious, but the sources for his convict novels were relatively few, less than three dozen according to one list.[32] As for Astley, both his private papers and the stories attest his use of parliamentary papers, newspapers, broadsides, books, pamphlets, diaries, letters, even the convict records themselves; and if his own collection was defective in any way he could use the public libraries, which by 1872 held a surprisingly large proportion of the transportation literature which is available to a modern student of convict history.[33] That Astley took advantage of the opportunity is confirmed by the fact that by 1891 he had been provided with a special table at the state libraries in Melbourne and Sydney, and had for several years been employing assistants to index newspapers and copy extracts from books and parliamentary papers.[34]

Nor did he confine his research to the written record, unlike Hay and to a lesser extent Clarke: often the written record merely supplemented what had already come from oral testimony. Given the initial impact of Graham's yarns it is not surprising that Astley valued this kind of evidence, which he had countless opportunities of gathering from old convicts and colonists during his travels around Victoria, Tasmania, and New South Wales. In 1899 he claimed that before he began writing he interviewed over eight-hundred people who had lived through the convict days,[35] and the claim is supported by evidence in his papers that he conducted three-hundred interviews in one year alone, and by the *Bulletin's* statement that even as late as the 1890's there were "marvellous collections of ghosts about Old Sydney . . . Astley was on hand-shaking terms with them all."[36] The record of four interviews has survived, though none, unfortunately, with ex-convicts. They reveal that Astley developed the practice of taking down on the spot a brief note of the personal history of this subject and then his recollections of various buildings, incidents, and historical identities. Thus the recollection of one old colonist in 1891: "Distinctly remembers Sir Thomas Mitchell, very choleric man, saw him jump one day in his hat"; "Wentworth slightly over the medium height, had an acrid, benevolent face."[37] The interview completed, Astley seems to have processed the rough copy by having self-contained parts of it typed up and by filing away the complete draft. Also in his files were the notes he took while fossicking around the former penal settlements—the only one he did not visit was Norfolk Island—and the letters he received from correspondents who by the late 1880's were scattered over three colonies. They answered bibliographical questions, gave leads to useful sources, told stories of their own experiences of the System, or recounted the experiences of contacts they had made.

The inevitable result of this research was that Astley gathered for himself a collection of material which, if not as massive as he claimed, was extensive enough and in danger of being unmanageable. Having accumulated his *pot-pourri*, gathering data from so many sources, even gleaning information from the same source in different ways, he needed to exert some control over it. Sensibly enough he reduced his material to a common form, so that notes collected from printed works or from documents were processed in much the same way as notes collected from interviews or from observations. Again, there are indications that he kept not only a variety of indexes but also an index to the indexes and, more significantly, that he correlated his material when preparing to write. Finally, that he was respected as a bibliographer and historian is indisputable: in the early 1890's he was commissioned to prepare part of a bibliography of Australia,[38] he helped booksellers notate their catalogs[39] of Australiana, and several times he was called upon to answer questions that had stumped collectors like David Mitchell. "I *happen* to have here the index to my Biblio: notes," Astley rather impishly wrote on one occasion, "and a casual reference tonight gave me the following": the "following" was a full bibliographical description of two rare pieces of Australiana.[40]

To sum up, then, even though very few papers survive from the period when Astley did most of the work which prepared him for writing his stories, it can be said with some certainty that he was interested in looking and listening as well as reading and recording, and that his research was so wide-ranging and comprehensive that he had had to take firm steps to organize his collection of data. By the late 1880's he was remarkably well-informed about the convicts.

VI *First Contact with the* BULLETIN

Just when Astley began to write about convicts, however, is much less certain. No stories were published under his pen name in any of the newspapers with which he was associated before 1890, although several of them had published historical tales by other writers at the very time he was employed as local roundsman or political writer.[41] It would seem that the *Bulletin* was the first outlet for his work, and to judge from a comment he made in passing in 1892 ("Two years ago I began to give literary form to my materials"),[42] his first contribution to the magazine, "How Muster-Master Stoneman Earned His Breakfast," was written not long before its publication on May 24, 1890. It is a moot point whether he had needed any encouragement in the first place from the *Bulletin's* editor, J. F. Archibald. Vance Palmer thought so, remembering how Archibald, the "pilot," had discovered Louis Becke and Edward Dyson and helped them to turn *their* fields of interest to literary profit.[43] But there is no notice in the famous correspondence column of the magazine to support such a contention, and it is likely that Astley made at least the initial contact.[44]

By 1890 the *Bulletin* was a decade old, an aggressive, brash, humorous weekly and already a name in Australian journalism.[45] It had overcome its precarious beginnings and under Archibald, and its business manager, William Macleod, had hammered out a consistent literary, social, and political philosophy which it stridently proclaimed week by week. The *Bulletin's* was a somewhat negative creed, isolationist economically and racially, antiBritish politically and culturally; in its early days much of its appeal had been generated by its nagging denunciation of what it felt to be antiquated values. But by the 1890's it was just as earnestly preaching a positive gospel, claiming[46] to be the "Premier Australian Literary Journal," the only one with a consistent "Australian National Policy," which it cataloged each week. It advocated a republican form of government, payment of members of parliament, a democratic franchise, land taxation, state education, penal reform, and "A United Australia and Protection against the World." It denounced sectarianism, foreign titles, the Chinese and Imperial Federation.

A significant part of the program was the cultural chauvinism fostered in the literary columns and art-work of the journal. In the drawings of "Hop" and Phil May the *Bulletin* sought to express its hopes for the future. Ranged opposite the rogues' gallery (the Chinaman, the Jew, Fat Man, John Bull) were the idealized Bushman, shirt-sleeved, lean-jawed and tenacious, and the Little Boy from Manly, the symbol of the emerging nation. In its literary columns were spawned folk heroes like Clancy, Joe Wilson, the Man from Snowy River, the Man from Ironbark, and, later, the "On Our Selection" scrubbers. They were all products of the outback environment toward which most contributors of prose and verse were encouraged to turn, and their virtues were those of the "Lone Hand," Archibald's original name for the *Bulletin:* toughness, honesty, sardonic humor, optimism, stoicism, mateship. As for the writers themselves, Archibald not only turned their attention toward Australian subjects but also bullied them into writing in a distinctively Australian way. One contributor who sought to please the proprietors was advised:

Well, be simple; be natural. Be brief; prefer a sentence to a paragraph, a phrase to a sentence, a word to a phrase. Don't beat your grain of gold over a column; nothing pleases the average writer more than to spoil a good par. in a bad story. Shun superfluous adjectives; stick to sturdy nouns. Don't over-elaborate; say what you have to say as tersely and as originally as possible, and quit saying. Come to the point at once, and stay there till you go. The best ideas pack in the least space. The *Bulletin* contains more concentrates than all the other Australian weeklies put together, and if we had time we'd put it in half-an-inch. [47]

The results of this advice were the many short "pars" about bush life which were packed into colorful columns like "Pepper and Salt" and "Aboriginalities," and on the literary pages a certain type of short story, the famous *Bulletin* "yarn," with its emphasis on originality, brevity, realism, and dramatic force.

The *Bulletin*'s cultivation of the stockwhip was not, of course, its sole literary interest. Nor did its policies necessarily guarantee good literature, as several critics have pointed out, the first being J. H. Greene, who complained in 1896 "the *Bulletin* short story works up to 'He is dead' or 'He is dead drunk'—this being a generalization of the two favourite climaxes—one some novel accident, the other a 'sell'." [48] Even W. T. Goodge, a contributor of popular verse who unmercifully exploited the outback environment, grew tired of

. . . the everlasting swaggie with his bluey on his back
Who is striking out for sunset on the Never-never track;
O'er the flat and barren country we can hear him tramping still
And he's Billy from the Darling or he's Murrumbidgee Bill;
And his togs are pretty rusty and his blucher boots are brown,
And his shirt ain't just the color of the drapers' clerks in town,
And he's looking for the station tank his water-bag to fill
And wherever you may find him
He's the same
Old

                        Bill!
There is Jim the dandy axeman who can chop six cords a day,
There is Micky from the Mulga who was ringer out at Hay,
There's McPherson, overseer at the Moonaburna shed,
And the bloke that belted Clancy, with a slip-rail, on the head.
There's the chap that struck the nugget when his credit at the
      store
Was so bad they stopped his tucker 'cos he couldn't pay his score,
And the jackeroo from England with his quarterly "remit,"
And whene'er you read the story
It's the same
                        Old
                        Skit!⁴⁹

But for all its faults the *Bulletin* did great service for Australian
literature. It was the first journal which consistently set out to use
indigenous material, and it produced a body of creative writing that
was often raucous but always defiantly Australian. Finally, it backed
up its policies with practical help. It paid for the contributions it
printed and issued a series of separate publications; its proprietors
were prepared to read new work and publish their criticisms in the
delightful correspondence column; and its contributors were assured of an Australia-wide reading audience. (By 1890 its circulation
had reached 80,000, it was known by such names as the Bushman's
Bible and the Laborer's Bible, and in the frontier town of Kalgoorlie
its arrival on Wednesdays made "Bully day" more commonly ob-
served than the Sabbath.)⁵⁰ With this kind of appeal it was inevitable that Astley should send his stories along for consideration. And
although in several important ways he never conformed to *Bulletin*
models, it did not take long for him to become a regular contributor.
His second and third stories were published in June and July 1890;
when the next, "Absalom Day's Promotion," appeared on August 9
the title "Tales of the System" was introduced, "Absalom Day's
Promotion" was numbered fourth in the series, and for the rest of
the year an installment was printed each week. The series finished
in the second issue for 1891; within a month two more, "Tales of Old
Sydney" and "Tales of the Old Regime," had begun their run.
"Price Warung" was by now entrenched as a *Bulletin* man.

VII *1891*

    Astley's career was to reach its peak in 1891. It was certainly his
busiest creative period, for in order to fulfill the contract for the two

series which were alternating from January, he had to write at least one story a week, to proofread installments which were in the process of being published, and to correct the typescripts of others being prepared for submission. Added to this were queries from readers for which Archibald demanded answers, a regular political column to write for the *Bathurst Free Press and Mining Journal,* and occasional political and historical articles for the *Bulletin.* Yet despite periodic bouts of ill-health he maintained this strenuous program of writing and an equally strenuous program of study, which included field trips to Blackheath and Tasmania and replies to dozens of letters from friends who were assisting him in his research. Inevitably there were setbacks, one being when Archibald, ever watchful for libel suits after his own experience in 1882, refused to publish two "Tales of the Old Regime" because they raised "Religious Questions."[51] Upset by Archibald's caution Astley took steps to sever his connection with the *Bulletin,* but capitulated when Archibald's associate, Macleod, prompted no doubt by the success of the stories with readers, paid £215 for limited rights to "Tales of the System," "Tales of Old Sydney," and "Tales of the Old Regime."[52] Under the terms of this agreement, signed in July, the *Bulletin* retained the book rights to these stories for five years, which explains why the selection of "Tales of the Old Regime," eventually published by George Robertson and Company, did not appear until 1897.[53]

For the next few months the peace was kept on both sides. Astley continued to supply copy for "Tales of Old Sydney" and "Tales of the Old Regime," which ended their runs in December, and for its part the *Bulletin* continued to pay him an average of five pounds for the magazine rights to each installment, gave over part of its correspondence column so that questions about the stories could be answered, and proceeded with the preparation of *Tales of the Convict System,* which reached the bookshops the following June. By the end of the year Astley's prospects had never looked brighter. He led friends to believe that he had a novel as well as a new series of stories in final stages, that he had completed the Tasmanian portion of a bibliography of Australia on which he was collaborating with G. B. Barton, and that he had already started his next project, a biography of John Dunmore Lang. As for his personal affairs, his health was good, he had made useful contacts with such leading politicians as Edmund Barton and Sir Henry Parkes, he was in demand as a negotiator around the hustings, and his financial posi-

tion seemed so secure that several times he had indulged his passion
for bookbuying. Little wonder, then, that in January 1892 a fellow
journalist, J. T. Ryan, ruefully compared his failure to earn "more
than pocket money" in Melbourne with what Astley had reported of
his success in Sydney.[54]

VIII *Disillusionment*

For Astley, however, 1892 was a year of mixed fortunes. The
separate issue of *Tales of the Convict System* was widely acclaimed,
but overshadowing this success was the steady deterioration of his
relationship with the *Bulletin*. The problem began when publication
of the fourth series, "Tales of the Early Days," was delayed for six
weeks while he haggled with Macleod over terms. Although, when
the series was established and the first of the "Ring" stories had
been published, Macleod wrote on behalf also of Archibald to
congratulate Astley "on your power of keeping up average quality
and dramatic interest,"[55] it was to George Robertson and Company
of Melbourne and not to the *Bulletin* that he sold the book rights
both for this series and for "Tales of the Riverine," which the *Bulletin* published intermittently between 1890 and 1894.[56] Nor was this
his only attempt in 1892 to escape dependence on the magazine: he
hawked his stories to Sydney and London publishers, he tried to
start a press agency and a manufacturing company, he campaigned
vigorously but unsuccessfully for the position of editor of the *Historical Records of New South Wales*. In time this involvement outside and its poor financial return produced such a strain that he
again became ill, thus limiting the amount of work he could produce. Inevitably the *Bulletin* management became impatient and in
October an irritated Archibald wrote, "Before sending in any more
copy we would like to have matter in hand completed. We hold
three paid for but unfinished stories . . . . And then you have
completely stopped the bushranging matter, the beginning of which
is now an affair of ancient history. Macleod tells me he holds order of
yours for £12 which is being pushed for."[57]

The bushranging "affair" is a well-known incident, several versions of which have been recorded. Astley is alleged to have arrived
at the *Bulletin* office one day with the last chapter of a history of
Australian bushranging which he was taking to his typist. After
much coaxing he was induced to let the *Bulletin* acquire serial
rights—"he left chapter XXV in Archibald's hands and took in

exchange the *Bulletin's* cheque for £50. Days and weeks passed; then it dawned on the horrified editor that chapters I–XXIV had never been written!"[58]

The account is only half-truth, for what were obviously the *first* three installments of a bushranging series were published in August and September 1892, and further evidence[59] shows that Astley was not expected to submit the bushranging articles other than in installments, as had been the practice with the convict stories. But there is also no doubt that his tardiness in submitting *any* copy (the last six "Tales of the Early Days," which completed its run in December, were extracted from him only after great effort, and Charles White, editor of the *Bathurst Free Press*, had similar trouble keeping him to his deadlines) meant a breakdown in the arrangements instituted with the *Bulletin* in 1891. The *Bulletin* paid for stories received (or promised) by honoring orders that Astley had taken on various firms. In November a curio dealer, James Smyth, complained that "I saw Mr. Macleod at 3 o'clock he said you were in this morning & never said a word to him, further that you owe the *Bulletin* upwards of £100 and until that matter is cleared up *he will not pay out another penny.*" A month later the solicitors acting for Dymocks, the booksellers, also threatened legal action if he did not pay for an order which the *Bulletin* had refused to honor.[60]

Thus it is not surprising to find G. B. Barton, himself in the midst of a dispute over ownership of some valuable historical manuscripts which Astley had acquired in Tasmania for Barton and refused to release, writing in his diary early in 1893, "Met M[a]cleod (of the *Bulletin*) yesterday in Bligh Street: talked about Astley, whom he doesn't like."[61] What Archibald thought is not documented, but A. G. Stephens called Astley a "sad rogue" and dined out on the story about the bushranging series.[62] It is unlikely, however, that Stephens had much to do with him, because by the time he arrived in 1894 Astley's link with the *Bulletin* was virtually severed. According to the magazine in 1911, the four series which it had published in three years had not exhausted Astley's "gleanings from the convict records—but the public had had enough."[63] More likely, given the disputes of 1892, it was the *Bulletin* management which by the end of the year had "had enough," particularly as Astley had written little for six months and a new face, Louis Becke, had arrived on the scene. Whatever the reasons, early in 1893 Astley was released from his obligations to the *Bulletin* so that he could become editor of the *Australian Workman*, the weekly organ of the Trades and Labour Council. The decision, apparently agreeable to both parties, meant that the leading contributor to the *Bulletin* from 1890 to 1892 had no more than three new stories accepted for publication there in the next five years.

IX   *Editor*

Astley's break with the *Bulletin* did not mean the end of his literary career. In 1891 Macleod had declined to serialize a political novel Astley had offered him, and it was probably this same work which Astley, as editor, now felt free to publish in the *Australian Workman* under the title of "The Strike of '95: A Story of the Passing Time." "The Strike of '95" has some historical interest as one of the first long pieces of fiction about the labor movement to be written in Australia.[64] After ten installments had appeared from February to June it was left unfinished, partly because of a dispute over copyright and partly because Astley became heavily involved in proposals to establish a labor daily. These involved meetings which were held all over Sydney and several country areas. Astley was among those who appeared on the platform to support the project, and he spoke of his plans for raising the finance with such eloquence and force that the youthful George Beeby fell completely under his spell: "he used to appear . . . as if he'd stepped down from some other world and was ready to give us the benefit of his wisdom. Well-dressed, good-looking and in some queer way 'distinguished'. Yet no suggestions of the charlatan about him. I used to follow him about: I'd never met a man who filled me with such admiration and positive awe."[65]

Perhaps as editor of the *Australian Workman* during the preliminary planning Astley expected a senior appointment on the projected *Daily Post*. But by the time it began publication in January 1895 his link with the labor press was long since broken. Ill-health had forced him to relinquish the editorship of the *Australian Workman* in November 1893; as for the *Daily Post* appointment, George Beeby recalled that when it was forced to wait throughout 1894 for capital to come forward a disenchanted Astley had "faded out of the picture."

X   *Publicist for Federation*

Astley faded out of most pictures for the next three years and not, ironically, until he left Sydney to visit Bathurst at the end of 1896 did he return to public notice. He had become increasingly agitated with the way in which the entanglement of Federation in the web of state and party politics had produced a widespread ignorance of the real issues at stake, and while at Bathurst he conceived the idea of holding a convention which would educate the man in the street and provide some index of popular opinion. The Bathurst People's Federal Convention was held in November that year. As its organizing secretary Astley labored strenuously to ensure that the convention conformed to his image of it, which meant ensuring that the delegates were drawn from all states and from all sections of the community, that the proceedings were fully reported, and that the mechanics of Federation (particularly the question of state rights) received close scrutiny. The convention was a huge success and, apparently now satisfied that Federation had a broad popular base, Astley was thereafter a zealous publicist for the movement, even though this meant compromising the beliefs he had held when writing on the issue between 1888 and 1893.

XI *Contributor to* Truth

In a roundabout way the Bathurst convention had important literary consequences as well as political ones, for it was there, in dramatic circumstances, that Astley was arrested and taken to Sydney to answer a charge of obtaining £15 by false pretences from another Sydney journalist, William Kitchen; although discharged then, he was committed for trial three months later. The case attracted much attention in the New South Press, particularly in *Truth*,[66] where Astley was vociferously supported by the infamous editor John Norton, who defended him by attacking Kitchen so trenchantly that a libel suit was instituted. (It had not been resolved when Kitchen committed suicide as a result of the disclosures about his private life.) Norton's sensational trial reports ("False Pretences! Kitchen Dished! Astley Honourably Acquitted") made sure Astley's innocence was publicized. Even more helpfully, however, he paid Astley's bail, sanctimoniously scolding the public for allowing "literary genius" to languish in Darlinghurst jail, and after the trial he commissioned Astley to write a new series of stories, "Tales of the Isle of Death," serialized in *Truth* in 1897 and republished by George Robertson and Company in 1898. The *Truth* stories were virtually the last new ones he wrote. In July 1897 Norton reported[67] that he had scooped the *Bulletin* and secured the rights for *In the Days of the Foundation*, a novel then being revised. But like *The*

Jewel of the Holy Death and *In an Empire's Dawn Light*, novels
allegedly completed in 1896,[68] it was not heard of again. So, too, a
fresh bushranging series of which there were rumors in 1899[69] did
not proceed any further. In fact, after 1897 Astley had only two new
stories published, a convict tale syndicated in the country press in
1898 and a short sketch about Sydney life in the *Bathurst Free Press*
in 1903.

XII *Decline*

Obviously the *Bulletin* was right in suggesting that longer work
was beyond him, and one of the reasons must have been his
celebrated addiction to drugs. "No! You can't consider Astley
without his Hag," warned Fred Broomfield, who helped Bertram
Stevens to nurse him, "and his 'Hag' was morphia," though another
contemporary suggested opium.[70] The addiction, which almost
certainly originated in medical treatment, left him chronically short
of funds; yet needing more to satisfy his "Hag" and not always able
to earn them, he was driven to questionable practices, like writing
postdated cheques, which caused him great remorse. Perhaps his
addiction also contributed to the wildness of his writing and increased his desire to remain an anonymous figure. But periodically
the physical effects were noticed: attacks of amnesia and insomnia[71]
and an increasing inability to withstand personal or vocational
pressures without nervous collapse. Was it withdrawal symptoms
which *Truth* noticed when it reported Astley's "horrible nervous
malady" when first charged with false pretences, and that when he
was eventually acquitted "he was in a state of terrible nervous
agony, and could barely respond to the utterances of his friends"?[72]

To judge from the amount of work Astley produced, the addiction
was more or less controlled until 1893. After that a pattern emerges
in his life whereby long periods of inactivity are punctuated by
bursts of strenuous labor. The ten days' work[73] which was all he
could manage in the three years after he left the *Australian Workman*, was followed by the rigors of the convention planning; his
nervous breakdown at the Kitchen trial was succeeded by the
energetic preparation of the *Truth* series, dictated to a typist in a
fortnight. Thereafter his movements become harder to trace, his
decline exacerbated by *tabes dorsalis*,[74] a degenerative and painful
disease of the spinal column which increasingly hampered him after
1891 and eventually caused his death in 1911. (Some eighteen years

before a similar disease had caused the death of a more famous writer of short stories, Guy de Maupassant.)

In 1898 Astley "blew in," in Robert Garran's phrase, to help publicize the Yes case at the referendum on Federation and stayed on to edit the *Clarion Call*, Edmund Barton's election newspaper, but he "blew out again" after Barton's defeat and did not return to assist at the next referendum. In 1899 he was trying to make another go of a press agency, in 1901 he applied to edit the *Westralian Worker* (the directors thought his name was Ashley),[75] and in 1901–3 he wrote several pamphlets to help Bathurst and alternative sites in the Western area of New South Wales expose their best sides to the committee selecting the site for the federal capital. He remained to become the first editor of the *Bathurst Argus*, but again chronic ill-health forced his resignation within a few months and his last years, of which there is virtually no record, were spent in poverty—without even the solace of books enjoyed by the old lag in "The *Henry Porcher* Bolter." (Astley's library, which may well have contained a run from 1803 to 1850 of the first Australian newspaper, the *Sydney Gazette*, had long gone to collectors like Mitchell when the other attempts to remain solvent failed. There are suggestions that in these dealings, too, Astley was less than honest.)[76]

In the first allocation of the Commonwealth Literary Fund, established in 1908 for the purpose of assisting old or sick writers and their families, Astley was awarded a pension of ten shillings a week.[77] He was penniless, however, when he was found wandering with amnesia in Sydney in December 1910, and he was eventually despatched to Rookwood Benevolent Asylum, where it took a fortnight for his friends to find him. They deposited him at his sister's house in Artarmon, but in September 1911 he returned of his own accord to Rookwood where he died on October 5.[78] The obituaries[79] were uncertain about what had happened to him in the last decade, but old acquaintances remembered him with some affection and turned up in large numbers at his funeral at Waverley cemetery.

XIII *Some Conclusions*

To this account of Astley's life what can be added? The comment, first, that although his last years were pitiful, they were no more so than the last years of many of his contemporaries. Victor Daley, Ernest Favenc, Louis Becke, to name just three, all struggled like him for a living and at the end had nothing. Perhaps as more is written about the *Bulletin* writers of the 1890's, some of the glow that still surrounds that legendary golden decade will be dissipated.

Secondly, the effect of Astley's struggle with his "Hag" should not be overemphasized. Compared with, say, Henry Lawson's alcoholism, Astley's drug addiction was a more spectacular vice but had less effect on the progress of the artist. There is not the deterioration in the quality of Astley's fiction as in Lawson's, simply a decline in output, which was caused more by *tabes dorsalis* and by the lack of a market after 1893. What should be emphasized is Astley's great dominance of the *Bulletin* from 1890 to 1892. The eighty-four stories he had published in those three years, more than a quarter of the total printed in the magazine, make him not only the most prolific contributor of the decade[80] but also one of the most prolific in the *Bulletin's* history, even though his career as a contributor was comparatively brief. The most obvious result of Astley's prodigiousness is that he wrote quickly and had little time to revise his work, at least as far as newspaper publication was concerned.

Thirdly, it should be emphasized that Astley was a writer of the *early* nineties, which means that he was one of the *Bulletin's* first "discoveries" and, more important, that he was Archibald's discovery and not the protegé of A. G. Stephens, the *Bulletin's* most influential *literary* editor. Most commentators see Archibald as a successful entrepreneur and good judge of folk writing but Stephens as the better critic. It is my belief that Astley was not simply a folk writer and that his work suffered from not having the benefit of Stephens's judgment. Finally, the account that has been given of Astley's life is inadequate as it stands, for more can be made of his involvement as writer and activist in the issues of his day. To assess the extent of this involvement it is necessary to look more closely at Astley's journalism.

CHAPTER 2

The Journalist and His Times

I "Good Work in Many Lines"

"ASTLEY was a brilliant journalist," said the *Bulletin* in its breezy obituary, "who in his day did good work in many lines."[1] Just how many lines there were even the *Bulletin* could not have known, for Astley worked on more than twenty newspapers and journals that we know about, and probably some others that we don't. He worked on large metropolitan dailies and small country weeklies, on radical journals like the *Bulletin* and conservative ones like the *Review of Reviews,* on dull trade papers like the *Storekeeper* and glossy art magazines like the *Australian Graphic.* Nine times an editor, he also had experience as a reporter, leader-writer, parliamentary roundsman, interstate correspondent, publisher, and press agent, and in the course of his career wrote everything from editorials to book reviews, literary notes, historical articles, social diaries, political chronicles, market reports, special features, answers to correspondents, and advertising blurbs.

Not all of this bread-and-butter journalism has survived,[2] and not all of what has is of much interest: reports of provincial agricultural shows and visits to horse studs and hop plantations,[3] even when Astley can be specified as the author, are of little relevance to his convict fiction. His most significant pieces of journalism are the political editorials, articles, and stories that he wrote in the decade or so after 1887. It was a period[4] of great social and political change, one which in New South Wales saw the development toward a modern system of party government and the emergence of the labor movement as a political force; in the six colonies, the growth of a national consciousness found a constitutional expression in the creation of the Commonwealth of Australia. On all these issues Astley made extensive comment; what he had to say was always lively, seldom impartial, occasionally wild and vindictive. But even the excesses in his political writing show how deeply he was involved in the great questions of his day.

II *Astley on the English*

One of the recurring themes in Astley's journalism, at least before 1898, is his antagonism toward the land of his birth. Perhaps this had its origins in the family tradition[5] that the Astleys were once well-connected in English society but had come down in the world to such an extent that Thomas was forced to migrate to Melbourne to make a fresh start. Perhaps also it was confirmed by William's research into the convicts, which convinced him that there were others who had been victimized. Whatever the causes of his resentment toward English society, he did not want such a society recreated in Australia and said so emphatically in the first editorials which can safely be attributed to him.[6] They were published in the *Bathurst Times* during the summer of 1887–8, at a time when the colony of New South Wales was celebrating the Centenary of its foundation. In keeping with the spirit of the festivities many colonists looked back in their speeches on one hundred years of progress and forward in their toasts to the continuation of a happy relationship with the mother country. For Astley, however, the Centenary celebrations confirmed that the

British interest in Australia is pure and unadulterated Imperialism, and, barely defined, appears as the desire to enmesh these colonies in the gilded net of Imperial federation. There is a fascination in the vision of a great world-covering union of the British race, but a federation which shall be a true union must be from the alliance of states co-ordinate in power and co-equal in political conditions. Between a country where the reins of power are held in the hands of men who are influenced by the traditions of caste and class, and a country governed by the instincts of democracy, there cannot be equality. A federation between such differing nations would be the sort that follows upon the absorption of the fly by the spider . . . . At this day the colonies are freer than England herself. Faulty though our democratic institutions may be, they still own the one great virtue that the people rule themselves, and are not ruled by class or classes. Imperialism, in its essence, hates democratic rule, and aims at concentrating power in the classes. It is simply an instrument for class aggressions, the gratification of class interests, and the attainment of class policy.[7]

Polemical in tone, rhetorical in style, with the texture of the prose shot through with striking images, this is a typical Astley editorial.

The specific target is the Imperial Federation League,[8] which until its collapse in the early 1890's voiced exaggerated fears of a foreign invasion in order to convince Australians that their best chance as a nation lay in becoming an integrated part of the British empire. The radicals saw this as fiction: the real danger (note Astley's use of words like "enmeshed" and "absorption") was that the Australian colonies would lose the identity they had fashioned during a century free of the "paralysing influence of vicious world institutions."[9] They would become ruled by caste and class, thereby mirroring English society where power was entrusted in the hands of the few. With the experience of his own family's history this was anathema to Astley. His alternative was to believe that democratic processes were already evolving in the colonies, and that at the proper time a new Britannia would emerge there free of the sins and internecine strife of the old, an egalitarian, socialist republic where all men would be free and equal (with the proviso, however, that they be white and Anglo-Saxon).[10] Such a nation, as events turned out, never really eventuated, but the vision of Utopia sustained Astley, and many of his contemporaries, throughout most of the 1890's.

III *Astley on the Politicians*

Not that the prospects for new Britannia seemed all that golden even in 1888, before strikes and depressions convinced socialists like William Lane that it would have to be founded outside Australia. If Astley's discussion of the significance of the Centenary minimized the faults in the way democracy operated in the colonies, the editorial[11] he wrote for Centenary day itself soberly advised the community to "analyse its blots, and not concentrate its gaze on its fancied beauties." The catalog that substantiated this warning indicted the judiciary ("which purchases its robes with huckstering so paltry that it would be contemptible were cabbages the object of barter") and a bureaucracy which, among other things, "fossilized" education and took it out of the reach of the masses. But the bulk of the criticism was directed toward the politicians. Inside the Legislative Assembly "democracy degenerate[d] into demagogy" (the alliteration is another typical Astley feature); outside it, portfolios were allowed to "fall into the hands of the peccant and venal," who then cavorted in the service of the colonial business establishment and showed deference to the aristocratic and commercial classes in England. By their actions they denied the people access to the new "Great Empire in the South."

So badly served did Astley feel the colonies to be by their political leaders, and so deeply did he feel that the job of the press was to "fearlessly assert" its warnings for the "welfare of the State,"[12] that his political writing over the next five years is characterized by a preoccupation with parliamentary malpractice. If the politicians had failed the people in 1888, their failure was more miserable in 1891, when they sat down to draft a constitution for the new nation. For Astley, now writing in the *Bathurst Free Press,* they were "ignorant," "prejudiced," and "traitorous" at the convention table, unable or unwilling to see that there were dangers inherent in the bill they prepared, and even more culpable when the Draft Bill was sent back to the state parliaments for discussion and amendment. In New South Wales, the "vital, momentous business of Federation" was plowed under parish soil as Sir Henry Parkes and George Dibbs, on either side of the House, manoeuvred their parties around the bill and argued its proposals "in the spirit which characterizes the contestants in a low-class Sydney boxing-ken." As for the corner-hugging Labor Party, which had entered parliament after the recent elections and carried Astley's hopes for honest government with it, its insistence on social reforms above all else meant that it had "let go the mackerel for the sprat." Federation was too large a question, the *Bathurst Free Press* concluded, "to be dealt with after the petty measures of party gauges."[13]

But their shelving of the Federation issue was not the only action of the politicians to displease Astley. Parkes was "headstrong" when he resigned abruptly as Premier later in 1891, in Opposition his attempts to regain power of his Free Trade party were dismissed as acts of vanity and malice. Branded a "mountebank," a "huckster," a "virago," a "fire-eater," and an "acrobat," Parkes was the "Old Man Malignant" whose degeneration tarnished the brilliance of his earlier contribution to the colony.[14] But if this decline meant that he stood at his death in 1896 only "Within an Ace of Greatness" (the title of Astley's obituary),[15] Dibbs, his Protectionist successor in 1891, was worse. The "congerie of blunderers" who took office under him were subjected to a steady sniping fire[16] throughout 1892, and early in 1893 it erupted in a major offensive,[17] when the government was accused of corruption and incompetence. To justify the abuse he heaped on Dibbs and his ministers—successively branded the "Flapdoodle and Fudge" ministry, "Ministerial Limpets," "The Pliant Ministry," "The Backdown Ministry," "The Government of Accident," and "The Hydra-Headed Ministry"—Astley cited their internal squabbles (the "snarling and jowling for the bones of office and patronage" of which he had earlier warned) and pointed to the willful mismanagement of several government departments. Most of Dibbs's ministers were singled out for treatment in a series of lead articles entitled "In the Midst of the Chaos," but the strongest words were reserved for Edmund Barton, later to become first Prime Minister of the Commonwealth. Where Barton had erred was in "Kowtowing to the Mumbo-Jumbo of the Hour"[18] by accepting the office of Attorney-General under Dibbs. This meant that although Barton was the one parliamentarian who understood and supported republican Federation, he procrastinated within a conservative administration to the point where Astley lost patience. In February 1893 he took his complaints to the *Bulletin*, which published his long open letter[19] to the "Fat Lord Justice of the Federation," the "Lord Justice Iscariot" as Astley called him in the draft. Barton was warned that in spite of his many virtues— "force," "generosity," and "ardor" among them—his association with the Dibbs government meant an association with "cronk balance sheets and sexual immoralities." More important, it threatened to convert his republicanism into Toryism, and if he continued to turn from the guidance of the "Star of the Republic" to "mingle with the Parasites of Imperialism," he would be enrolled among the "Iscariots of history"—hardly the kind of warning to justify Vance Palmer's description of it as "austere though friendly."[20]

In our present era of strict libel laws Astley's thrusts at the politicians make entertaining reading—if he spoke as he wrote it is not hard to understand why he was a popular orator. But how valid are his criticisms? And how relevant are they to his fiction? It should first be noted that if he was stronger than most in condemning what he took to be the corruption of governments (though the *Bulletin*, for one, was just as vehement) he was not alone in his disapproval of the way contemporary politicians conducted themselves. Although something like a modern party system was starting to emerge, the feuds and conflicts hanging over from the earlier days of faction politics were still in evidence. The offices of the New South Wales parliament were popularly known as the "bear-garden," and the citizens of Sydney had several opportunities in the early 1890's to witness public brawls between parliamentarians overwrought by personal animosity;[21] in 1895 even the staid *Sydney Morning Herald* compared the Legislative Assembly with a bullock team which seemed unable to move without a copious use of bad language.[22]

And yet Astley, unable to grasp the concept of party allegiance, was ambivalent on the issue; his attack on the three parties for their internal feuding did not keep him from censuring individuals like Barton, who is now usually acquitted of procrastination over Federation, for not exerting their independence enough. Moreover, when his own conduct is considered, it is obvious that he was far too severe on the politicians. In his personal dealings with them he was at best erratic[23] and sometimes downright hypocritical, exchanging vituperation for high praise when the financial necessity for patronage demanded it. (At the very time, for example, that he was attacking Parkes, Dibbs, and Barton in the Bathurst press he was courting their affections in Sydney.) Similarly, as editor of the *Australian Workman* and involved in the establishment of a daily organ for the workers, he railed at most metropolitan newspapers because they were "servants of plutocracy,"[24] but this did not stop him either from offering material to their editors, or, when it was accepted, publicly recanting an earlier position. His most spectacular capitulation was to John Norton, a minor politician as well as a journalist. In 1892 Norton, the "nominal proprietor of that notorious repository of filth called *Truth*,"[25] was judged by Astley to be a scandalmonger impelled by base motives. In 1897, after "Tales of the Isle of Death" had commenced serialization, Astley compared Norton with Thomas Paine and judged him to be a man who, "at once publicist and tribune, is both reformer and pioneer," a man who had "fearlessly subordinated his powers and private interests to the common good."[26]

Such a compromise, in fairness to Astley, should be seen as economic rather than philosophical. As a free-lance journalist with recurring ill-health of one kind and another, he was seldom in comfortable circumstances, even during his association with the *Bulletin*. Perhaps his disappointment—or his guilt—at having to become a "mercenary of the enemies of democracy," as he put it,[27] is one explanation for the wild rhetoric he used when free of their clutches, though there are other possibilities: for example, the disorientation stemming from drug-addiction; the puritan standards acquired from a nineteenth-century upbringing (which may have given him exaggerated notions of honor and increased his embarrassment at his own instability); or the fact that even in a calmer mood he could become intoxicated with words. Whatever the reasons, his political writing was seldom cool-headed and constructive, and too often the value of his criticism diminished as it degenerated into sneering abuse of individuals. Astley's own conduct should have made him more tolerant; but even if, as he suggested, Parkes *was* guilty of malice, or Barton of hypocrisy, or Dibbs of incompetence, neither they nor their contemporaries deserved the hysterical epithets he regularly cast in their direction—"vice-breeding vermin," "harpies on the public purse," "parasites of office," "treacherous tools that may slip and cut the hands that clasp them," and so on.[28] Astley's Bathurst editor, Charles White, was a strong enough opponent of Dibbs, but even he pleaded of the "Flapdoodle" editorials, "Pray do not get too warm," and correctly censured a vulgar attack on the most famous political larrikin of the day, the rumbustious W. P. Crick, "We would have been better pleased if you had dealt with the subject in a somewhat more dignified style."[29] It is not a lack of dignity, or even of tolerance that is relevant to Astley's writing. Simply, the wildness of so much of his political journalism reveals how easy it was for him to lose the professional virtue of detachment. And a lack of detachment also limits the achievement of the convict stories.

IV *"The Strike of '95"*

The other problem with Astley's rhetoric and his preoccupation with personal attack is that they camouflage what he really thought of his society and the forces that shaped it. Behind all his condemnation of the politicians is the idea that power corrupts, but the implications of this belief were seldom spelt out, even when in 1892 a member of the New South Wales Legislative Assembly was actually convicted and jailed for fraud.[30] His political journalism is riddled with catchcries and aphorisms (" 'Distrust the Politicians!'—Take that for your watchword and your battle cry!"; or, "the Legislative Council is an asylum for the politically obsolete"[31]), but only once did he come close to providing his readers with anything like a summary of his credo. That was in 1892 when, in answer to his rhetorical question, "what is the function of the politician?", he replied: "The good of the people, their relief from poverty, the diminution of crime, the addition to what constitutes a nation's real splendour, the enlargement of national values."[32] Finally, the job of piecing together a statement of Astley's beliefs is made more difficult by the fragmentation of his work.

Fortunately, however, there is "The Strike of '95," Astley's unfinished serial which, like William Lane's better-known novel *The Workingman's Paradise*, was inspired by Bellamy's utopian romance *Looking Backward*.[33] "The Strike of '95" is a poor piece of fiction, and as with the journalism the problem is a lack of detachment. Astley insists on weaving editorial comment into the texture of his plot to such an extent that there is an almost total lack of narrative progression or depth of characterization. Yet it is precisely because Astley refuses to curb his tongue that "The Strike of '95" is so useful, not as a novel but as a tendentious tract in which he analyzes the imperfections of the present and signals his hopes for the future. Both these intentions are implied in the subtitle, "A Story of the Passing Time."[34]

The protagonist of "The Strike of '95" is Edward Warner, a democrat earnest for social reform who does a number of odd jobs to supplement the pittance he receives clerking for the Honorable Frederick Dutton, a member of the New South Wales Legislative Council and one of Sydney's wealthiest and most influential men. Though the first three installments have not survived,[35] Astley's summary reveals that they were set in Dutton's house. Warner arrives with a letter from the Colonial Secretary containing information which upsets a land-grabbing scheme concocted by Dutton, the Secretary, and several public servants. In order to save the situation Dutton enlists the aid of Warner, whose democratic predilections he abhors but whose acquiescence he hopes to buy with gold or with the favors of his daughter Ethel. After studying the attractions of Ethel over lunch, Warner is ostensibly drafted into service, but when he leaves the house he calls an emergency meeting of the League of the Emancipation, a workers' secret society which has its parallel in the convict stories in the brotherhood of the Ring. The League, told of Dutton's plans, decides he is an enemy of the state and has his name added (in bold white letters on an appropriate blue background) to the Scroll of the Infamous, a list of men who have betrayed the democratic national interest into the hands of "the caste-builders, the privilege-mongers, the monopolists."

So ends the first book, "The Rumbling of the Volcano," and so ends the novel: the promised sequel to "The Rumbling of the Volcano," "The Explosion," did not eventuate. Conveniently, however, Astley left a plot summary of what he had *intended* to write. Dutton, corrupt M.L.C. and captain of the Plutocrats, and Charles Hughes, President of the League and captain of the Democrats, were to meet in the electoral arena and then on "a bloodier field," where presumably the action suggested by the title of the novel was to take place. After the confrontation New Australia would arise: not, according to Astley, in Paraguay, where his old friend Lane was about to found a socialist commune, but "within the borders of the old." Warner, however, was to be sacrificed: he was to become "confused in the tangled issue of life . . . duty and desire, love of woman and love of country. He became a pawn in Dutton's game, after all, and in so doing destroyed himself. But yet—for such is life; in the moment the hand snatches the fruit of victory it turns to ashes—Dutton lost the game."

How does "The Strike of '95" summarize Astley's beliefs? First, perhaps, in the picture it presents of the alignment of the characters. In one corner is Dutton, gout-ridden in the early chapters of the novel, the bloated capitalist and corrupt politician ensconced in a "finely-situated mansion at Darling Point" while he plots to extend his influence and expand his income. Opposite him we have Edward Warner, who has more than his surname to link him with his creator. Like "Warung," Warner is an abstainer, to the surprise of Miss Ethel, who "had always heard them spoken of as faddists and cranks and bigots." Again, Warner writes a column for a country newspaper just as Astley was the political correspondent for the *Bathurst Free Press,* and he contributes to the *Blisterer,* obviously a fictitious *Bulletin.* Understandably, Astley preaches through Warner. When Ethel suggests that something like the French Commune could never exist in Australia, he retorts, "Who can say, Miss Dutton? . . . we have certainly no corrupt Imperial system to eat away at our nation's robustness"; later, he defends his work for the *Blisterer* by claiming, "When a man's in public life his character is public property. It is by virtue of his character, or rather what is known of his character, that he presumes to enter public life."

Like Astley, finally, Warner is unobtrusive: as secretary of the League and anonymous contributor to the press, he hugs the corner of the stage. A more public opponent of Dutton and the vehicle for most of "Warung" 's polemics, is Charles Hughes, the President of the League. Just as Dutton is Fat Man so Hughes is another allegorical figure of the times. He is the noble worker, a cousin of the *Bulletin*'s noble bushman, and as such is sentimentalized and idealized by Astley. He is tall, "massive of frame," has hands "that had wielded hammers and had worked drills but . . . could also caress a child, or fasten with a gentleness of touch a sick woman's bandage," and has sober habits which are emphasized by his dark suit cut plain and his "simple, brown felt hat." He is an example of "how great and glorious a possession manhood might be made," and his nobility is such that his head "might properly, with its profuse curls of grey hair, have been faithfully copied in marble by any sculptor who was moulding . . . the ideal form of a Hercules or an Agamemnon."

It is in Hughes's long evangelical address to the League (which meets over four episodes in a room of "republican severity") that Astley's editorial intrusion is most blatant and his narrative grinds completely to a halt. With a missioner's zeal Hughes rails at the enemies of the workers, the businessmen who cripple the economy by floating wild-cat mining companies, the self-interested politicians who, like the squatters in the past, have alienated the land from the people. Among the sinners named aloud are the Queensland politicians Thomas McIlwraith and Samuel Griffith. The Scroll of the Infamous, then, is the precursor of a special kind of national monument that Hughes envisages as part of the landscape of New Australia. Alongside a shrine commemorating the national heroes will be built a second, he warns, "of sombre ashlars, in which every indentation made by the mason's chisel will be the expression of . . . a curse": "That shall be Australia's Temple of her Infamous sons—the men who would have bound her to the chariot-wheels of the Reactionaries for ever, who would have sapped her popular liberties in order to aggrandise the classes, who, upon a foundation of serfdom, would have constructed the vile edifices which are the palaces of the king, the aristocrat and the land-thief."

Of ultimate victory Hughes is in no doubt. Like Astley, he looks to a nation independent, prosperous, stable, and, it seems, honorable. Although the national debt has been incurred by the economic machinations of the capitalists, it is his view that it be repaid, chiefly because of the "reflex effect upon the national character which would result from the manful bearing of a burden involuntarily assumed."

"The Strike of '95", then, is a synopsis of Astley's radicalism, a synthesis of the doctrines presented piecemeal in his previous work. Up to this time he believed in and propagated a democratic future free of the authoritarianism, the "Caste" and "Privilege" as he called it, which was endemic in a monarchistic and aristocratic society,

England being the quoted example. Federation meant a new nation, and in his version of New Australia Astley invested his hopes for the creation (whether by evolution or revolution, he was not sure)[36] of a society where wealth and power would be taken from the few (the "Plutocrats" or "Monopolists," as they were called) and given to the many (the "Democrats" or the "Workers"); stated always in these general terms, the alternative to capitalism was some form of socialism. It was because the promised land still had to be attained in the early 1890's that Astley subscribed to his iconoclastic theology. Like the *Bulletin* he saw himself as a missionary in the wilderness, whose responsibility was first to identify the wealthy few whose attempts to gather more wealth about them led to the corruption of politicians and civil servants, and then to make public the collusion and the corruption.

V *Astley and Federation*

Yet the feeling which went into the propagation of this credo should not be allowed to disguise the fact that Astley was not a deep thinker, nor, when his political writing *after* 1893 is considered, was he a particularly consistent one. On issues like penal reform and tertiary education his interest was longstanding and his stance progressive, but his habit of being affected by the enthusiasms of the moment meant that often he took up a cause for a time and then dropped it. His decision to become editor of the *Australian Workman*, for example, merely regularized a relationship with the labor movement that had been intensifying for several years; after he left the newspaper he cut himself off from the movement, preferring to devote himself to Federation. But even with this cause, in which he retained an abiding interest throughout the 1890's, he was capable of accommodating himself to changing moods. Before 1893, as we have seen, he was a staunch believer in republicanism and a fervent opponent of imperial Federation. In 1891, in a scholarly and uncharacteristically calm analysis,[37] he opposed the first Draft Bill for the Commonwealth precisely because it failed to preserve the rights of the states in the projected senate, which left the way open for unification under a strong central authority, including a judiciary responsible finally to the English high court, as an alternative to Federation. After the Draft Bill went back to the states for discussion and ratification he attacked the New South Wales parliamentarians for their failure to see the weaknesses in the bill, for their refusal to keep the issue free from the taint of party politics, and for their collusion with the Imperial Federationists.

But somewhere between 1894 and 1898 Astley's republicanism and his Anglophobia moderated as he became more and more a publicist for the Federation movement and less and less a critic of the way the politicians were leading it. His republican principles were still important enough in 1896 for him to insist that the Bathurst Convention be a *people's* convention, open to all sections of the community; to insist that there be just one convention register, where millers, saddlers, masons, and butchers could enter their name in the professions column beside the doctors, lawyers, and politicians; and to insist that the state rights clause of the 1891 bill be the main topic of debate. In 1898, however, as a member of the press committee established to publicize the Yes case at the Federal Referendum he wrote most of the paragraphs and articles which went out to country newspapers known to be in favor of the constitution drafted at the 1897–8 Federal Convention. In contrast with the "democratically defective" constitution of 1891, the new one was, he now argued, "in its essentials, as well as on the surface, Progressive, Liberal, Democratic"—even though the senate still did not possess the powers that in 1891 he maintained were essential for its democratic operation, the proposed federal executive was potentially as autocratic, and the link with Britain would obviously remain. In answer Astley marshalled a number of unrelated arguments: any problems would be rectified "in due course"; the "Tory Spirit" was dying anyway; there were urgent problems of defense (an important plank in the platform of the Imperial Federation League); it would be a shame to waste the efforts that had been made; the destiny of a now free people had arrived. "Does a ship's master," he wondered, "setting out on a voyage which must be undertaken, refuse the only chart available because he fears its obvious defects, because in some places the currents are unmarked, the coast lines undefined, and the shallows unsounded?" The advantage of the bill was that it was "a chart to steer by in the national voyaging across seas necessarily in parts unknown."[38] Just seven years had elapsed since Astley had warned of the danger of consummating a "hasty marriage which will have to be repented of at leisure."[39]

How far Astley was to move from the uncompromising republican position he maintained up to the publication of "The Strike of '95" can only be gauged by his actions on December 15, 1900. He made a special trip to the Gap to watch the *Royal Arthur* pass through the heads of Sydney Harbor; on board was the first Governor-General, Lord Hopetoun. Less than a decade had passed since he had been Governor of Victoria and Astley had described him as a man who "since his arrival here has performed with accuracy certain functions which a wax figure with a phonograph in its interior could have performed with equal grace and a corresponding dignity."[40] Now Hopetoun and the attendant symbolism—"Sea, Sky and Circumstances were sublimely auspicious"—moved him to write a jingoistic panegyric, "The Opening of the Gates."[41] It is sentimental claptrap, like most of Astley's verse and like most of the occasional verse written to commemorate the Commonwealth. The point, however, is that its publication in 1893 would surely have put his name on the Scroll of the Infamous and meant that he could be branded, with Barton, as a parasite of imperialism.

It must be realized that this *volte-face* was by no means abnormal. Republican nationalism ebbed and flowed, in the 1880's and 1890's, in proportion to the threat of imperial domination, and so many writers and politicians[42] were caught up for a time in the ground swell of Anglophobia that for Astley to be entrapped was almost an act of conformity. Nevertheless, it must be realized that his attachment to causes like Federation and socialism (and their exponents and opponents) was emotional rather than intellectual, utopian rather than practical, and this also explains some of the apparent inconsistencies in his political writing. His analysis of contemporary events, even in the cautionary tale "The Strike of '95", was superficial: stripped of the verbiage and the vituperation, it reduces itself to slogans like "distrust the politicians," the refrain of the political leaders. His prescription for the future, stripped of contradictions, reduces itself to mottoes like the one he borrowed for the Bathurst People's Federal Convention—"Foedere facto aequamur," "One People, One Destiny." The sentimental idealism which informed this vague thinking was part, as I have already suggested, of the Australian dream of the period. But it was not so much a vision as a mirage, and perhaps this was another reason why "The Strike of '95," a story of the *passing* time, had to be left unfinished.

VI *"The Strike of '95" and the Convict Stories*

One last word about "The Strike of '95": of all Astley's political work it has the closest links with his convict fiction. However "taw-

dry and scandalising"[43] some of Astley's contemporaries may have
found its specific references to people and institutions, it still claims
to be fiction. Thus Astley's lack of control is more relevant to his
convict stories than his lack of professional detachment in the
journalism (though they stem from the same angry commitment).
Furthermore, the past and the present are as inextricably woven
together in the convict stories as the present and future are in "The
Strike of '95"; if the latter is a story of contemporary times in which
Astley looked forward to the future, the convict stories are the
means by which he looked back from the vantage point of the
present. These perspectives result in parallel groupings of
characters: Dutton is the physical and spiritual descendant of the
colonial aristocrats in "Tales of Old Sydney," while the ancestors of
Hughes, the noble worker, are obviously the convicts, who are seen
to be the victims of an authoritarian society. If some of them lack
Hughes's dignity and humanity, it is precisely because, Astley
suggests, they have lost it under the yoke of the System. The
common enemy of the noble worker and the noble convict is the
English Boss.

The links with the present are made clearer in the convict stories
by Astley's habit of interspersing his narrative with parenthetical
asides which are reminiscent of his editorial comments in "The
Strike of '95." Captain John Piper was a "great hand at accounts," we
are told in "Andy Webster's Last Will and Testament," he "would
have shone in these latter days as a director of an investment
company"; or, "The System . . . [was] . . . invented by the Devil
in his mundane residence at No. 14 Downing Street"; or, most
pointedly, when Astley talks of the "chasm from the Old to the New
Regime, the measureless distance between the Twenties and the
Eighties."[44] Perhaps the asides influenced a London publisher to
reject the stories in 1892 because they "would not attract the major-
ity of English readers of fiction at the present day";[45] certainly they
appear in sufficient quantities for an Astley selection to be suppressed during the Second World War in case the enemy used it as
propaganda.[46] However, it is in the preface to *Tales of the Convict
System* that Astley shows most clearly how his convict fiction is
grounded in the beliefs that emerge from his political writing. To
neglect the convict beginnings was foolish, he warned:

The Transportation System has knitted itself into the fibres of our national
being. There is not a single Australasian province (and this includes Vic-

toria, South Australia and Maoriland [New Zealand]) whose character was left unvitiated by the methods England adopted for the disposal of the criminals she had bred; in three provinces the existing legal systems bear the marks of the convict-mould in which they were fashioned; in two, peculiar land-tenures obtain which, the corollary of the conditions of penal settlement, blight the whole population today. The convict past of Australia cannot be shut out of sight. No man can put his finger on the date when it ended, for the reason that it glided imperceptibly into the vigorous and splendid, if still imperfect, present.

Vigorous and splendid, then, because potentially egalitarian, socialist, and democratic; imperfect, because of the corruption of the capitalists and politicians like Dutton, who is trying in "The Strike of '95" to create a new regime, to perpetuate the kind of society which produced such suffering for the convicts under the old one. So "The Strike of '95," however useful as an appendix to Astley's journalism, is more than that; it is the bridge by which we can move from the political writing to the convict fiction. It was Astley's way of showing how the sins of the fathers were in danger of being visited upon the children.

CHAPTER 3

The Literary Milieu

WHATEVER Astley's political writings may reveal about his attitudes towards society, they do not reveal much about his literary values, in particular the conceptions about literature that he brought to bear on his convict fiction. It is here that Astley's occasional journalism (even when the occasion is parochial), his stories of Riverina life, and his literary criticism are more useful: the last because in commenting on other writers he exposes some of his own attitudes; the first two because they give some indication of the relationship between his critical principles and creative practices.

I   Astley's Reading

All of Astley's writing, however, tells us something about his reading, for scattered throughout his journalism and fiction are dozens and dozens of literary references. Some of these are to writers of only passing popularity (Edward Bulwer-Lytton and Bret Harte, for example), but more often they suggest that Astley's tastes were, by modern standards, sophisticated. They were also cosmopolitan: although he alludes very little to the classics, to list the authors to whom he refers in one form or another is to catalog almost a who's who of English, American, and European literature. He knew his Elizabethan, Romantic, and Victorian poets, well enough, in the case of the Romantics, to be invited to help organize a Shelley Centenary in Sydney;[1] though not as enthusiastic a Jacobean as Joseph Furphy, he enjoyed quoting from the plays of Shakespeare and Jonson, and perhaps most interesting of all, he was familiar with most of the great novelists and critics: Defoe, Fielding, Sterne, Richardson, Samuel Johnson, George Eliot, Thackeray, and Dickens among the English; James, Twain, and Melville among the Americans; Pushkin, Dostoyevsky, Cervantes, Heine, and Mann among the Europeans.

It is tempting to anticipate for a moment our discussion of the convict stories and consider what Astley learnt from these authors. Did Defoe, for example, teach him the value of corroborative evidence? Or Fielding and Thackeray the technique of editorial intrusion? Or Twain the usefulness of a vernacular idiom? Perhaps. But no firm answer can be given to these questions because most of Astley's references to his authors take the form of brief quotations or passing asides. A characteristic example is his comment in the open letter to the *Bulletin* that Barton should be wary of the "hee-hawing idiots" in the Colonial Office, who owed their positions "to the circumstance that Becky Sharp has sold herself once again to my Lord Steyne."[2] Or to move from the political writing to the occasional journalism, we find Astley concluding a report of the Governor's visit to Warrnambool, "When will Warrnambool see the like again? The garish flags of all colours, from the 'sooty flag of Acheron,' like to that which Milton spoke of. . . ." A month later Milton returns in this comment on Marcus Clarke's life: "There can be, however, little doubt that 'the vintage of the full-glob'd grape' would have been 'bodied excellence' indeed. But it was not to be. 'The thin-spun life' was to be 'slit by the abhorred shears' ere the prime of manhood had been fully entered upon." Then it is Dickens's turn: Astley solicits contributions to a gossip column he is establishing and promises to print everything he receives, "always providing that that most autocratic of autocrats, the Editor, is like Barkis—'willin'.'" At the end of that issue an item is concluded with another reference to *David Copperfield*: "If this doesn't make us what Uriah Heep called 'umble', nothing will"[3]—and several years later the novel is again alluded to in one of the convict stories, where Astley, careful to avoid the possible anachronism, reports that one of his characters "was applied to, and intimated, like the then uninvented Barkis, 'that he was willin' '." Elsewhere in the stories, finally, are such statements as, "And the poor stricken lady, distraight for love's sake like Ophelia," and a young man "not completely emancipated from the Byronic stage of manhood had wandered in the precincts of Newstead Abbey, and had spouted 'Don Juan' and 'Childe Harold' to the wondering and unapplausive deer."[4]

It should not be thought that such a literary inheritance as this was unusual among Australian writers in the nineteenth century. Furphy was an "incorrigible Shakespearian," Lawson read Dickens "over and over again," Boldrewood called Scott "the Magician," and

Clarke was not only a wide reader but also something of a scholar, contributing several pieces to *Notes and Queries*.[5] But in Astley's case what cannot be missed, even in the few examples quoted, is the care he took to make sure readers knew of *his* learning. To be sure, the literary reference was a staple technique of nineteenth-century journalism,[6] but time and time again, particularly in his early journalism, Astley self-consciously paraded these references. It is as if he felt that mentioning famous authors gave his work a cultural seal of approval.

The origins of this self-consciousness stem, I suspect, from the lack of a formal education past the early days of his youth. Much regretting this deficiency, perhaps he saw a knowledge of books as one way in which it could be repaired. But he could not wear his learning lightly: it was paraded to companions at mutual improvement society meetings in Richmond, and it continued to be paraded once Astley began writing. It emerges not simply in his name-dropping of the masters and his quotations from their works, but in a more general way in the mannered literariness of his style, his prediliction for an unnatural vocabulary, euphemistic and ornate. The most obvious contrast is Lawson, who remained uncorrupted by his reading and "fell into a natural stride from the beginning," to quote Vance Palmer.[7]

A second effect of Astley's self-consciousness is an uncertainty of judgment which helps to explain the excessive amount of documentation and editorial intrusion in the convict stories, and which can also be detected in some of his early pieces of humorous journalism. "I cannot use the rapier myself," he was to write some years later in a not so humorous attack on A. G. Stephens, "and so I have been driven to adopt the club."[8] A fairer statement about a satiric piece he wrote in 1888[9] is that he was uncertain about which weapon to use—and so employed both.

The occasion, as might be guessed, is the Centenary of the colony of New South Wales. Astley was in Bathurst, and as there was no local celebration on Centenary day to write about he invented one, using the fictitious report as an opportunity to mock parochial festivities in general. His best moment is when the procession begins to form: "It may here be remarked that the Salvation Army had originally wished to be ranked next the clergy. On it being pointed out by the marshalls, however, that, in this case, they would have to precede the press, the Army objected to being placed in the demoralizing contiguity of the newspaper men, and requested that they might be associated with the Fire Brigade, for the reason that the latter body was as instrumental in saving property from the burning, as they themselves were souls from conflagrations of another sort." Though this was only a small-town affair, the rapier has been deftly used. The effects of the club can be seen elsewhere, most clearly when Astley, having written "Scarcely had the notes of Handel's (improved) great work died away . . . ," immediately weakens the impact of his jibe at the rural orchestra's rendition of the *Messiah*, by adding "when the marshals—always there when death's about—assisted the orator of the day . . . to mount the platform." And he was so uncertain whether readers of the *Bathurst Free Press* had got the point that he italicized the aside.

II *"Art is nature concentrated"*

If the whole body of Astley's writing tells us which authors he felt he had to quote from, it is his literary journalism that gives us the clearest picture of his critical beliefs. As with the political journalism there are problems of identification and fragmentation, but enough evidence survives to provide an outline of his views—several book reviews, and parts of a column which he ran in the short-lived Sydney magazine *Spencer's Weekly*, in which he analyzed current literary trends and assessed new books.[10] The evidence confirms, incidentally, that he admired the authors he quoted—"genius" is one of the most used (and abused) words in his critical vocabulary.

Central to all his criticism was the idea that the study and practice of literature was a serious business. In jocular mood he could write that the "main end of fiction is amusement" but normally he was more somber. The value of literature was in the way it could mirror life; art, at its best, was "nature concentrated." The picture of society presented in most contemporary drawing-room novels was, he believed, artificial; labelling one of them "lady-like," he then proceeded to dismiss it in this characteristic way: "There is the usual amount of love-making, more or less delicate; the usual episodes which mark the course of true love which does not run smoothly; the usual lord; the usual lady with a bye-name; the usual happy ending. All is neat and decorous in style, with the usual neat and decorous Italian or French phrase, neatly and decorously interpolated into sentences which it would be difficult to parse and impossible to analyse." In contrast, he admired the novels of Dickens for their complexity, their social "realism."

The brand of realism to which Astley subscribed, however, had certain limits: it did not extend to the naturalism of some contemporary European fiction. If "chastity of treatment" distinguished the study of sexual relationships in George Eliot's *Romola* and *Adam Bede*, Zola's *Nana* was characterized by "sordid sensuality," and *The Ladies' Pleasure* by "corrupting sensuousness." Novels like these were "crude" and "unwholesome" (two more favourite words), part of what he called "the literature of the decadence," or, more scathingly, "the erotic, neurotic and Tommy-rotic." "I for one", he wrote in *Spencer's Weekly* in 1895,

do not relish the transfer of the apparatus and "subjects" of the dissecting room to the boudoir and the study. There is the realism which describes a Phryne in her congenial surroundings, or a moral and physical leper in his lair; and it is conceivable that the literary artist may, by the obligations of his art, be sometimes driven to be brutally true to certain morbid aspects of life. But there is, besides, the realism of the heroic and the good in human existence, and of the glorious in nature, and he who cannot discern the preponderance in the scheme of things of what is wholesome and what is admirable over what is the reverse, must be myopic indeed.

The irony in this is that Astley had already drawn the criticism that *he* was myopic and morbid: not because of sexual explicitness (he was honest enough not to shy away entirely from the sexual corruption of the convicts, but his diffidence made him use euphemisms of the day like "the sin of the cities of the plain" to describe homosexual attacks on young convicts): but because of his preoccupation with evil. Even one of his firmest admirers confessed that "I should like to see your work relieved by a few instances of noble self-sacrifice . . . which cannot be found wanting in the history of the convict settlements,"[11] while Sir Henry Parkes suggested that *Tales of the Convict System* "do not supply the field where a healthy soul would seek enjoyment. Our moral world is made up of passions, good and bad, straining for the mastery. Our noblest efforts are only strainings to the right side." In reply Astley pointed to Parkes's strong opposition to transportation in the 1840's and protested, "I do not make my subject. All I sought to do was interpret it. As my themes become different so, I trust, will my work become healthier in kind and effect."[12] But as the convict stories make up the bulk of the fiction, and the rest is just as gloomy, this promise was not fulfilled.

III   *The Reality of Romance*

The second way in which Astley's realism was qualified can be guessed from his statement about "the realism of the heroic and the good in human existence, and of the glorious in nature." Perhaps the darkness in his own life made him preoccupied with evil, but at the same time it helped, paradoxically, to make him an uncompromising romantic. If Marcus Clarke espoused the "romance of reality," as a recent critic has suggested,[13] then Astley might be said to have sought solace in the reality of romance. And if this belief led him to admire the poems of Burns, "whose simplest notes breathe LIFE—the truest, the wholesomest, the tenderest,"[14] it also meant that he admired more "melancholy" writers (that is, writers of his own temperament) for their "strength." Such words as "melancholy," "strong," "vivid," "power," "dramatic," and "graphic" recur in his criticism. Marcus Clarke is admired for his "power of vivid conception" and "vigorous execution," Pushkin for his "power of analysis" and "graphic vigor of portraiture," Zola for his Parisian scenes which provide the setting for a drama, "which, though terrible, is *real*."[15] (Astley's emphasis) Given these assessments, it is no surprise to find him laboring over the construction of his convict stories to make them as dramatic as possible. A carefully organized plot leading up to a sensational climax was for him just as much a representation of reality as any documentation and factual detail he might provide.

The problem is that sentimentality and melodrama were an integral part of this romanticism, and that Astley's creative writing sometimes succumbs to these traditional weaknesses of Victorian fiction can be seen in the rampant melodrama which pervades every paragraph of "The Strike of '95." But had this serial not survived, there is ample warning of the danger in some of his criticism: for example, in his assessment of Burns, in his description of Bret Harte's "touching lyrics,"[16] or, perhaps most clearly, in his review in *Spencer's Weekly* of a contemporary drawing-room romance called *Two Strangers.* Another "lady-like" piece of fiction, Astley found it unremarkable for the most part. What distinguished it was the "admirable vividness of description" to be found in the climactic scene, "in which Bertram, although stricken with anguish at the

departure of his wife and daughter, yet laughs hysterically when
Mr. Wradesley, alone and, as he thinks, unobserved, places Tiny's
crushed forget-me-nots in his pocket-book, under the impression
that they have belonged to her mother." If Astley's taste was so
defective that he could single out this scene for special praise, little
wonder that he should consider the other "situations" in the novel as
"not too" melodramatic.

The paradox that must emerge from this description of Astley's
critical attitudes, and from a catalog of his reading, is that, for good
or bad, he was influenced more by overseas literature than by
Australian literature. Or to put it more strongly, given the
perspective of his political writing, his ideas about literature and
about how to express himself were formed from his acquaintance
with the culture of a country he so often professed to despise, more
than from his acquaintance with the emerging, immature culture of
a country in which he had placed his hopes. It should not be
thought, however, that this kind of paradox applies only to Astley: it
has also been detected in the work of equally fervent nationalists
like Lawson and Furphy. The latter's *Such is Life*, suggests John
Barnes, is "unmistakably Australian in its created life, and unmistakably English in its literary origins."[17] As for Lawson's stories,
they seem unmistakably Australian both in their created life and in
their literary origins. But according to Brian Matthews at least the
apparatus of romance and melodrama was a "ready made source of
inspiration" for Lawson, part of his "sensibility." It was only in his
early work that he controlled the "natural sentimentality and
romanticism to which he was attracted"; later, he was to "peddle
traditional melodrama dressed up as bush stories."[18]

IV *Astley on Australian Literature*

That Astley was not much influenced by Australian literature does
not mean that he found nothing to please him in the work of his
predecessors and contemporaries. Although he seldom quoted local
writers, he admired the poetry of Kendall, Gordon, Paterson, and
Brunton Stephens, the journalism of Julian Thomas (the "Vag-
abond"), and the novels and articles of Marcus Clarke, whose close
research he admired as well as his powerful effects. Toward the
Bulletin he was somewhat inconsistent. He thought Archibald an
"epigrammatist who could coruscate in choctaw"[19] but disapproved
of some of the articles written for the Red Page after his own de-

parture from the magazine. In 1901 A. G. Stephens was dismissed with characteristic invective as "the Paladin of the New School of Criticism urging on, with his Britannia-metal spurs (Brummagen manufacture) his noble steed—the advertising draper's donkey borrowed for the occasion—launching himself in dreadful onset against windmills, like Cervantes' Don."[20]

His most extensive and most interesting comments, however, were about Henry Lawson, a "young writer" who he thought in 1895, had "done some very remarkable work in his brief career— work that would have given him an enviable repute had it appeared originally in English or American journals."[21] The significant use of international comparisons is confirmed later in this notice by Astley's hope that the projected publication of Lawson's stories and poems would "ensure him that large audience which he merits." Nevertheless, he saw Lawson's success as good for *Australian* literature and it was in these terms that he began his review[22] of *While the Billy Boils*, published by Angus and Robertson in 1896:

> The publication of this volume marks a new date in the annals of Australian Literature. Novels and volumes of collected short stories have been published in good style in Australian cities before now, but the appearance in exceptionally handsome form of a native-born author's prose sketches, with the *imprimatur* of an Australian publishing-house, with well-drawn plates by a native-born artist . . . [Frank Mahony] . . . is a fact that distinguishes, with a note of originality and suggestive importance, the time and place of its issue . . . . In these young communities it has been held impossible, except under rare circumstances, to enrich the pages which have come from the pens of local *litterateurs* with the accessories of elegant type and artistic binding, the plea being that the cost of production in Australia would make publishing ventures of that kind unremunerative. This volume from Lawson's pen, following upon the success of the experiments with Paterson's (Banjo's) and Lawson's verse, conclusively demonstrates that the day has gone by when a plea could be advanced by a publisher with a reputation for enterprise and intelligence. That is what attaches unique interest and importance to this volume. Proof is now supplied that Australian readers are numerous and enlightened enough to appreciate local literary work of fine quality to an extent that justifies the concentration, upon publishing enterprises, of large capital and of high-class typographical and book-binding skill.

The bibliophile's approving voice can be heard loud and clear, and so can the literary patriot's; it is as if the care which had gone into

the making of the book was one measure of the seriousness with
which Australian literature was finally being taken. But what of its
contents? For Astley, Lawson's stories were to be admired for the
way they portrayed the variety of Australian life:

> [This volume] gives us Australia in a hundred phases of character, of
> episode and of scenery, and notwithstanding that there is more than an
> occasional recurrence of type, and a monotony of tone not always agreeable,
> taking the volume as a transcript of things Australian, there is scarcely a
> passage of ten consecutive lines which I should like to see expunged. We do
> not yet, we Australians, know our country. Most of us know a corner of it,
> and the people resident in that corner, tolerably well; some few more know
> also a few score other places; few, indeed, can be truly said to have formed
> any accurate idea of the myriad facets and characteristics, the huge variety
> of interests, the discrepant conditions between existence here and existence
> there, the subtle differences between class and class, people and people,
> township and town, bush and city, or of the congeries of phenomena which
> make up our country and the life of our country. To most Australians,
> indeed, the acquirement of such an idea by process of actual observation is
> beyond the bounds of the possible, and therefore, considering the whole
> collection of sketches and stories from a non-critical point of view, and
> simply as they appeal to every lover of these lands, their republication
> should be heartily welcomed. So regarded, there is scarcely a superfluous
> half-page. The very *ephemeridae* have their suggestions; the bald sketch,
> scribbled on the rude and shaky editorial table—perhaps an inverted gin-
> case—of a back-block newspaper for five shillings, the payment of which
> might precipitate the newspaper into insolvency, its importance. For when
> the sketches have not the artistic worth of a picture, they have, at least, the
> value of a cleverly executed photograph. He is gifted, indeed, who knows
> his Australia as Lawson knows it; and as in the nature of the case, such
> knowledge and such men must be rare, we who are not among the gifted
> ones must rejoice that Lawson brings within our reach the teeming richness
> and inexhaustible fertility of the life beyond our ken, and crystallises for us
> into easily grasped compass the possibilities that lie in the wide spaces of
> our land. Whatever else may be said of it, certain is it that this book must
> make Australians know their Australia better.

A long paragraph, but it continues to consider the collection from a
chauvinistic and, as Astley himself suggests, "non-critical point of
view." It is clear, though, that whatever the merit of Lawson's
"transcript" Astley was not entirely happy with Lawson's technique.
The criticism hinted at in the aside about "bald sketches," like,
presumably, "Enter Mitchell" and "Hungerford," he took up
elsewhere in more detail:

There is too much here of the merely ephemeral or the paltry—of the odd scrap written with the urgent need for the guinea, or, may I say, without belittling the literary calling, for the casual half-crown? Rigid editorial revision, had it been exercised, would have strengthened the author's just demand upon the attention of the critics, and have possibly rendered unassailable his title to fame as a genuine prose-writer. As a contribution to literature, strictly so-called, the book would have had its value intensified had Lawson understood the duty an author owes to himself of putting a large portion of what he himself has written and published in newspapers or magazine journals, even though one of the latter be the *Bulletin*, into the fire, in preference to republication. Few writers appreciate the potent influence of the waste-paper basket as an auxiliary to their reputation.

There were, then, too many sketches which were "merely ephemeral," rambling on in an inconclusive, inconsequential way. However accurate they might be as photographs, they lacked "artistic" shape. They had insufficient plot to sustain them, which meant a "frequent lack of balance" and "an absence of constructive or analytic power"; in other words, they lacked the manufactured "strength" for which Astley usually aimed in his own fiction. The irony is that it is precisely these "faults" which critics like Palmer and Matthews have much admired in Lawson: his apparent casualness led Palmer to talk of his "natural stride," his slightest bush sketches were seen by Matthews to be among his best; for many critics *While the Billy Boils* represents the peak of Lawson's achievement. In contrast, Astley's preference for strong effects is one reason why his convict stories have become period pieces.

V *"Tales of the Riverine"*

As a final introduction to those convict tales, it is useful to see how Astley's literary values emerge in his own bush stories, most of which were first published in the *Bulletin* as installments of the series "Tales of the Riverine" and reprinted in *Half-Crown Bob and Tales of the Riverine*. The subject-matter of the tales grew out of the years which Astley spent at Echuca, a Victorian town separated from New South Wales by the Murray River, and at the time of his residence the focal point for a flourishing border trade, chiefly in wool, which was conducted by paddle steamers travelling up and down the Murray, Murrumbidgee, Lachlan, and Darling Rivers to the back-country of South Australia and New South Wales. Astley was only one of several writers[23] to be attracted by the romance of the rivers and by the legends that clustered around the boats and the people who manned them. But there is little room for nostalgia, even of a romantic kind, in his recreation of riverboat life. The rivers were full of snags, the surrounding country was barren and isolated, and its inhabitants were constantly threatened by the harsh realities of drought and flood. It is this darker side of things which his melancholy temperament leads him to emphasize, and whereas a central theme in the Norfolk Island stories is the way evil men can transform a natural paradise into a hell for the innocent, an "Isle of Death," a recurring theme in the Riverine stories is the way nature contributes to, and often creates, the suffering endured by Astley's victims. Thus "The Snagging of the Saucy Nell" demonstrates how nature bursts "into one of those grim, ironic moods with which she occasionally tempered her tyranny over the Far West of the Riverine"—"as though", continues Astley in an attempt to be playful, "Peter the Cruel sought his recreation in wearing the mask of Voltaire, or Torquemada that of the mocking Heine." As the story unfolds, flood replaces drought, the Saucy Nell is snagged trying to get a load of wool down from a back-country station to Echuca, the load is lost, the banks foreclose, the station owner commits suicide. The other stories follow a similar gloomy narrative path, most ending in death ("Jim the Rebater") or disillusionment ("Brocknell's Prodigal") or destruction ("The Doom of Walmsley's *Ruby*"), and occasionally in all three. In "In Pugga Milly Peach" the skipper of the small steamboat *Jessie Jane* forfeits his chance to win a race to pick up a cargo which promises him solvency because he makes a detour to take a sick child to hospital, only to have the child die, the mother accuse him of tardiness, and, finally, the boat blow up with him on board. Again, when Archibald, noting that "Everybody in Xmas issue last year *died*,"[24] asked for something more cheerful for the 1892 Christmas number of the *Bulletin*, he was supplied with " 'Bess o' the Rivers',," which opens with the accidental death of a riverboat deckhand. His mates raise a subscription to provide a start in life for the sweetheart he planned to marry and to whom he was sending his savings. The representative of the rivermen journeys to Melbourne to give her the money—and discovers that she is a prostitute.

The point to be noted is that the pessimism in this recreation of Riverine life is conventional and literary, not the "ruthless pessimism "[25] pervading the picture of outback life that we get, to repeat, in the best of Lawson. Astley falls victim to his belief in manufactured power and to his desire that each of the Riverine tales be an expression of a particular "theme." (He jotted such phrases as "tragedy," "crime and deceit," and "trickery and gold" beside titles of stories that he was planning to write.)[26] To achieve these dramatic effects he relies on the situational clichés and banalities of nineteenth-century popular fiction. One result is a rash of self-indulgent sentimental asides: "each square mile has its tale of some human soul going to wreck on its sea of grey plain"; "In the life of every human being there are arcana that may not be unveiled, experiences that may not be narrated."[27] Or having at the start of "Jim the Rebater" described how the logs which start their journey in the Australian Alps sweep down the river and end up as treacherous snags, Astley extends the comment into a swooning metaphor which is the epigraph for the story: "And the soul, too, goes downstream with the mass of wood stuff, and after its journey of a few hundred miles it too falls a victim to the vicious undertow of life, and becomes in its turn a snag, which shall wreck another soul."

Most of these weaknesses can be found in "The Idyl of Melool Wood-pile," which reads like a parody of a sentimental serial. A poor but honest member of an aristocratic English family, whose fiancée has married his rich cousin, Lord Erskine, has cut himself off from society and has been living a solitary life as the keeper of Melool woodpile, his only human contact the crews of the riverboats he supplies with fuel. His seclusion is disturbed when the former fiancée, now a widow, comes upriver. She has been scouring the world to find the woodkeeper and tell him that she only jilted him to save her father from ruin and that now he can inherit both her and the title. Her journey, however, is in vain, for she is the victim of an ironic reversal of fortune. Is his love dead? she asks:

"No", he answered, slowly and painfully. "No, Heaven knows it is not dead. But it is worse than dead—it is useless now. You are too late, Bess!"

"Too late?" she repeated.

He replied to her question by another.

"Do you remember, Bess, how we read *Locksley Hall* together years ago?"

"Yes," she replied.

"You said then that you would have a greater respect for the hero had he carried out his threat to 'mate with a dusky maiden' when he was jilted by his love. Well, I have done that. I have married—legally married, you understand—a half-caste girl from the Maloga Aboriginal Mission Station. Come, let me introduce you to my wife, the other Lady Erskine."

It is the stories with most "plot," then, which are, with one exception, the least successful. Astley writes best when informed by his own experience, and the point is nowhere better made than in the contrast between the exotic, "literary" climax of "The Idyl of Melool Wood-pile" and the first page of the same story, where the reality established by a terse opening sentence ("The time was 3:50 on an August afternoon in 187–") is confirmed in succeeding lines by an uncomplicated description, firmly grounded in fact, which introduces and authenticates the story:

The old *Pride of the Murray*, trustiest of river steamers, was making ready to swing into the stream for another of her profitable trips from Echuca to the Darling. Captain "Bill" Davies, senior and most respected of the river skippers, and the most encyclopaedic of authorities on snags and shallows, currents and channels, and all other details of riverine science, had just stepped into the pilot-house; a deckhand was paddling across to the old and stolid red-gum stump in Air and Westegard's boat-building yard on the Moama bank, to fix the warp to guide round her head; the huge steamwheel had just beaten the turgid water into foam with a preliminary clash and lash; the Custom-house officers had performed the solemn task of clearance; and the crowd of wharf loafers and stevedores' men were canvassing the relative chances as to whether "Old Bill" would let his barge drop through the punt first and then pick her up, or whether he would adopt the quicker but riskier proceeding of taking her in tow. All these things were happening or had happened when one of the clerks attached to the office of McCulloch, the big shipping agent, came rushing up the wharf.

Though the story degenerates from the time Lady Erskine enters to beg Captain Davies to take her to her lover, Davies himself, introduced here and discussed later in more depth, remains a credible character, as firmly placed in the story as is the stolid stump in the boat-building yard. He is not an importation from an overseas romance, but one of the "thousand-and-one types of humanity"[28] who made up what was a cosmopolitan community during Astley's time in the Riverina. Astley cannot write about the suffering and the deaths of these upcountry indigenes without succumbing to sentiment or contrivance; but they *are* convincing when he relaxes with them, picturing them not as the victims of some manufactured disaster but as people who survive by living on their wits or by accepting their misfortunes as "part of things." Perhaps it is too fanciful to suggest that his writing is more controlled because he is chronicling their acceptance; what is more certain is that he knew them *enough* to accept their strengths and weaknesses, and therefore to write of them as people and not as posturing villains and heroes like Dutton and Hughes in "The Strike of '95."

Most of all he is successful with the eccentrics, the itinerants Dictionary Ned and College Bill, or the agent whose particular idiosyncracy is captured in the opening sentence of *Half-Crown Bob and Tales of the Riverine:* "Big, burly Tom McGrundy, with the thirst of a sponge, the features of a red, red nose, the heart of an angel, and the financial genius of a Wilkins Micawber—his I.O.U.s and P.N.s would have covered the Old Man Plain with a pavement of tesselated indebtedness—drove up to the boats as they were raising steam for the trip to Echuca." This is one occasion when Astley's inflated style is effective. The jawbreaking extravagance of the aside and the reference to Dickens are controlled by the syntax and the ironic allusion to Burns. Elsewhere the prolixity makes for ironic understatement or for gentle satire, as when Astley tells what happens when a new arrival refuses to come and meet the goldfields identity Half-Crown Bob:

The tent-pegger was an old Pacific Slope man of the picturesque "Forty" period. Many a muss had he been into and got out of with credit to himself and damage to his adversary, and the "beads" he had drawn and the men he had "dropped" formed not the least despicable amongst the records of the duello as practised by the Argonauts. As he rose to his full length, a very ugly customer he looked. During the exhortation to come and be "interdooced" he had shortened his grasp on the billet of firewood which served him for a mallet; and, as the exhorter ended in what were doubtless intended to be persuasive accents, but which, unfortunately, suggested formidable consequences in case the invitation was declined, the billet flew straight for the exhorter's head. It was followed by a condensed Commination service. Despoiled of its objurgatory ornaments, the language of the service implied that the billet thrower hadn't the slightest idea of "coming 'long"; and, what was more, he would make it particularly hot for anybody who persisted in asking him.

What was the sequel will take longer to tell than it did to happen. It was Bill the Smelter who, wishing to be neighbourly, had proposed to "interdooce" the latest arrival. It was Bill the Smelter who had made the exhortation above reported. It was the same Bill the Smelter who, owing to old-time expertness at "mid-on" in the cricket-fields in his native Kent, had caught the piece of wood as it hurtled fearfully close to his head, and let the sender "have it" before the lapse of a second full on the left leg, a couple of inches below the knee.

"I think yer'll come 'long now an' be interdooced," said Bill, as the ex-Argonaut fell (the limb was broken), easing his descent by more extracts from the damnatory clauses. And the ex-Argonaut was introduced straight away, being carried to Half-Crown's claim in his own blanket, from a fold of which Bill took the precaution to remove something known in camp parlance as "shooting-irons".

The similarity to Furphy in such phrases as "condensed Commination service" and "Despoiled of its objurgatory ornaments" is all the more remarkable when it is realized that " 'Half-Crown Bob' " was published at least[29] five years before *Such is Life*.

Unfortunately " 'Half-Crown Bob' " is spoilt, to return to an earlier comment, by Astley's insistence on plot. It is subtitled "A Sketch, A Story, and A Letter," and the sardonic "sketch" of life on the Grampian goldfields is entombed within a conventional narrative, part epistolary, which tells how the untainted Bob has to give up fame, fortune, family, and fiancée to live on the goldfields and die rescuing his mates from a collapsed mine. And one inevitable consequence of Astley's dependence on melodrama and romance is that the illusion is lost that he has control over his idiosyncratic prose style.

The stories where Astley sustains his control longest are "Dictionary Ned" and "The Incineration of Dictionary Ned," which both grew out of his experience of Riverine life. Dictionary Ned, so christened because of the treasured dictionary he keeps as a means of self-education, is reminiscent of two other characters in Riverina fiction: the bullock-driver Dixon in Furphy's *Rigby's Romance*, who keeps a dictionary in his wagon for the sake of the Latin phrases at the end and translates "non omnia possumus (adj.) omnes" as "there ain't no (adj.) possums in the ole country," and the sundowner Bralga in J. A. Barry's *A Son of the Sea*, who spends each night by the campfire reading his dictionary from go to whoa and can't understand the difference between "iron" and "irony."[30] It is surely likely that some Riverina identity was the source for all three characters and that Astley had heard of him; at least he led his readers to think so by adding a documentary footnote about Ned's original. Similarly, the incident which became "The Incineration of Dictionary Ned" has some basis in fact and is still remembered in the area.[31]

Perhaps because he is on familiar ground, Astley strikes the right sardonic note in each story. He is the omniscient author, casual and detached, settling into the role in the opening sentence of "Dictionary Ned": "Emerson says somewhere that it is an achievement of high eloquence to confer an expressive nickname, but no particularly fine quality (oratorical or otherwise) was needed to attach a bye-name to Ned—Ah, now I'm stuck!." He can't remember Ned's real name, so concludes that he's never heard it. But this doesn't matter—even the least oratorical person in existence ("a Victorian-shire councillor") naturally would have used the name Dictionary Ned to refer to the man who has long carried about with him a dictionary complete with a glossary of slang and foreign phrases and an " 'Analytical History of the Growth of the English Languages' (in two pages)." After ten years he has got to the V's, to "that page that begins with 'vital' and ends with 'votive' " (a temptation to a reader to see if his own dictionary is the same), learning the words and their meanings by heart—ten words a day minimum, a hundred on holidays, Sundays devoted to the glossary.

What surprises Astley is that all Ned's "grinding away at vocabularies never seemed to tinge by the faintest degree of refined colour his vigorous colloquialism." Nor is it clear, as we move easily to the end of this first section of the story, "why he hadn't begun 'larning' before he reached middle age. Once he was interrogated on the point, but the answer, though apparently conclusive, does not appear a sufficient explanation now that we can look back." In order to clarify this deliberately vague statement Astley relates, in simple fashion, the central incident in the story, in which Ned gets the better of the inebriate layabout College Bill, who for the amusement of his fellow sundowners tries to get a rise out of Ned one Sunday by wondering aloud why an itinerant bushworker, whom he rechristens Dictionary Dick, should want to be educated. Ned stands on his dignity, however, and shames College Bill with the rejoinder that he is only trying to make up for his lack of opportunities and that College Bill should be condemned for wasting his education. The section ends with Bill being rechristened God Almighty's Mistake (the new nickname derives from a phrase Ned has used during his attack) and with Astley adding a footnote to explain how God Almighty's Mistake had once cadged a drink from the British politician Sir Charles Dilke.

Up to this point the story has meandered steadily along. But perhaps to prevent it from rambling to an inconsequential (and for him an unresolved) conclusion, Astley tacks on a melodramatic ending. Ned decides one day to get his tattered dictionary rebound in Melbourne, frets during its absence, and in his excitement at its return doesn't watch what he's doing, is crushed by a passing boat and dies after a reconciliation with College Bill, who has given up the drink after Ned's remonstrance. This later part is contrived, but the slip back into convention doesn't really destroy the verisimilitude of the earlier portion, and Astley recovers his poise with a nice touch right at the end. Since Ned's death Bill has remained reclaimed, his only relapse being when he stood for parliament, but having won popular respect he was not elected.

Moreover, Ned's death allows Astley to write the sequel, for Ned's coffin and its contents are used as fuel by the *Currency Lass* to win a race with a rival boat, the *Pride of the Darling*. In comparison with its predecessor "The Incineration of Dictionary Ned" has a tighter plot but the success of the story derives not so much from Astley's macabre ingenuity (Ned is only on board because he had expressed a wish to be cremated) or from the ending, which he gives away twice. It again stems from his cool detachment, which allows him to be gently cynical and helps him to control his style. The introduction is too long, perhaps too "thematic," but it does outline with something approaching impartiality the way in which the river people were inevitably drawn into the battle over land between the selectors and the squatters. After this Astley only has to make a brief comment (of all the men and things involved in the dispute "the most singular item was the corpse of Dictionary Ned") before proceeding to the main part of the action. With Ned on board ("the sight of that elongated object was touching—and a splendid excuse for drink"), the *Currency Lass*, skippered by an independent owner, is cheered out of Hay. She meets on the way to Echuca the *Pride of the Darling*, which has on board Samuel Darke, M.L.C., a squatter, who refuses to allow the boats to race until the *Currency Lass* takes on a group of selectors at Balranald and he sees an opportunity of "breaking the ————". "This was an occasion," Astley notes (and again before the publication of *Such is Life*), "when his old-time bullockese was of distinct value as a mode of expression."

The challenge is accepted, the problem of stakeholder is overcome after a "colonial experiencer" ("*en route* for his mother's Kensington drawing-room") and a bush missionary travelling to Melbourne to drink away his collection, have been rejected, and the conditions are finally agreed upon. In reporting these conditions, Astley blends nicely his asides with his detail:

Each boat to have a representative on the other.
Day and night running.
First through the punt at Echuca.
The boats to start from the foot of Yuranigh
Street, called after Sir Thomas Mitchell's
famous black Yuranigh (whose grave enclosure
was for some time used by a distinguished
legislator as a cow-bale).
No warping over pinches and shallows.
Fair heel-and-toe work all through.
Fuel, cord for cord, taken in at Balranald
and no stoppage for refilling at woodpiles permitted.
And—fuel not supplemented from cargo.

The race proceeds with first one boat and then the other getting
ahead until Darke "effervesces" with "(bullockese)" and "(more
bullockese)" when the *Pride of the Darling* runs out of wood. So
does the *Currency Lass* and it is then, with both boats drifting
slowly in sight of the finishing line, that her skipper grants Ned his
cremation in order to provide his boat with enough fuel to win the
race. The selectors claim their winnings from the stakeholder, who
overrules Darke's objection that Ned was cargo, and as in "Dictionary Ned" Astley ends on a gently mocking note. The Methodist
Cornish Jim, a deckhand on the *Currency Lass*, who had earlier
objected to having Ned on board because it "worm't natural," now
thinks that the Almighty knew what He was doing after all. Like
most men, Astley concludes, "Cornish Jim approved of the Almighty's dealings with him when he was on the winning side."
    Whether Astley's own preference would have been for something
less artless and more "artistic" like "The Idyl of Melool Wood-pile,"
"Dictionary Ned" and "The Incineration of Dictionary Ned" are his
best Riverine tales, the only two which are not for the most part
traditional melodrama dressed up as bush stories. They rank with
the best convict stories and are convincing, to repeat, because
Astley allowed himself to write of what he knew, to be informed by
his experience and imagination rather than by his reading and by
literary convention.
    With the convict stories, however, the issues are less clear-cut.
Because they were pieces of historical fiction, Astley had to take
account in some measure of his reading; his experience of the convict system was at best second hand. Moreover, the very nature of

the System meant that there was little chance of avoiding melodrama, even in the lighter tales. The extent to which the convict stories are also convincing (and that is an important question in an assessment of any piece of historical fiction) depends in no small measure on how well he resolved these additional difficulties, given the conceptions about literature which he brought to bear on all his creative writing.

CHAPTER 4

A Survey of the Convict Stories

IN all, Astley wrote ninety-four stories of convict life,[1] and any survey of them must recognize that with few exceptions[2] they were first published in one of five series: the *Bulletin*'s "Tales of the System," "Tales of the Old Regime," "Tales of Old Sydney," and "Tales of the Early Days," and *Truth*'s "Tales of the Isle of Death." These were all self-contained series with significant differences among them, particularly in the number of stories included (ranging from thirteen "Tales of the Isle of Death" to twenty-five "Tales of the System") and in the locations which Astley used. Thus the setting for most "Tales of Old Sydney" is obviously Sydney, the setting for most "Tales of the Old Regime" is Tasmania, and the setting for most "Tales of the Isle of Death" is Norfolk Island. (In the other two series the net is cast wider.) Similarly, there are different central characters in each series because there is a regular cast for each geographical area. Commandant Scragge and the Anglican parson, Taylor, dominate the Norfolk Island stories and therefore "Tales of the Isle of Death"; the colonial club loungers Flicker and Warphy, forger Pounce, and magistrate Slyde dominate the Sydney stories and therefore "Tales of Old Sydney"; soldiers Banks, Darrell, and Rossell dominate the Port Arthur and Macquarie Harbour stories and therefore "Tales of the Old Regime," with the exception of the Hobart stories, in which another Anglican parson, Theophilus Ford, usually makes an appearance.[3] Finally, the environment of the stories influences the way Astley brings the System into focus. In "Tales of the Old Regime" and "Tales of the Isle of Death" he is primarily concerned with its operation at the closed institutions, Norfolk Island, Macquarie Harbour, and Port Arthur, while in "Tales of Old Sydney," "Tales of the Early Days," and "Tales of the System" he is just as interested in its operation within the framework of an emerging free society.

71

These differences are obvious enough, yet they should not be allowed to conceal more important similarities in the five series. That there are different characters in each series is less significant than the fact that in each characters appear again and again: thus Scragge, who appears in all but one of the "Tales of the Isle of Death," occupies the same role as Pounce in "Tales of Old Sydney" and Bankes and Rossell in "Tales of the Old Regime." Again, that there were *five* series of stories is less significant than the fact that the stories were part of *a* series, and that all five series were organized along parallel lines—the same titles, the same internal groupings,[4] and so on. Not that this is surprising as far as the *Bulletin* stories were concerned, for they were concentrated into the years 1890, 1891, and 1892, and in one of those years two series alternated; what is interesting is how little different the *Truth* stories are.[5] Finally, although Astley moves from the free settlements to the secondary punishment centers, his convicts endure similar experiences whatever their location and social position, assigned servant at one end of the scale, incarcerated felon at the other. In all his convict stories Astley is preoccupied with the evils of the convict system. In broader terms, he is preoccupied with the suffering which results from man's inhumanity to man.

I *Astley and Clarke*

Such a preoccupation can partly be explained by Astley's determination to score a political point, to show that the convicts were an oppressed social class. But a more obvious explanation is that the convict system *was* brutal and inhumane; indeed, the brutality and inhumanity it generated have fascinated all the novelists who have turned to Australia's "ballad-like and tragic history," as William Hay put it.[6] Evil and suffering are important themes not only in Astley's stories but also in Caroline Leakey's *The Broad Arrow*, in James Tucker's *Ralph Rashleigh*, in Hay's *The Escape of the Notorious Sir William Heans*, in Clarke's *For the Term of his Natural Life*, in J. B. O'Reilly's *Moondyne*, in Hal Porter's *The Tilted Cross*, and in Thomas Keneally's *Bring Larks and Heroes*, to name the most important convict novels.[7] The difference between these works and Astley's stories is that in each of the former the central character is usually a convict,[8] whereas no one convict (with the special exception of forger Pounce)[9] detains Astley's attention for long, and in many stories his main character is not a convict but a penal official

(Scragge, Arthur, Maconochie, Slyde, for example). The convict novel which is so like Astley's stories in theme and emphasis that it requires special mention is *For the Term of his Natural Life*.[10] So great was its effect on Astley that he dedicated *Tales of the Convict System* to Clarke's memory.

For the Term of his Natural Life has a documentary basis which undoubtedly encouraged Astley to make liberal use of his own evidence, and it has several characters who have their counterparts in an Astley story. The pairings include Clarke's parson, Meekin, and Astley's chaplain, Ford, the cannibals Gabbett and Tooth, the convict constables Troke and Franke, and the penal officials Frere and Scragge; in more than one case these pairs of characters are based on the same historical figure.[11] But *For the Term of his Natural Life* is closest to Astley's stories chiefly because, for all Clarke's "affirming vision," which for one critic amounts to an imperfect attempt to show that imperfect man is capable of re-demption,[12] the lingering effect of the novel is the terror and pity aroused by the suffering of Clarke's protagonist Rufus Dawes, the most famous Australian convict of them all. Dawes suffers in many different ways in the course of the novel. Once his sentence is commuted to transportation for life, he has to endure the privations of the prison ship, and then in Australia he spends terms at each of the secondary punishment centers, Macquarie Harbour (where part of the time he is in solitary confinement on infamous Grummet Island), Port Arthur (where he is part of the chain gang), and Norfolk Island (where he is leader of the convict Ring). Under his treatment Dawes degenerates: he is first broken and then brutalized by his suffering, which is both physical and spiritual and is made keener because he is innocent of most of his crimes, because he is vic-timized by tyrants like Maurice Frere, and because he has several opportunities to compare his life-style with that of the free colonists.

The same things happen in Astley's stories, which are illuminated even less by an affirming vision than is Clarke's novel. Astley is a pessimistic and melancholy guide conducting his readers on a tour that wanders through almost perpetual darkness. That this tour encompasses a wide geographical and sociological area, from Southern Tasmania to Norfolk Island, from penal settlements to assignment and probation centers, from female factories to courts, from isolated rural farms to private homes in the metropolis, really does not matter. The convicts whom Astley visits face the privations that Dawes is forced to endure, though with one important difference. Whereas most of the evils of the System are distilled into the dehumanizing experience of Dawes, Astley's convicts are captured at a specific point of their degeneration; his stories are fragments in which particular evils of the System are brought to our attention. Yet when the fragments are put together, not in any rigid chronological sequence but like pieces in a jigsaw, it is clear that the collective suffering of Astley's many convicts is identical to the suffering of Clarke's most important single convict.

II *The Jigsaw*

In the first vignette to be published, "How Muster-Master Stoneman Earned His Breakfast," Astley takes us to Oatlands in Northern Tasmania to meet convict Glancy, already under sentence of death for the murder of his road-gang overseer. Glancy has been amusing himself on the evening of his execution watching the construction of his scaffold, his pleasure only interrupted by the long-winded ministrations of Chaplain Ford. Next morning it is discovered that Glancy has escaped, having murdered the sentry on duty. Muster-Master Stoneman, in charge of the execution and surprised that Glancy has departed when he seemed only too glad to be executed, is about to organize a search party when Glancy returns with a defiant explanation that he escaped in order to desecrate the overseer's grave—an action which, since he is about to be hanged, cannot involve him in further punishment. Stoneman, however, has the last laugh: as magistrate of the district he has powers which he can now use to destroy Glancy's triumph. To the surprise even of another petty tyrant, Sheriff Ropewell, Stoneman has Glancy severely flogged for the escape just before he is hanged for the original offense. Having been forced to exercise his judicial and administrative functions to the full, Stoneman can feel that he has earned the breakfast which he leaves his office to enjoy at the end of the story.

In several ways "How Muster-Master Stoneman Earned His Breakfast" is a representative story. Although there is more straight narration than is usual, the ironic ending and Astley's satiric asides, and the way he captures one or two moments in a convict's life, are all characteristic. More important, the story presents a typical picture of Astley's convicts and penal administrators. The first thing we are told about Glancy, apart from his name, number, and ship, is that he was "originally under sentence for seven years for the theft of a silk handkerchief from a London 'swell' "—that is, his first crime was a minor offense not deserving the punishment it received, a predicament shared by many Astley convicts. Indeed, as a petty thief Glancy is even more guilty than most of those whose original crimes are discussed. In "Andy Webster's First Will and Testament" Astley suggests that Webster ("a rank republican and a believer in Tom Paine") is the victim of political oppression, like Overseer Cook in "In the Granary," transported for "some aimless ranting in a London street over the Peterloo Massacre." Others who became convicts, it is reported in "A Bathurst Field Day," were forced by starvation or suffering to steal "a faggot valued at one shilling, or a bunch of turnips of the price of twopence"—and some, at least, were innocent of any crime. John Dale, the central character in the two stories which followed "How Muster-Master Stoneman Earned His Breakfast," could not establish an alibi for the crime leading to his transportation because, like Rufus Dawes, "to have done so would have been to blast the fair fame of a woman." In all these stories Astley states the so-called crime, usually as an aside, and leaves it at that, but in "The Evolution of Convict Hendy" and in "Convict Smith the Second" the incidents leading to the transportation of the protagonist form an important part of the narrative. Both convicts have been high-spirited youths caught up in youthful escapades: Hendy takes part in a poaching adventure led by an elder brother, Smith borrows a horse to complete a surveying assignment and is charged with theft. As with Glancy, the sentence far exceeds the seriousness of the offense. Both might have received a far lighter punishment, Astley suggests, had it not been for the severity of the magistrates before whom they appear.

Whether petty thieves, political agitators, penniless citizens, or exuberant youths, Astley's convicts are presented always as the victims of a harsh criminal code; so in "Bob Warphy's Kindly Deed" "the summer Assizes and the Old Bailey Sessions" are pictured as "working harmoniously together in the good work of freeing Merrie England from the rabbit-poachers, the turnip-stealers, the pocket-handkerchief-'nippers', and similar hardened ruffians." The political implications in all this are periodically discussed, but there is another reason why Astley is insistent about the original innocence of his convicts: it accentuates their suffering and degradation in Australia. Smith's account of his original offense is made more poignant, for example, because it is narrated to a prison chaplain preparing him for execution. And as Astley depicts it, convicts like Smith suffer because unlimited, naked power is thrust upon men like Stoneman and Ropewell, the penal administrators in "How Muster-Master Stoneman Earned His Breakfast."[13] These are Astley's villains, "Men of the System" he christens them, who rigidly adhere to or abuse the penal laws, in particular the penal regulations, a codification of evil which Astley derisively refers to as the Bible and the Catechism.[14] Thus Stoneman uses his magisterial powers to revenge himself on Glancy in much the same way as Price, in "John Price's Bar of Steel," revenges himself on the convict Danny Duncan, who has taught Price's child an offensive prayer, by secreting a needle in Duncan's clothing so that he can be charged with carrying a bar of steel. In stories like "A Bathurst Field Day," where two magistrates dispense 1825 lashes in a day's sitting, or "For His Child's Pleasure," where a convict is summarily tried and hanged for interrupting Governor Foveaux's afternoon nap, even the letter of the law is flagrantly abused, while in others the rigidity of the law binds tightly those few administrators who retain any instincts towards humanity. Lieutenant Aichison in "The Burial of Govett's Leap" cannot save the young convict Benjamin Tinsley from homosexual attack in the chain-gang caravans because the regulations expressly forbid a convict to be at large after dark, nor can he as Major Aichison in "The Flogging of Fergie" save from punishment a soldier who has refused to shoot an innocent prisoner.

If the book of penal regulations is the symbol of the authoritarianism of the System, the lash is the System's chief instrument of degradation. Many different tortures are described in the course of Astley's fiction: the spread-eagle, the silent cells, the underground mines, the chain gang, and the human tramway, all of which Henry Graham saw at first hand. Even more unpleasant are the branding-iron which gouges the flesh of a female convict in "The Torture of Jane Applegarth," and the iron tube-gag which springs open when inserted in the mouth of convict Robbins in "Lieutenant Darrell's Predicament," thereby widening his mouth a quarter of an inch each side. Again and again, however, Astley returns to the effect of the lash. It is the punishment feared by all convicts, one that brings a pallor to the cheeks even of the incorrigible Glancy. More commonly it is the real reason why so many convicts succumb. Phil Hendy's deterioration, his "evolution," begins with his "introduction to the gory triangles" in Tasmania and only ends when he is deceived by the treacherous Scragge into attempting an escape from Norfolk Island. John Dale, on the other hand, suicides as soon as he is flogged, despite knowing that his pardon has arrived in the colony.

But the most detailed study of the effect of the lash is the suffering of Edgar Mann in the two stories later grouped as "The Pegging-out of Overseer Franke." Mann, "gently-born," transported because he was "probably bearing the brunt of some rich or great man's crime," has the misfortune to be consigned to the gang in charge of Phillip Franke, an emancipist overseer who has sold his birthright to the System. Mann resists Franke's taunts and insults because he knows that "he was done for once the cat stung him. He would no longer be a man—a human being; he would be an animal that cringed before such a creature as Phil Franke, or he would be a desperate, blood-craving beast." In time the prophecy comes true: Mann is flogged when he goes to assist a fellow convict, and once flogged he becomes a revengeful animal. When Franke is overpowered it is Mann who leads the convicts as they torture their overseer, and it is he who then devises the ingenious plan, a refinement of the torture practiced on the overseer, Huggins, in *Ralph Rashleigh*,[15] to leave Franke pegged out with a trail of sugar leading from the bullet wound in his wrist to a nearby anthill. By leading the revenge Mann, too, denies his birthright; not only is the plan brutal, but its fulfillment means that he has dishonored his promise not to kill Franke. And when Franke accuses him of this cardinal sin of a gentleman, the reply is despairing: "Blast you—yes! You cut the gentleman out of me with the cat. You die!"

Like Dale in " 'Egerton of Ours'," Tappin in "The Commandant's Picnic Party," and Reynell and Felix in "Secret Society of the Ring," Mann is a sacrificial offering to the System: he kills himself to avoid falling further. Convict Glancy, however, is evidence that many convicts became degraded and Astley does not gloss over the bestiality and subhumanity to which they could be reduced. As he admits in "The Wooing of Convict Denham," "Convictdom . . . was liable to freaks of bloodthirstiness" and capable of "downright devilish ingenuity," which is surely part of the explanation for Glancy's escape. So "How Muster-Master Stoneman Earned His Breakfast" is only the first of many vignettes which show the degradation of the convicts. There is also the perverted sexuality of the lime diggers in

"The Torture of Jane Applegarth" and the road diggers in "The Burial at Govett's Leap"; the brutality of the convicts who, like Franke, join the administration and become convict constables, overseers, and police runners; the mob violence of the probation gang in "The Ross Gang 'Yarner'-ship," who make new arrivals run the gauntlet; the cannibalism in "The Wearing of the 'Shoes of Death' "; the treachery in "The Liberation of the First Three" and "The Liberation of the Other Three." But the treachery, corruption, and cruelty are perfectly understandable to Astley. They demonstrate "how dreadful a Thing the System had made."[16] They are inevitable when such power is entrusted to some people that they can treat other human beings as animals, to be worked or brought to heel and if recalcitrant to be lashed, leg-roped, or corralled. To be treated thus is to be denied basic human rights.

Astley's use of animal imagery constantly emphasizes this denial, and he is nowhere more emphatic than in "Mr. Slyde's Auction." The title of the story refers to the private auctions which Ernest Slyde regularly holds for the benefit of those sections of the free population whose corruption is revealed in the early scenes of the story. The goods to be auctioned are the newly-arrived female transports selected by Slyde for disposal as mistresses to his commercial and governmental colleagues. (The residue he then assigns by normal legal processes.) So as to be adequately prepared, Astley tells us, Slyde goes down to the convict ship to make his preliminary inspection of the stock, drafts "a list of likelies," and has them sent to his barracks the next day. On their arrival they are paraded in twos several times so that the onlooking buyers can compare their relative merits, then paraded singly, the cackling matron Lucrezia explains, "that the gem'men can size you better, my dears." On this last circuit Slyde's clerk calls out the lot number and a description of the goods (name and length of service), after which the auction gets underway:

"Now, gentlemen," said Mr. Slyde as he took the chair ten minutes later at the head of the table in his own office, "Let's to business! You all know the terms and conditions? The lots will be put up one by one. The bidder of the highest premiums will have the lot knocked down to him. Gentlemen in authority now present agree to facilitate the routine of formal assignment of the transport to the highest bidder, in due course and premiums to be devoted, gentlemen, to the sacred cause of charity!" A smile from every one! The Charity invariably was a tip-top spread to the patrons of the auction, at Mr. Walker's famed Parramatta hostelry!

"Lucy Jamieson, gentlemen," called Slyde, (the clerk was shut out of these proceedings), "a brilliant brunette, buxom, with a duck of a waist, but a devil of a temper if her eyes speak truly."

"I'd risk her temper," said Lieutenant Stewart. "I rather like a bit of a vixen—but I'd like to know her crime."

Slyde touched a bell. His clerk came in. "Find out what Lucy Jamieson, lifer, was convicted for?"

In two minutes the clerk was back. "Murder, she says, sir. Killed her lover because he struck her. Condemned to death, reprieved and commuted to transportation for life."

"Ah, thanks!" said Stewart.

And Lucy Jamieson was passed in. Lieutenant Stewart's admiration for spirit didn't go so far as her engagement.

Although there is no buyer for Lucy Jamieson, Elizabeth Gurtin's golden hair brings a price for her of five pounds, and Rosaline Lodge is knocked down to the rascally Captain Woode after Slyde pulls out of the bidding at three fifteen.

The obvious parallel in all this is the American slave auction, and the point Astley's satiric narration makes is that natural order is as much in chaos in the Australian colonies. It is not surprising, then, that moral order decays among the convicts. Death is a release, welcomed by the condemned in the four mass hanging stories, "The Bullet of the Fated Ten," "Absalom Day's Promotion," "The Hanging of the Eighteen," and " 'The Hanging of the Eight'." It is Glancy again who sums up the attitude of most convicts toward the gallows when he jerks his head at the scaffold and exclaims, "But do you think I was going to run away when I was so near Freedom as that?" The humanitarians like Maconochie, Aichison, Willson, and Taylor, the heroes in Astley's sharply defined world, can do little to alleviate this despair, and in "Secret Society of the Ring" and "The Whaleboat Plot" their specific attempt to instill hope causes destruction; such is the strength of the System. In the former story the success of Maconochie's humanitarian program with convict Reynell brings down the wrath of the Ring on the head of that convict, and it is Maconochie who in fact delivers the Ring's judgment of doom. In the latter, Scragge opens the letter which the kindly Mrs. Taylor has written for Hendy, and with the aid of a hymnal supplied by her decodes the escape plans which Hendy has incorporated into an apparently innocuous text.[17]

The Ring, a convict secret society with its satanic ceremonies and argot, is the clearest manifestation of the denial of the moral order. As in *For the Term of his Natural Life*, it flourishes at the secondary punishment centers, its members preferring the inversions of the society to the perversions of authority—and since, in the words of one Astley convict, "There ain't no God out 'ere—we all left God behind us in th' channel,"[18] the Devil becomes their God and evil their good. In addition, the Ring helps to break the dulling routine of labor and supplies an outlet for the natural justice so consistently denied by the authorities. Some historians[19] have found in Astley's Ring stories an early expression of mateship, that traditional ingredient of the national ethos. Yet Astley is not sentimental about the Ring. The old lag in "The *Henry Porcher* Bolter" tells how his desertion of his mates leads them to swear the Ring's oath with all its awesome power, while in "The Liberation of the First Three" and "The Liberation of the Other Three" the actions of the three coalmine cannibals, who kill the three prisoners with whom they have sworn allegiance and then kill each other, make a mockery of mateship and transform the convict oath into a statement of grimmest irony.[20]

But whatever the System might do to the convicts, its effects are just as damaging for its perpetrators; as Astley suggests, "If there was scarcely a convict whom the System and the Régime did not spoil more or less, neither did they spare the officials."[21] The Ringer in "Secret Society of the Ring" is prepared to go further: the System "finds 'orl its orf'cers men," he taunts Maconochie, "an' leaves 'em orl brutes! Orl o' we don't get 'ardened, but there ain't one 'o *yer* wot doesn't." That is hardly a fair assessment of Maconochie, but accurate enough for Price and Darrell, who rank with Bankes, Rossell, Slyde, Foveaux, and Scragge as the most vicious and hardened of Astley's penal administrators. Darrell, created by Astley "to stand for many who lived and are forgotten," has "the stuff of hero" in him, Price is brave, efficient, and intelligent; the System feeds both through its "dehumanizing press" and renders them calloused brutes. The nobility of Price, for example, is transformed into pure evil, though even he is accorded a rough justice. "The life," Astley writes, "that might have ended at the doors of Westminster Abbey was miserably let out by a felon's hand on Williamstown Pier. He whom the System created, died by the System."[22]

III *Astley's Techniques*

It should be clear from even this brief description that Astley's tour of the early settlements of Australia is indeed a melancholy one and that his convicts inhabit a dark, hellish world. So do the convicts in *For the Term of his Natural Life* and *The Tilted Cross;* Hal Porter, no less than Marcus Clarke, insists on the fact. Porter's convicts live in Van Dieman's Land (Tasmania), "an ugly trinket suspended at the world's discredited rump" as it is described in the opening sentence of the novel. But not only is this the bottom of the world in geographical terms, it is a moral underworld as well. Porter's convicts live under a tilted cross in the sense that they live under the Southern Cross, a famous constellation of the Southern hemisphere skies, and also in the sense that they inhabit a region where moral values, if not inverted, are at least "tilted."

But whereas Porter, the novelist, explores these themes by means of imagery and allusion,[23] Astley, the short story writer, is primarily concerned with incident. Even more than Clarke he was attracted by the extremes of the System, the dramatic highlights. The sensational incident appealed to his artistic temperament, as we have seen, and the sensational effect largely governed the way in which he constructed his stories. Some of them are tautly written, to be sure (parts of "The Bullet of the Fated Ten," for example), while others seem to be inconsequential and peripatetic in the bush yarn tradition. The best of these is "The Felicitous Reminiscences of Scourger James," in which Astley appears as the historian collecting testimony from the inmates of an old men's home in Launceston. And because his main informant has had extensive experience of the System, Astley guides him back through his memories:

"What was the naval cat like? It was different from this?"

"Oh, lor, yes! Three feet o' rope tarred an' resined—eighteen inch rove an' boun' round with sail-thread, an' 't'other eighteen inch in six tails sometimes, an' sometimes nine, with three knots on each tail. It war the easiest to use—long way nicer than the Settlement cat or the Harbour cat. And when I'd done on the *Rainbow* an' got my glass of grog, an' Cap'n Rous'd told me I war an artist—lor' sir, how he larfed as he said it!—I arxed his Honor for the cat, an' he guv it me, quite pleasunt-like an' gen'el'manly. An' I kep' it for a long time, an' used it at Port Arthur once or twice till Capt'n Boote—him as followed Dr Rossell, sir—said as its use war quite illegal, 'cos it war more destructive than *our* cat—'it war 'tensifyin' punishmunt beyond the demands of justice'—them war his wery words, sir—'cos a dozen with a man-o'-war's cat war ekal to fifty with ours, an' fifty with the man-o'-war cut a man up more'n two hundred of System's floggin'."

"Well, that was genuinely kind of Captain Boote!"

"That's as it may be. Wait till ye hear all.

"It war Monday. Com'dant Rossell used to flog most o' Sunday, but Boote was more religious—'it didn't give a chap, who was at the triangles at eight o'clock, much chance of attendin' church at ten in a good frame o' mind'— them are his words agen, sir—an' so he made Monday his princ'pal floggin' day, an' John Price, sir, he liked Monday best, too, scourgers war flasher, he used to say, after Sunday's rest—but there, I'm ramblin', wot war I goin' to say?"

The casual effect, deliberately planned, is repeated in those stories where Astley occupies the same role as James and has to remind himself where he is: "But we are rambling—and Forger Pounce is waiting to be introduced to the Captain"; or, "Here let us digress to remark . . . [a long paragraph later] . . . This is, we say, a digression. And having ended it, we proceed to state that . . ."; or, "But we are digressing. We left No. 6006 reading the documents he had withdrawn from the now unsealed pack."[24]

Yet however loose Astley's narratives might appear to be (and it must be admitted that sometimes the story gets lost),[25] they are nonetheless carefully organized around a number of static, striking scenes. Normally it is possible to distinguish three parts to an Astley story, which is introduced by a varying mixture of topographical description, recapitulation (if the story is a sequel), thematic exposition, and character analysis (or assassination). "How Muster-Master Stoneman Earned His Breakfast," "The Whale-boat Plot," "Convict Smith the Second," and "A Day with Governor Arthur" are good examples of Astley's preference for one of these ingredients in his opening, while in the opening of "Secret Society of the Ring" the ingredients are combined in more or less equal proportions. Then comes the story as such, characteristically unfolded through a number of fixed scenes in which the narrative develops from dialogue as well as from incident, or from Astley himself, who is usually hovering around to intersperse editorial comments. These central scenes, strung together by further editorial descriptions, stage directions, or brief pieces of reportage, accumulate into a dramatic climax which can, as in "The Liberation of the First Three," be the end of the story, though more often there is a short narrative denouement.

It would be wrong to suggest that the stories conform *exactly* to these specifications. "Marie Antoinette's Fandango," which by Astley's admission consists of "a centre-piece and four panels," has only asterisks to partition the scenes; there are many more stories with only one set;[26] there are even some where Astley tells a story rather than sets a scene.[27] Again, quite often the clock is turned around so that the beginning can be dramatic, as in "Lieutenant Darrell's Predicament":

Lieutenant Darrell, of the –rd Regiment, second officer of the detachment stationed at the Hell's Gates of Macquarie Harbour, V.D.L., was in a predicament, in which the element of strangeness while considerable, was much less than that of mortal danger.

Lieutenant Darrell was the victim of reversed conditions. In place of commanding a prisoners' guard, he and his guard were in charge of a score of prisoners. That was the singular thing in this situation.

And the prisoners who had so defied the King's Majesty and all the proprieties as to suppress the liberties of Lieutenant Darrell, instead of ordering themselves humbly towards the officer (as the Catechism urged them), and obeying him with abject slavishness (as the Regulations commanded them) had just placed him in such a position that his life was literally depending upon his own toss-up of a coin. That was the dangerous element in the case.

He stands now in the centre of the rough, large dormitory, with forty fierce, unpitying eyes fixed upon him. He is stripped to the waist—a good specimen of the well-fed English middle-class boy of 19 or 20; and he evidently has the courage of his years and race. He balances a guinea on his thumb-nail preparatory to flipping it into the air with all its heavy burden of destiny on its glittering surface, and, save that his face is a trifle paler than usual, not a symptom of fear is discernible about him. He would rather that the wretches who are environing him with their bodily loathsomeness and the putrescence of their tainted spirits, should definitely fix his doom themselves. He had said as much to them, and that was his solitary attempt at influencing them as they played their murderous game. They had rejected his suggestion. They wished, by a refinement of cruelty, to constitute the young officer the arbiter of his own fate, and their leader had told him so. And the blanching of his cheek had followed upon the convict's retort. A natural and not unmanly question, surely, for what man is there who would not sooner receive his doom from the hands of another, than choose it himself after ten minutes of the dreadful suspense that "fluctuates 'twixt blind hope and blind despair"?

A circle of steel points—bayonet tips! is pressing upon Darrell as he stands there. The stocks of the muskets are held by convicts' hands, and so close are the weapons held to his naked body, that the action of his arm in tossing the coin, causing as it does a momentary protrusion of his back, drives his flesh on one of the points.

The coin ascends—shimmers a golden ring for a moment on the sight—and falls duly to the earthern floor.

The parti-coloured figures—some grey, some brown, some yellow and black—stoop over it, and there is a cry of "Heads! He goes by the left door!"

The encircling bayonets are withdrawn a few inches to let the officer face to the left. The chief of the felon-gang picks up the guinea, and tenders it to the Lieutenant. The plucky boy takes it, and flings it into the other's face with a taunt.

"Here, keep it," he sneered. "You'll be the sooner dead because of it. It's an even chance that any one of you would murder another for a single shilling. It's therefore twenty-one chances to one that you'll be killed now you've got a guinea."

Then he strode down to the door behind which his fate was lurking for him. At the sixth or seventh step he paused, and wincing as his sudden stoppage brought him on to the bayonet again, cast another gibe at the convict: "That's the first guinea, I'll swear, you ever had in your possession that you didn't steal!"

But even here it is only the order of things which is being changed, not the fundamental structure of the story. Having given his readers a taste of the sensational and built up their expectations, Astley has Darrell move to the door and then says, "but, perhaps, we ought to have begun at the beginning"—from which point he now starts afresh.

Another Astley story, and one which illustrates his more "normal" method of proceeding, is "Parson Ford's Confessional." It opens in the leisurely manner of "Dictionary Ned", with Astley introducing the characters and the setting: "It is beyond question," he begins, "that Parson Ford's resolve to keep up the amount of his fee for performing marriages was responsible for the annoyance which visited him on the occasion of our story." It can already be guessed that Ford is going to be more than "annoyed," but the manner of his discomfort is put aside until we are told more about him. Ford's fee is eight pounds sterling, a marked rise on the three pounds charged by his predecessor Knopwood, who being an inebriate was often relieved of it anyway. Ford, in contrast, is "steady, pure, and sober"—though not necessarily a man to be admired, because he is also pompous and acquisitive. The contrast between his personality and Knopwood's means that he is in conflict with a community "in which the heads liked to be drunk by mid-day, where matrimonial arrangements seldom were entered into except for the purpose of securing an additional grant of land or a right to other property, and where it was unsafe for a person to be out of doors after nightfall, because of his liability to be robbed, if not by unofficial criminals, by the men of the watch." In deciding to raise the fee Ford has placed "the coping-stone to the edifice of his unpopular life," though as to the reason why "people who disdained marriage should have been thus irritated" Astley feigns ignorance.

So far, it might be thought, Astley has merely indulged himself in a character assassination of Ford and the frontier community of Hobart in which he lives. But the prologue has more point than this, for with the central conflict of the story now established the curtains can be raised on the first scene, in which Ford and Governor Davey argue about the wisdom of raising the fee. Davey suggests that the fee might prove an impediment to marriage. Ford counters that the previous charge did not produce a headlong rush to the altar, though if it will produce a reduction of Davey's own extramarital activities he'll reduce it. With Davey not taking up the offer, Ford stands by his resolve and is bowed out of the room. The scene is short because the dispute about the fee is to lose its importance in the story. But it has served the purpose of alienating Ford from Davey, who vows to seek revenge for the insult which has been paid him. It is not that Davey is normally vindictive, writes Astley as he resumes the role of commentator, but he does like a joke, and "when by the same stroke he could have both his joke and his revenge, he would have fallen below the level of his drunken, rollicking, immoral old self if he had refrained from applying it."

The mocking continues into the next scene, again a short one, where the Governor is shown plotting with his two mistresses the embarrassment of Ford. Just what the plan is is not fully revealed until the end of the story, but it involves Davey feigning a reformation which induces Ford to preach a strong sermon against immorality the following Sunday. Taking as his text a verse from

Ecclesiastes, "And I shall find more bitter than death the woman whose heart is snares and nets," Ford denounces the iniquity of irregular connections, draws tears from his audience by his description "of the conjugal felicity which prevailed in the palace of the Sovereign" ("he was discreetly silent as to the Regent," interrupts Astley), and concludes with a "most touching peroration": "With eyes alternately directed to the roof and upon the viceregal pew, he thanked Heaven that he had it from the best, he might say the *very best,* authority that *henceforth* the Local Representative of that pure and pious Personage whose virtues added lustre to the Crown of England, contemplated reflecting *in his person and establishment* the example of his Gracious Sovereign."

The sermon disturbs those residents of Hobart who have long followed Davey's example but pleases the wives of two officers who have long objected to the lax morals of the rest of the garrison. They invite Ford to tea, and he, in turn, after they have gossiped about the Governor, invites them to accompany him to the Female Factory, where all three are to extract from the newly-arrived (and pregnant) prisoners the identity of their partners in sin. But the plan comes unstuck, for Davey has already bribed the prisoners to reveal that the parson himself has caused their ruin. To the horror of Ford and his two guests and to the tarnish of his reputation the promises are boisterously fulfilled:

Humming a hymn, Parson Ford walked up and down. His back was to the line of women, and consequently he did not see the startled looks which were bestowed upon him and then upon each other by the two ladies. By the time, however, he turned in his walk, each interrogator had examined her second girl, and as she obtained a reply, she glanced so strangely at the clergyman that he could not help but notice her manner. He put the singularity of the look down, however, to some surprising revelation. "Revelations" under the like circumstances were so common, that they had long since ceased to be surprising to him.

As Mrs. Bobbin interrogated her third girl, Mrs. D'Ewes finished the examination of her fourth. They exchanged a look of horror—then moving simultaneously into the centre of the room, they exclaimed together—

"Oh, Mr. Ford! You wretch!" called Mrs. D'Ewes.

"Mr. Ford, you're a hypocritical villain!" cried Mrs. Bobbin, and she hysterically searched for her handkerchief.

"Ladies!" exclaimed Parson Ford, not believing his ears.

"Yes, sir, I'm glad I came to-day to unmask a scoundrel! Each of these four girls says *you* are the father of her child!" cried Mrs. D'Ewes.

"Madam!"

"And–oh–infamous!–these three girls all say–they–owe–their–ruin to you!" gasped Mrs. Bobbin, in tears.

"And I say the same!" said a girl as yet uninterrogated.

"He's the father of my child too!" said another.

"And of ours!" cried the rest in chorus.

Under this terrible avalanche of accusation Parson Ford was dumb!

Although this is the climax to the story, Astley returns briefly to tie up the loose ends of the plot and to finish with a lovely anecdote about how, fifteen years later, Governor Arthur unwittingly referred to Ford at a birthday dinner as one of the "fathers" of the colony.

With its leisurely beginning, its scenes of dialogue, its sensational climax, and its short denouement, "Parson Ford's Confessional" is a typical story. It illustrates the essential feature about Astley's mode of construction, that he is less interested in *telling* the harrowing story of the convicts than in presenting his indictment through a series of vivid pictures. Most of all, perhaps, it illustrates how deeply Astley becomes involved with his indictment. He is very much the omniscient narrator and editor, who here is confidential and sardonic and elsewhere is informative, pompous, scornful, loquacious, scurrilous, or bitter as the mood takes him. But whatever tone he adopts Astley is seldom very far from his stories, even when, as in "Absalom Day's Promotion," he only whispers his presence like a television commentator nudging our attention toward the significant parts of a procession. Normally, he is much more garrulous, a participating author who assists, explains, and comments, who revels in the opportunity that he has created for himself to set the scene, to record his impressions of the events in his pageant and the characters who enact them, and occasionally to tell his readers a story.

That Astley is so obviously orchestrating the action, and that his stories are so obviously an indictment of the penal system, means that we must immediately suspect their historical accuracy. Not that Astley shied away from the issue, quite the reverse: if at times he came close to admitting his bias, he was equally careful to point out that he had studied the convict system in great detail. This study was not just a necessary preparation for writing historical fiction but part of a massive historical project. The convict stories were only the firstfruits of Astley's labors, "preliminary chapters," which were to be followed by others covering "the whole field of Australian life."[28] Thus at different times in the 1890's he was planning to write about churchmen, governors, bushrangers, explorers, politicians, miners, pastoralists, and Pacific traders as well as about convicts.[29] Some of these studies he intended to be biographies, some conventional histories, and some dramatic, semi-historical (or semi-fictional) "narratives," but the differences in these forms are not as important as the similarities. Although living in an age in which historians were becoming more and more interested in the scientific basis of history, Astley believed that history should also tell an exciting story. Therefore he saw his convict stories like his unfinished bushranging articles and his series of articles on Sir George Grey (the only other historical works he managed to get started): less as literary creations in their own right than as "applied" literature. He saw himself, then, as a "litterateur," a word he used often, making a perfectly respectable contribution to convict historiography. However far *Tales of the Convict System* might "fall short of the standard of graphic story-telling," Astley wrote in the preface to the volume, "the writer feels that he can honestly claim that he has sought to communicate the quality of historic truth. His principal aim throughout has been the preservation of the appropriate local colour and the historic atmosphere, and not the mere presentment of dramatic episodes. To this end he has directed analytic research and systematic industry, and if he has erred in his attempts to describe the subjects of The System as human beings and not as chattels–things–numbers, the fault cannot be attributed to an indifference to the obligations which bind the historian."

Cautious words, some of them. Phrases like "the quality of historic truth" are vague and noncommittal; even the most casual, the most "fictitious" writer of historical fiction aims to preserve local color and historic atmosphere, and usually claims to have been systematic and industrious. But the gist of the argument is unmistakable: several times in the extract Astley asserts the sovereignty of his history over his fiction, and at the end he is less guarded about the obligations stemming from his commitment. Nor was this statement about his historiography an isolated one. In private he was happy, even anxious, to discuss the matter, for he did not need to be so careful and could make quite unambiguous statements like, "Faithfulness to fact is incumbent upon every historian, but considering the extraordinary nature of our Early Institutions accuracy becomes obligatory upon the Australian annalist to a peculiarly impressive degree."[30] And even if he periodically qualified himself in print, the sheer quantity of evidence which he continued to supply about his historiography in later prefaces, in footnotes, and in the stories themselves was such, as we shall see, as to convince most of his contemporary readers and subsequent critics.

Yet any assessment of Astley's historiography does not end but only begins with the conclusion that he claimed his stories were sound history. That he and others believed his picture of convict life to be accurate does not mean that it *is* accurate, or that its accuracy is uniform. (The familiar bias of the political journalist, for a start, is surely implied in Astley's use of such emotive phrases as "chattels–things–numbers" in his preface to *Tales of the Convict System.*) Again, any assessment of Astley's use of his sources does not end but only begins with the conclusion that he was well prepared to write about the convicts. Such a conclusion does not get us very far in deciding just how he wrote the stories; that is, how he arranged and incorporated the material that he had so painstakingly studied, and where his preferences lay within the range of sources that he had at his disposal.

It is to these questions that we must now turn.

CHAPTER 5

"The Average of Things"

I Astley and the Convict Legend

THESE days it is not difficult to measure, at least in general terms, the accuracy of the convict stories. Despite Astley's insistence that he was a "faithful historian striking the balance of things,"[1] his picture of convict life is distorted, whatever excuses may be made in his defense. The distortion is best illustrated in the way he presents the convicts. Half of them are prisoners at the secondary punishment centers, Norfolk Island, Macquarie Harbour, and Port Arthur, where conditions are uniformly grim, and the rest do not fare any better simply because they are in contact with a free society. In the Hobart and Sydney tales their frustrations are increased because freedom seems that much closer.

A typical Astley convict is Philip Hendy, the protagonist of "The Evolution of Convict Hendy," "Mrs. Taylor's 'Letter-Day,' " and "The Whale-boat Plot," a useful example to study because he is seen in several locations and because his development is traced in more detail than that of any other convict in Astley's stories. An innocent youth caught up in a poaching adventure in England who is only transported in the first place because of the harshness of the magistrate before whom he appears, Hendy develops into a monster in Australia because of the suffering to which he is subjected. His degeneration begins when he is assigned to a cruel free settler who inevitably introduces him to the lash. From this point his record becomes "continuous and varied": at Port Arthur, where he is part of the human tramway, he has "the very vilest reputation as a man of unconquerable passions and the most violent impulses."[2] Predictably, he ends up at Norfolk Island, where he is shot after being tricked into attempting an escape from his degrading incarceration.

But although Hendy's treatment conforms to the legend that the convicts were more sinned against than sinning, more victims than villains to repeat an earlier statement, recent research[3] has established a far different picture of the typical convict. For a start, he was more an urban thief than a village Hampden (like Hendy) or a political martyr (like other Astley convicts). He was previously convicted at least once before transportation (Astley's convicts are invariably first offenders who either are totally innocent or have stolen in order to feed their starving families). He was relatively well-treated on the convict ships to Australia (Astley's discussions of this subject state the opposite), and on arrival he was usually assigned to a free settler (the greatest proportion of Astley's convicts are sent direct to the penal settlements, sometimes by mistake, or are already there when the story opens). As an assigned servant the typical convict had several masters, some of whom were kindly (the kind settlers in Astley's stories are still bound by the law, which forces them to inflict punishment). Although punished several times during his service he was not likely to be flogged (very few of Astley's convicts escape the lash) and had less than one chance in six of being sent to a secondary punishment center. Finally, he usually secured a ticket of leave within three years and if his behavior was fair he was granted a conditional pardon before the expiration of his full sentence. (Some of Astley's convicts receive pardons, but most lose them before the end of the story; others receive pardons to which they are not entitled or, more characteristically, do not receive pardons to which they *are* entitled.)

The experiences of the run-of-the-mill Australian convict, then, were far less severe than those of Astley's run-of-the-mill convict, Philip Hendy, let alone the experiences faced by Astley's most durable convict, Jane Applegarth, who in the first of three unforgettable stories[4] is sent to Macquarie Harbour by mistake after the records have been doctored by a commandant in search of a fresh mistress. Her refusal to be seduced and her spirited ducking of the commandant when he approaches her so enrage him that she is successively charged with assault, convicted without trial, flogged, branded "W" for "whore," shaved, and then raped; having thus supped full with horrors she murders the commandant and escapes! Nor does Astley merely chart too pessimistic a course for his convicts, underestimating their original culpability and overemphasizing their later suffering. His broad historical lens can be shown to be distorted in numerous other ways.

Yet even if Astley is not telling all the historical truth, he is at least telling one side of the story. If Jane Applegarth's suffering is so unabated as to be unconvincing and ultimately ludicrous, the kind of treatment which Philip Hendy experiences is not without documentation in transportation literature. As 'one historian has written, transportation "could become a very severe punishment, which it was meant to be,"[5] and for some convicts it was a nightmare. Some *were*, like Hendy, innocent of the crimes that caused their transportation. Some *did* suffer on the voyage to Australia, as Astley in "Janet Guilfoyle's Delusion," Marcus Clarke in *His Natural Life*, and Caroline Leakey in *The Broad Arrow* all show. Some convicts *did* degenerate under the lash, like Hendy or Edward Mann in "The Pegging-out of Overseer Franke," and many of those who were flogged degenerated to the point where they were sent to Norfolk Island, to suffer privations which made them wish to be freed from a worse-than-death existence. Some, indeed, committed capital crimes to earn that freedom in much the same way as the ten convicts awaiting execution at the beginning of "The Bullet of the Fated Ten" have committed murder on Norfolk Island in order to get a "free" trip to Sydney for their execution. Finally, it is generally agreed that at such places as Norfolk Island too much authority was given to the penal administrators, some of whom were vicious brutes like Scragge, and that similar evils were perpetrated on the mainland because convicts were allowed to be assigned to free settlers whatever the disposition of the latter. Assignment *was* a lottery, not a few masters turned nasty in the way that Hendy's master Dilton turns nasty, and their charges suffered great hardship as a result.

So Astley's problem as a historian seems to be one of balance, not one of complete fabrication, and even against a charge of bias he offered a defense: "It is always nice to take the average of things," he protested on one occasion, "when extremes lead to the drawing of unpleasant inferences."[6] Modern Australian historians might not agree with the implications of that statement, particularly those who in the last two decades have established enough historical truth about the convicts for the darker side of transportation life to be seen in perspective, and for the convict legend to be "dropped overboard for the simple reason that . . . [it] . . . is just untrue."[7] Not everyone has chosen to follow this directive: it conflicts with the increasing desire of many Australians to claim an early ancestor. Any convict is preferable to an ancestor more respectable but more recent, but so much the better if that convict is a victim rather than a sinner. Even Tasmanians, who have been sensitive about their state receiving the greatest proportion of convicts, now support a flourishing Broad Arrow society.[8] And, to return to Astley, although the historians have finally provided the information which allows us to say that he did not write balanced history but perpetuated a romantic legend, what is more important is that he did not present a new interpretation of the convicts. He consolidated and perpetuated the legend about them which he had inherited from his sources.

II *The Flight of the Legend*

He inherited it, first, because he was so willing to listen to oral testimony. His comment in 1892 that he had written his stories "from the press or from personal narratives"[9] was an overstatement of his dependence, but in support of his claim are the notes from interviews which survive in his papers, and also, in the stories, a number of anecdotes and asides like that which ends "The Skeleton Banquet." Astley has just finished telling how in the 1820's a champion Sydney racehorse was killed and eaten by a gang of convicts:

Three years ago, the host at a small friendly dinner-party in the Bathurst district, pressed another slice of the sirloin upon the writer.

"Take another! 'Tis Blackdown beef—*you* have not often tasted a juicier morsel!"

There was an emphasis on the pronoun that induced us to reply: "Why, have you?"

"Lord, yes! When I banqueted off Skeleton! Did I never tell you that story?"[10]

It is possible that Astley is not telling the truth here. Just as the old lag in "The *Henry Porcher* Bolter" is evidence that he sometimes invented informants (or at least markedly changed their identity) for dramatic effect, so he may have invented an informant for this story to preserve the illusion that he was writing a typical *Bulletin* "yarn." But even if he is an unreliable witness about all his witnesses, many stories that he did *not* suggest were derived from personal testimony are the kind of mixture of fact and fiction that must have come to him by word of mouth.

A good example is "The Rationing of the Sentinels," in which two

escaping convicts are eaten by sharks, the "sentinels," off Eaglehawk Bay near Port Arthur. Although several convicts escaped
from Port Arthur in this way, and although shark attacks further
south than Bass Strait have never been corroborated, the story
persisted that Eaglehawk Neck was "looked after," in the words of
Marcus Clarke, by "a commissioned officer, with a subaltern's guard
(and a rationed shark, as legends go)."[11] One writer, having traced
the legend back to early penal officials at Port Arthur who tried to
discourage escapes by circulating the story that man-eating sharks
were encouraged by feeding to frequent the waters, has complained
that it has no foundation in fact—if sharks were fed they wouldn't
have been hungry for the swimmers, and in any case the official
records do not show any allowance of meat for feeding purposes.[12]
The logic may be impeccable but is irrelevant; one wonders how
many versions of the story Astley heard from his Tasmanian informants.

The point at issue is not the precise number of Astley's stories
which were written *directly* "from personal narratives" (my own
calculation puts it at about a third[13]) but the extent to which those
narratives influenced his attitudes toward the convict system. His
subjects who had been convicts emphasized or exaggerated their
suffering, understandably enough, but not only they had gory tales
to tell of the past. Astley's papers suggest that most of the free
colonists whose reminiscences of the System were gathered by or
passed on to him felt sympathy toward the convicts and could
remember scandalous incidents like the first South Australian
hanging. The following account of it was sent to Astley by Charles
White:

Father says . . . [it] . . . took place at some distance from where Gvt. House
stands to the best of his recollection, and he thinks the body was buried
near the river bank. The man was convicted of shooting at the Sheriff, and
was taken to the spot—a tree being used as the gallows—on a cart, to which
a drop table had been affixed. The Sheriff was a kindly gentleman, he says,
and was in great dread lest he should have to act as executioner. By paying a
goodly sum, however, he induced a man to undertake the job, although he
(the Sheriff) had to read the death warrant; and in doing this he wept like a
child. The rope was adjusted and the drop fell as the cart moved off. But it
wasn't a neat job, for the man's hands had not been pinioned properly and
as he fell he jerked them from the cords and caught hold of the rope—
getting his fingers between it and his neck; and lifting himself up he cried

"Murder!" As soon as he had fallen, the executioner, who was masked to hide his identity, jumped on his horse and was galloping away, when he was recalled, and as he came back to finish his task, some of the spectators cried out to stone him; upon wh. the order was given for t[he] marines in attendance to "present," and fire if any attempt was made to injure t[he] man, who at once seized the criminal's legs and hung on to them until he ceased to struggle. Father says it was a horrible scene, death not ensuing for nearly twenty minutes—I am sorry Father's memory is so halting, but a long time has elapsed. . . .[14]

Moreover, evidence of this kind of suffering was not confined to personal history but confirmed in the written record, even though the written record was sometimes contradictory. The contradictions existed because during the transportation era itself, when most of what can be called transportation literature was written, the convict was an ambivalent figure, despised by some, pitied by others.[15] He was one of the great subjects of public discussion in the period between 1820 and 1850, when immigration was changing New South Wales and Tasmania from giant jails into free colonies, and those who wanted this development to proceed unimpeded argued for the abolition of transportation. As a central part of their argument some writers cited the degrading influence of the convict and the equally degrading influence of his brother emancipist on the emerging free community. The convicts were regarded as "branches lopp'd for their rottenness from the tree of British freedom," as the celebrated autocrat James Mudie wrote;[16] or as an anti-transportation ballad written in Tasmania in the 1840's put it,

> Shall fathers weep and mourn
> To see a lovely son
> Debas'd, demoraliz'd, deform'd
> By Britain's filth and scum?[17]

Strong words; but not strong enough, or written often enough, to sway Astley. Instead of being convinced by the writings of the free colonists that the convicts were vicious, despicable, and immoral, he held fast to the idea that it was the free colonists and colonial aristocrats who were despicable, vicious, and immoral. Sydney society, he suggests in "Marie Antoinette's Fandango," "was born in corruption, and moved on wheels of bribery, blackmail and hush-money," which is why forger Pounce, the central character of "Tales

of Old Sydney," is so much in demand with the Slydes and the
Warphys. As for Mudie, when Astley wants to indicate the extent of
Kate Latchford's cruelty in "Miss Latchford's Overseer," he has one
of her victims exclaim, " 'Why, Miss Latchford, you're a Mudie in
petticoats!' "

Nor were the attitudes of Mudie shared by all his contemporaries.
There was as much emphasis on the suffering of the convicts in the
polemics written by abolitionists as on any taint that they may have
given to the colonies: the vehement protests of the Mudies
were more than complemented by the vehement protests of the
Ullathornes, the Murrays, the Willsons, and the Wests,[18]
humanitarians who abhorred the degradations suffered by prisoners at the secondary punishment centers. A second group of
writers,[19] including Alexander Maconochie and the Quaker mis-
sionaries Backhouse and Walker, was concerned that the convict
system, if not repealed, should at least be humane and corrective in
its operation. The sympathy which the humanitarians and the
reformers felt toward the convicts was most widely publicized in a
famous specimen of transportation literature, the report of the select
committee on transportation, presented to the House of Commons
in 1838 and usually called the Molesworth Report.

The committee's report, and the minutes of evidence taken from
many sources, are documents containing a detailed description of
man's inhumanity to man under the guise of criminal punishments;
together with other parliamentary papers of the period they undoubtedly provided Astley with abundant and sickening confirma-
tion that the convicts had indeed been scapegoats and victims. If he
needed any further evidence there were the convict writers
themselves, for a steady trickle of reminiscences written (or allegedly written) by such as James Hardy Vaux, John Mortlock, and
Henry Savery[20] flowed through colonial and English presses in the
nineteenth century, even up to the 1890's, when Astley was asked to
oversee the publication of Mark Jeffrey's *A Burglar's Life*. These
memoirs, usually racy and colorful, "emphatically picaresque" as H.
M. Green so well said,[21] were often wildly distorted in their rep-
resentations of convict life, exaggerating the innocence of the author
and the punishments he suffered. But they reached a public in
whose folksongs, ballads, and broadsides a special place had been
reserved for the convict beset with tribulation and oppression. It is
true that many songs and ballads about transportation which are

extant today ("Botany Bay" is the one best known to Australians) do not tell stories of hardship and despair. Most folklorists agree, however, that these frothy entertainments arose in the music halls of London and not on the shores of Botany Bay; and further, that there *were* genuine convict songs and ballads, most of them expressing a fervent hatred of the System, which did not survive in large numbers because they were issued ephemerally or because as treason songs they were suppressed by penal authorities. One long piece which managed to escape into the twentieth century is "A Convict's Tour to Hell," which Astley used and quoted extensively in the story "The Ross Gang 'Yarner'-ship." Another is the well-known "Moreton Bay," which presents a radically different convict to the one abused in the anti-transportation ballads. He is no longer one of Britain's filth and scum, but one of the oppressed and the despairing:

> Early in the morning, as the day is dawning,
> To trace from heaven the morning dew,
> Up we started at a moment's warning
> Our daily labour to renew.
> Our overseers and superintendents—
> These tyrants' orders we must obey,
> Or else at the triangles our flesh is mangled—
> Such are our wages at Moreton Bay.[22]

III *The Legend and the 1890's*

In suggesting that Astley inherited a romantic legend from his sources, we are also suggesting that his sources were weighted in a particular way. In accepting this emphasis, however, he was only reflecting the attitudes which his own age held toward the convicts, for the legend embedded in transportation literature survived the cessation of transportation. In the following period the infant colonies grew to political adolescence and the first histories of Australia, the first interpretations of the foundation years, were written.[23] Looking, as the free settlers before 1850 had done, at the present and future prospects, the authors of these histories were faced with a predicament. How could they write about the past when their main theme was Antipodean progress, and one of their main intentions the seduction of emigrants from America and England to the land which gold had made plentiful? The solution was quite simple: write about the first sixty years in such a way as to minimize the importance of the embarrassing convict origins. As the Melbourne *Argus* put it, "Australasia has been branded already sufficiently with the convict stamp . . . . One of the plain duties before us is to efface this stigma."[24] For the Victorian journalist and historian David Blair this meant, "Better, a thousand times, would it be for the world, if the entire record were buried in eternal forgetfulness"; and he applied his theory in a thousand-page history of Australasia published in 1879. The convicts were given only an introductory note with the justification that "as a repetition of the story here would tend to no good purpose, it will be passed over as lightly as the exigencies of true narration will permit."[25]

Blair's revisionist tactic meant that he did not clarify what specifically about the past he wanted to forget: that the convict forefathers had been criminals, that the convict forefathers had been oppressed, or that the authorities had been harsh. But neither are any distinctions significant. With so many choosing to remain silent (including, Russel Ward suggests,[26] the new settlers after 1850, who quietly and tactfully agreed to spare the feelings of older colonists) and with some authorities taking more positive steps to forget the past by destroying the official records,[27] the climate, though apparently oppressive, was, ironically, such as to allow the convict legend to take root and flourish. With few historical works to correct the balance, the literary recreations of convict life came to be accepted as historically accurate. The spectacle of suffering provided in Caroline Leakey's *The Broad Arrow* and more importantly in *For the Term of his Natural Life* was accepted, in the words of Brian Elliott, "as the naked truth of history." So popular did *For the Term of his Natural Life* become, Elliott claims, that it once graced every cottage library shelf in Australia, taking its place alongside Shakespeare, the dictionary, and the Bible.[28] Soon there were very few people who did not believe in the convict legend and who did not accept, therefore, that Astley's stories were accurate, since they presented the convicts from the same point of view as *For the Term of his Natural Life*. Even those who did not want to discuss the past came to accept, or perhaps to emphasize, the innocence of the forefathers. This explains why the following exchange could take place in the New South Wales Legislative Assembly around the time that Astley's stories were published:

Mr. Dacey: I wish to ask the Colonial Secretary whether it is a fact that the person who is editing the public records of New South Wales has power to suppress whatever he deems right?

Mr. See: I am not aware of the fact, but I will cause enquiries to be made. After all, perhaps, there are some matters in connection with the history of New South Wales which it is just as well not to perpetuate. I think certain documents might very well be burnt. I know that the late Sir John Robertson ordered the destruction of a lot of old records.

Mr. J. C. L. Fitzpatrick: He made a great mistake.

Mr. See: I do not think he did. I do not think that the sins of the fathers should be visited upon the children. I do not think that the children of the men who were sent to this country, perhaps, for taking a halter or a lolly out of an old lady's lolly shop, should be branded as the descendants of felons for all time.[29]

For John See, Premier as well as Colonial Secretary, it was wrong to exhume the past if it embarrassed contemporary Australians, even though the convicts had only stolen lollies. For others, it was right to exhume the past if it embarrassed the English or their Anglophile lackeys in the colonies. And when in the late 1880's and early 1890's it looked as if the imperialists were going to determine the course of the emerging Federation movement, the republican nationalists gave the convict legend a political interpretation to help them in the fight against imperial domination. The most outspoken of the republican nationalists was, of course, the *Bulletin*, which held that a federal union under Great Britain amounted to Australians "giving up our cottage" in order to "go to share the mansion of the leper"[30] and which saw the Centenary of the first settlement in 1788 as a wonderful opportunity to give vent to its Anglophobia. In this regard the convict was a useful symbol, whose dominance of the "magnificent Centennial number," as the January 21, 1888 *Bulletin* was sardonically advertised in preceding issues, can be gauged by some of the titles of the major pieces—"The Day We Were Lagged," "Our Centennial Criminal Code," and so on.

For the *Bulletin*, the point was not whether the convict was an innocent—as part of the "festering vileness of England"[31] he could not be entirely blameless—but that his jailers had been guilty of "tenfold more loathsome crimes," and that all had been cast ashore by an English government to "putrefy upon the coasts of New South Wales." The inheritance was not a free society but one tainted by corruption in government and business and one which retained a judicial system as harsh and a criminal code as brutal as those which operated during transportation. In other words, the descendants of the convicts were still the fettered bondsmen of the imperial taskmasters, their incarceration brilliantly captured by Phil May, the *Bulletin* cartoonist, in two drawings placed side by side under the title "The Same Old Tune (And a Bad One at That)." In the left, marked 1788, he depicted a convict (still a villain, to judge from the heavy jowls and close-set eyes) dancing in chains to music provided by a military piper. In the right, marked 1888, he depicted a bushman, wearing a hat with the letters N.S.W. on the crown and chains marked with the word "Imperialism," dancing to music provided by a smiling, fat, florid John Bull playing a concertina. So clear-cut was the point May had helped to make that the editors hardly needed to offer their bitter toast: "We drink to the institutions of the colony—to the Centenary of blood, and the plague spot of the civilized world. New South Wales owes much to its forefathers." The Centenary was soon a dead issue, but the *Bulletin* remained rabidly opposed to any imperial link and continued to cite the convict past as supporting evidence. Throughout 1888 it published its first long series of articles, "The History of Botany Bay," republished in 1889 as the first of the *Bulletin* books. It was the *Bulletin*'s repudiation of the official interpretation of the foundation years, a self-styled "record of the hanging and flogging customs of the early days," deliberately intended to outrage public sentiment because "such record explains the genesis of our own existing Australian customs."

Perhaps now it is obvious why Astley first published his stories in the *Bulletin* and not, say, in the *Bathurst Free Press*, and why he started writing those stories around 1890. Apart from being attracted by the *Bulletin*'s reputation and by its policy of paying contributors, Astley had been provided by 1889 with clear evidence that the journal was interested in publishing material on the convict past. Astley not only had the same attitude to the convicts as the *Bulletin*, he had the same attitude, at least at that time, on such related questions as corruption in government and business and imperial Federation. For example, just a week before the *Bulletin* had argued that imperial Federation amounted to Australians being infected with a leprous taint, Astley had characterized the relationship in the *Bathurst Free Press* in terms of the absorption of the fly by the spider.

As for Archibald, it should be equally obvious why he was so pleased to receive Astley's contributions. What remains to be explained is why for so long he encouraged Astley to look backward, and why he exercised so little control over the material Astley submitted. Why did Archibald allow four series of the stories to be published when he normally objected "to lengthy or serial matter"?[32] Why did he make so few of his famous "repairs" when Astley's copy, invariably longer than his contemporaries', was submitted?[33] And why, finally, did he allow these expansive, rather old-fashioned historical pieces to dominate the *literary* columns of the *Bulletin* for three years at a time when most contributors were required to be folk writers wielding the stockwhip in a no-nonsense fashion?

CHAPTER 6

A Charge of False Pretences

IF Astley was so conditioned by his sources and by the attitudes of his age that he can be forgiven his bias, perhaps acquitted on the grounds of diminished responsibility, one further complaint about his historiography remains to be considered: the possibility that he was guilty of false pretences. Despite intermittent statements that the stories were "essentially historical"[1] (that is, fair but not perfect copy), more often he insisted that the incidents he had recreated had *actually* happened, and that in his commitment to the obligations binding him he had been not merely scholarly in his research but rigorous in his methods and above all careful in his documentation. The statistical estimations of his research which he loved to compile for editors, publishers, and skeptics were invariably applied to the stories: this, for example, to give the editor of the *Evening News* "some idea of my methods of working up historical matter": "On the average I refer for the bare detail of each narrative, to 50 volumes in M.S.S."[2]

The most convincing arguments, though, came from the stories, where Astley waged an energetic and intensive campaign to win the confidence of readers about their historical truth. One favorite technique was to introduce identities from the past, many of them well-known. They appeared under their real names (Maconochie, Marsden, Macquarie), under thin disguises ("Ford" for Bedford, "Nellathorne" for Ullathorne, "Taylor" for Naylor), or under disguises a little more subtle but with enough strands left loose to tempt readers with initiative to do their homework, make the connection, and become satisfied that the stories rested on a firm historical foundation. In his first story, for example, Astley has Muster-Master Stoneman involved in an incident which took place at Oatlands, Tasmania, "on a September evening, 55 years ago"; that is, in September 1834 or 1835, depending on when the story was written. Any *Bulletin* reader pursuing these leads through the relevant sources would have had problems with the Oatlands and September clues but might still have discovered that in April 1835, in Hobart, Muster-Master Thomas *Mason* was involved in an incident very like the one depicted in "How Muster-Master Stoneman Earned His Breakfast."

For those readers not able or not diligent enough to decipher these codes, there were further assurances of familiarity. Almost all the tales formed part of a series, and within each were characters who reappeared, sequels for regular readers to follow up, and a number of cross-references for the itinerant or forgetful. Thus Astley's informant in "The Felicitous Reminiscences of Scourger James" recalls that he went to Port Arthur in 1832 to work for the commandant, Dr. Rossell:

> "Ye've heard of Rossell—him as flogged his own bastard boy to death?*— but I had no hand in that. An' there I grew more an' more of a dab. I larnt to cross-cut there. So!"

> The Super., for experiment, had lent us an ancient five-tailed scourge— one of the pattern invented by Ernest Augustus Slyde, godson of the Duke of Cumberland, sometime Police Magistrate of Sydney, and distinguished scoundrel+—and this pretty joy James James cuddled lovingly before he combed out the tails.

The reference marks directed readers to attendant footnotes in which Astley specified where, in back issues of the *Bulletin*, the relevant stories could be found: "Convict Jerrick's Death-Mask," in which Rossell has the convict Benjamin Jerrick, in reality his illegitimate son, flogged to death; and "Convict Rudde's Proposal of Marriage," in which Rudde is forced to marry the convict Rosaline Lodge and thus legitimize the infant product of her liaison with the promiscuous Woode, who bought her at Slyde's auction.

Added to these assurances of familiarity were assurances of documentation, for like many writers of historical fiction in the nineteenth century Astley never lost an opportunity to surround his stories with the scriptural proof of his research. Each convict with at least a walk-on part was identified, and although Astley admitted that the names used were fictitious, the numbers and ships' titles that he also assigned to most of these convicts were supposed to be genuine. Also genuine, he suggested, were the reproductions of the documentary record of the System which studded his texts and were typographically arranged as in the original—gazette notices like the one reproduced in "The *Henry Porcher* Bolter," lists of penal regulations, assignment passes, conduct registers, quotations from newspapers, even illustrations. These "particulars," he stressed in footnotes,[3] were copied from actual documents, many of them in his possession. At other times the footnotes explained "flash" vocabulary (the convict jargon which had been incorporated in conversations), amplified incidental textual information, developed into chatty exposés of the inadequacies of fellow historians,[4] or detailed the anachronisms he had introduced, which were minor and intentional and therefore to be excused. After a forger named Sparkler Ned is mentioned in "Marie Antoinette's Fandango," Astley admits in his footnote that "Sparkler Ned, an artist in the substitution of paste diamonds for the real thing, did not leave London, under banishment, for two years after the date of Mrs. Chester's ball"; that is, for two years after the date of the incident he is in the process of recreating. His defense is then submitted: "Nevertheless, as Mrs. Kent's diamonds, lent to 'Marie Antoinette' as genuine, were returned as paste, it is to be presumed that Sparkler Ned had a predecessor in Sydney."

Periodically, then, Astley discussed in this half-oblique, half-direct way the accuracy of his stories. And just as "the search of historic truth" had "forced" him when writing about the bushrangers "to divest the subjects of . . . [my] . . . narratives of some of their more brilliant achievements,"[5] so he had had to be careful when using personal testimony in writing about the convicts. Only when he came across "an old tattered manuscript in a Hobart bookshop" did he believe the story of Jane Applegarth's tribulations, which he had heard years before in "garnished phrase" from an old Tasmanian convict.[6] Further examples of this propriety are the two stories in which Astley appears as an interviewer, "The Procession of the Buttercup" and "The Felicitous Reminiscences of Scourger James." In the first he tells his hostess, an early settler, that he has formed an unfavorable impression of Robert Knopwood, the first Tasmanian clergyman, and presses her to correct the balance: "You know I am gathering material for literary use by-and-bye. And if the incident is evidence of Mr. Knopwood's humanity, by all means, it should be told." In the second he states that the "one almost certain method of detecting whether an ex-convict is lying or not in a narration of old-times, is to suggest at the first *lacuna* in his story some imaginary name or date or incident, and if the fellow is a liar he will instantly adopt the suggested 'fact'. The dodge," he concludes, "if not quite moral, is efficacious," though ex-convict James, who is about to be tested, does not fall for the trap.

Finally, to add to the accumulation of "evidence" and to the display by Astley of his command over scripture, there was Archibald, happy to add his own editorial assurances to Astley's, and even happier when he had installed Astley as the *Bulletin*'s resident historian and could scribble notes ("Dear Astley, do you know what this refers to? I don't," or the more urgent "Astley!")[7] that sent correspondence about Australian history away to be answered. Astley's prompt and accurate replies[8] meant Archibald could suggest, in August 1892, "Write 'Price Warung,' care of *Bulletin*, who will, no doubt, supply the information." Or, when a reader a week later brazenly challenged the *Bulletin* on one of its facts, "M.B. (Camden): 'Price Warung' says that the original Margaret Catchpole *did* die at Richmond in 1819."[9] In return, Archibald passed on snippets of historical information that came his way, gave over part of the busy correspondence column for Astley to answer questions about the stories, and made periodic statements that the stories were faithful to fact.[10]

Most contemporary reviewers agreed with Archibald, even conservative newspapers which were somewhat nervous about the reclamation of the past. "These tales by Price Warung," wrote the *Australian Star* of *Tales of the Convict System*, "are, we question not, founded on fact." "There is far more that is strictly true than is usually to be met with in such publications," thought the *Daily Telegraph*; Astley had not "drawn upon imagination to a much greater degree than in the alteration of names and dates, so that needless pain should not be given to worthy persons now living."[11] Such assessments suited the temper of the 1890's and were confirmed by some historians in the first two decades of the twentieth century. The rehabilitation of the convict had continued to the point where the foundation Professor of History at the University of Sydney cited *For the Term of his Natural Life* as evidence of the suffering endured by the forefathers and felt justified in asking, in a way quite reminiscent of Astley, "Does anyone now consider that the labourers who sailed to Australia with the convict brand upon them surpassed in moral wickedness the politicians, lawyers, and bishops who put that convict brand upon them? Is it not a fact that the atrocious criminals remained in England, while the victims, innocent and manly, founded the Australian democracy?"[12]

What is surprising is how well Astley's history has fared since the 1920's, when the convict legend has been under examination. The stories have been used by three recent historians[13] to illustrate the workings of the convict system and as source materials by Eric Partridge, a leading collector of underworld talk.[14] Literary historians in Australia, happy—or obliged—to work under these seals of approval, have been led by appearances, have seen the stories as "scrupulously based upon recorded fact,"[15] as Brian Elliott put it in 1957. "After the manner of a scientist," Astley has a "mode of presentation which was severely objective;"[16] his work has "a succinct, unadorned quality";[17] he is not a romantic like Clarke but an "uncompromising realist"; he is "concerned only with a recreation of the facts."[18] Critical comment has incorporated the thesis that he simply wrote up the records: he is assessed as a reporter or recorder rather than as a creator, a documentary writer who at best "soundly handled" his documents, "made sparing comment upon them," had "a sense of form that kept his abundant material in place,"[19] but a writer whose passion for accuracy and detail could limit his imagination as the *Daily Telegraph* suggested in 1892. At times Astley's "subservience" to the facts "almost defeated the role of a raconteur."[20] Or to juxtapose two comments of Nettie Palmer made twenty-three years apart: Astley's "trees do not hide the wood"; "one of the drawbacks of the stories as fiction was the author's reverence for literal fact."[21]

Admittedly some of these comments are taken out of context. Brian Elliott, for one, went on to suggest that Astley was not an objective writer and that he conveyed an artificial impression about the convict system. But the only critic to really question Astley's reverence for fact and his apparent ingenuousness as a documentist is F. T. Macartney, who long ago pointed out that he was selective and garrulous. But even Macartney did not go far enough, and although his assessment is sound enough (Astley's method "is to take some phase or occurrence of convict life, supported sometimes by quotations from original documents, and to reconstruct it imaginatively and indeed freely")[22] it underestimates just how free, ingenious, and unscrupulous Astley was.

I *Astley's Methods*

There is no doubt that the first part of Macartney's assessment is often true, in that many of Astley's stories can be shown to be reconstructions of a specific incident in convict history. In this way "Parson Ford's Confessional" is based on an incident in 1839, when the original of Ford, the sanctimonious clergyman William Bedford, was insulted by a group of female prisoners; the Jane Applegarth stories are based on an incident at Macquarie Harbour in 1828, when a tyrannical overseer was held under water by a gang of rebellious prisoners; and "The Whale-boat Plot," the last of the Hendy series, is based on an attempt by several convicts to escape from Norfolk Island in 1842. Or to take Astley's first story again, "How Muster-Master Stoneman Earned His Breakfast" is based on an incident in April 1835, when the convict Joseph Greenwood absconded from a road gang, stabbed a constable sent to arrest him, was sentenced to one hundred lashes for absconding, and received his punishment just prior to being executed for the capital crime.[23] In Astley's hands Mason becomes Stoneman, Greenwood becomes Glancy, the date is changed, and the sequence of events is altered slightly. (Glancy, it will be remembered, is already awaiting execution for the murder of an overseer when he escapes to desecrate his victim's grave. Only when he returns to mock Stoneman is he flogged as well as hanged.)

For some of these stories it is not possible to locate the source which Astley used, either because his reconstruction is too free or simply because he did not indicate any preference for a particular source. So in the case of "How Muster-Master Stoneman Earned His Breakfast" his source may have been the Tasmanian newspapers, which reported the case, but he may also have used the London newspapers, personal recollections, and John West's *The History of Tasmania*, which were sources of similar "potential."[24] And the difficulty of locating sources is magnified for those stories which do not seem to be based on specific incidents but are recreations of recurring situations in convict history.

With all these problems, it is still possible to locate the source for many stories. Sometimes it can be located by default, as it were: the idea for "John Price's Bar of Steel" seems to have come from a well-known transportation pamphlet relating to the dismissal from

Norfolk Island of the Anglican minister Thomas Rogers, because in it is contained a reference, the only one to appear in print, to John Price having punished a convict on the frivolous pretext of having a needle in his possession.[25] For other stories, similarly, a specific source emerges from the clues Astley left in his letters and jottings, in *Bulletin* correspondence, in footnotes, and in the stories themselves. Astley specifies one of the sources for the Jane Applegarth stories (the old tattered manuscript found in the Hobart bookshop) in reply to a *Bulletin* correspondent as the journal of William Schofield, an early minister at Macquarie Harbour.[26] A clue in Astley's jottings reveals the source for "The Ross Gang 'Yarner'-ship" to be the old convict ballad "A Convict's Tour to Hell," text supplied by fellow-antiquarian Thomas Whitley.[27] And a clue, finally, in the prologue to "The Procession of the Buttercup" reveals the source for that story to be the reminiscences of an old Launceston pioneer.[28]

Some of these clues are questionable, particularly the textual ones, as we already have discovered with "The *Henry Porcher* Bolter." And as for the Jane Applegarth stories, even if Astley used Schofield's journal,[29] Jane herself is an invention, for no female transports were ever sent to Macquarie Harbour. Yet the fact remains that when writing some stories Astley relied heavily on his sources. One publication which served him well was an 1841 report from Alexander Maconochie to his superior Governor Gipps, which Astley probably read at the Sydney Public Library and which he quoted almost *verbatim* in "Captain Maconochie's 'Bounty for Crime.' " Another was William Ullathorne's *Memoir of Bishop Willson*, first published in 1887, which proved valuable for two Norfolk Island tales. In one part Ullathorne wrote this of Willson's tour of the island in 1846, when Joseph Childs was Commandant:

The military on the island were horrified at what they saw of the suffering of the convicts, and on one occasion, when a corporal's guard was marching past, the soldiers detached one of their number to let a Bishop know that a man had just been condemned to severe punishment for stealing a bit of bread. This, as the Bishop represented, was a dangerous state of things. Major Harold, an admirable officer, who had command of the troops, after a conversation with the Bishop, with uplifted hands, exclaimed, "For God's sake, go home, and let the British Government know the truth." This the Bishop resolved to do.[30]

"The Crime of Convict Cunliffe" and "The Consequence of Cunliffe's Crime" evolved from this paragraph. In the first story Astley describes the suffering of Cunliffe, spread-eagled in the open during a bitter winter night. Next morning he is discovered by Private Smithers, who has been detailed to find Bishop Willson and "express the views of the soldiers as to the state of things that existed in the Establishment." The sequel ties up the threads: Smithers fetches the Bishop and when the convict reveals that his only crime was to "take some bread, sir, from one of the tables of the 'ospital," Willson smuggles Cunliffe back to his quarters and informs Commandant Scragge that evening of his intention to use the case to convince the Colonial Office that Norfolk Island should be abandoned.

But if Ullathorne's memoir gave Astley both the idea and most of the plot-line for the two Cunliffe stories, it also gave him a description of Willson which he incorporated in a characteristic way. Ullathorne wrote:

No one could come into Father Willson's presence without being sensible of his calm, dignified, and self-possessed manners. Of middle stature, and somewhat portly, he had led too active a life to become a ripe scholar; but he was a man of keen observation, unusual good sense, and great knowledge of human nature. His lower features were squarely set, and indicated strength of will; his mouth was firm yet gentle in its lines; his grey eyes vivid under their firmly marked brows; but the imposing feature of his countenance was his brow. Square and well advanced above the eyes, the upper part presented an extraordinary development, which rose like a second small brow upon the first . . . . Spurzheim was lecturing on phrenology in the Town Hall of Nottingham when Father Willson came in, removing his hat as he entered. The celebrated phrenologist interrupted his lecture, and asked, "Who is that gentleman? He has the largest development of benevolence that I ever saw on a human head."[31]

Astley's version is:

Spurzheim, one of the fathers of the pseudo-science of phrenology, lecturing one night in the town hall of Nottingham, England, stopped in his discourse, as a gentleman entered the hall and took his place in front of the platform. The lecturer turned to one of the persons seated by him and asked—"Who is that gentleman? He has the largest development of benevolence that I ever saw on a human head . . . .

The man who approached . . . was dressed in ecclesiastical garb, very slightly over middle height; a certain dignified portliness of presence, and a manner of walking at once slow and graceful, conveyed a sense of dignity which, when associated with a remarkable conformation of head, spoke emphatically of an elevation of character, and both the capacity to exercise, and the necessity to exercise, distinguished authority. The lower features of the face were set square; firmness characterized the mouth, yet softness and gentleness reposed in its curves; grey eyes, possessing a resilient quality, indicated at once the power to flash their way into the heart of the wronger, and to moisten sympathetically at the woes of the wronged . . . . the most remarkable characteristic of his face was the . . . second brow. The brow proper, prominently thrown out above the eyes, was almost rectangular in outline, but above this again rose "a smaller but extraordinary development," forming, as we say, a second brow. Uncovered when the man bared his head, the whole formation and expression of the features would command respect and inspire tenderness in any human creature capable of being controlled, at one and the same time, by both feelings.

This man was Robert Willson, head of the Roman Catholic Church of Van Dieman's Land, and the man to whom, humanly speaking, the destruction of the vile penal system can be, without fear of contradiction, ascribed.

These opening paragraphs of "The Consequence of Cunliffe's Crime" show that Astley has reworded and rearranged his original to convey a particular impression: that Willson is dignified, impressive, yet gentle and kind. So instead of having "grey eyes vivid under their firmly marked brows" he has "grey eyes . . . possessing a resilient quality," meaning that his gaze can be alternatively steely or sympathetic. More noticeable than the rewording, however, is the rearrangement: instead of the anecdote about Spurzheim's response to Willson coming at the end, almost as an aside, it is placed at the beginning where it becomes an emblem for the story.

(It is unlikely, incidentally, that Astley is being disparaging when he talks of the "pseudo-science of phrenology." To judge from descriptions in other stories it was precisely the kind of pseudo-science he believed in. He writes of Governor Arthur that "the wrinkles of the brow and the crevices between the eyebrows tell that he is a precisian," and of a convict leader that "An intrepid brow and fearless eyes surmounted lineaments indicating powers of organization of command, but a defiance of society could be read in their lower contour."[32] Similarly, he adapts Ullathorne's description so as to emphasize more fully the "phrenological" significance of Willson's unusual features.)

It is clear that in writing these two stories Astley has relied heavily on a specific source, which he has paraphrased and reordered without being irreverent or even particularly ingenious. But it should not be thought either that Astley was normally this reverent with his sources or that Ullathorne's memoir was his only source for the Cunliffe stories. The ubiquitous Henry Graham was on Norfolk Island in 1846, the year of Willson's visit, and the Cunliffe stories are part of the series for which he was the "main informant on the 'inside' official life at Norfolk Island."[33] If the statement is accurate, then Graham is an obvious source for the last part of "The Consequence of Cunliffe's Crime," where Willson confronts Commandant Scragge.

So the two Cunliffe stories do not illustrate a technique whereby (to paraphrase Macartney, other critics, and Astley himself) Astley characteristically took some phase of convict life, reconstructed it, and in the reconstruction quoted or paraphrased certain specific documents. The two Cunliffe stories illustrate what truly was his characteristic technique—one where he took a phase of convict life, reconstructed it (often very freely), and in the reconstruction incorporated material that he had collated from a number of sources—material, moreover, which had been recalled and imagined as well as recorded. This technique was useful when information in his sources was duplicated and essential when his sources contradicted each other, but it was a technique which he employed for almost every story, even if it meant collating materials which had little connection with each other.

II *The Collating Technique*

Any number of stories can be used to show Astley's collating technique in operation. The Jane Applegarth saga, in particular "The Immersion of Captain Bankes," may well have been based on a minister's journal as well as on personal testimony, but Astley incorporates into the first of the stories extracts from private letters and government memoranda. Again, the gist of what became "The Skeleton Banquet" Astley may well have heard at a dinner party in 1888, but in the story there are quotations from two manuscript sources and references to no fewer than six newspapers—*Bell's Weekly Messenger*, the *Sydney Gazette*, the *Australian*, the *Times* (London), the *Morning Chronicle*, and the *Monitor*. To take one final example, "A Bathurst Field Day" may well have been based on the diary of the pioneer settler George Suttor (called "Suchor" by Astley when he quotes extracts in the story), but there are contextual quotations which reputedly come from a manuscript court report, a "footnote to a printed copy of the magisterial court report," the *Sydney Gazette,* and the *New South Wales Magazine.*

In each of these stories it looks as if Astley has had a principal source from which the story derives and a number of subsidiary sources which he used in passing. But this assessment is only correct if Astley's word can be relied upon, which has already been shown not to be the case. In "The Immersion of Captain Bankes" and the two Bathurst stories Astley's reliability is not really significant, for the additional documentation (the newspaper quotations in particular) is there to authenticate, or to seem to authenticate, what are only minor details. But in other stories which can be used to show Astley's collating technique in operation, the reliability of his word is much more important.

Take "A Day with Governor Arthur," Astley's recreation of a typical working day of Colonel George Arthur, who is presented as a stern, inflexible autocrat, a good representative of the System. He is "supreme over the destinies of 32,000 human beings, and he looks capable of dealing justly with 32,000 blocks of pine or gum-wood," Astley writes in his prologue to the story. "That, possibly, is why he is Lieutenant-Governor of His Britannic Majesty's Colony and dependency of Van Dieman's Land. A man with a heart would have been out of place in that chair." The story opens with Arthur's decision to review applications for tickets of leave with the Comptroller-General of Convicts, James Fubster, and, in keeping with the theme Astley has established, these two officials proceed to reject the six applications which are discussed in detail. Two convicts are refused because they have not served the requisite period of assignment, two because they have not demonstrated their reformation, one because he has smuggled a letter out of the colony, and another because Arthur and Fubster consider that a mistake has been made in the transcription of his record onto the application (for which the supposedly guilty convict clerk is ordered to be punished). The review completed, Arthur discusses with Fubster the phrasing of a dispatch he is drafting to Viscount Goderich, the Colonial Secretary, about the abandonment of Macquarie Harbour and the relocation of the educated convicts at Port Arthur. The story ends with the installation of Richard Johnson as hangman, who swears the executioner's oath as administered by Fubster and is dispatched dramatically with the concluding words, "Get thee Hence, Wretch!"

In plot and theme "A Day with Governor Arthur" is a typical story. It is unusual because Astley went to some trouble to separate some of the material which he had gathered and used in the story. "This narrative," he wrote in a long introductory footnote,

is mainly founded upon conversations with a prominent official—he died only the other day—who was for some years immediately associated with Colonel Arthur. Documentary evidence is, in addition, extant for nearly every statement made in the course of the tale, and the words put into the mouths of the characters are mere paraphrases of utterances of their originals. The "police reports" and convict "records" quoted are authentic in every particular; "Longden's" letter is that of a veritable convict. In the wording of the Executioner's Oath, the author has followed his informant instead of transcribing another form which he has in his possession, which, however, does not differ very materially from the former. "The Sheriff's bidding," which concludes the administration of the oath, was uttered, it is asserted, on as recent an occasion in England as the appointment of that late honoured servant of the state, Calcraft.

Just who the mysterious informant was Astley does not make clear, though if he died just before the story was written[34] he must have been a young man during Arthur's term as Governor of Tasmania (1824–1836), and probably was not an intimate associate. A more likely possibility is that Astley got most of his insights into Arthur not from any penal official but from his father-in-law John Cape, a Launceston merchant who recorded his impressions of Arthur three months before the story was published, and who died, coincidentally, the day it was published.[35] If this conjecture is correct and Cape is Astley's informant disguised as a former penal official, then it explains why the description of Arthur's working habits is not accurate. (Arthur was not in the habit of starting work punctually at ten in the morning.) It also means that Astley probably had just one form of the executioner's oath in his possession and that his statement about using a similar text provided by his informant is an attempt to mislead us about the identity of that informant.

What sources are we left with? Personal testimony still, perhaps, though gathered not from a penal official who was close to Arthur and gave Astley the idea for the story and sundry details, but from an old man whose impressions were formed at a distance. A more important source, the one on which the story was in fact "mainly founded," was an 1834 British parliamentary paper, a collection of correspondence dealing with secondary punishment to which there is reference in Astley's papers.[36] The collection contained several dispatches from Arthur to Goderich, including one in February 1833 which provided him with most of the comments which Arthur makes to Fubster about Macquarie Harbour and the educated convicts. Preceding the dispatch was a return for November 1832 of applications for tickets of leave: from this Astley extracted the police reports and convict records of five of the six convicts whose applications Arthur and Fubster discuss. The original listed one hundred applications: the 43rd, 42nd, 24th, 61st, and 99th are those on which, respectively, the applications of Astley's first four and last convicts are based. In each case the preliminary details read out by Fubster have been accurately transcribed, with Astley restricting himself to slight changes of format and to alterations in the names of the convicts and the numbers of the documents. In each case, similarly, the subsequent discussion between Fubster and Arthur is a paraphrase of official comments which were recorded in the original applications. In the main Astley again restricts himself to changes in punctuation and paragraphing, so that for all intents and purposes the discussion between Fubster and Arthur is, as he suggested, "mere paraphrases of utterances of their originals." The application of Cole in Astley's story, for example, is based on the forty-second application in the original, where the following comments of Spode (the model for Fubster) and Arthur are recorded:

> I can only regret that this man has been allowed to join the police. The circumstances attending the rape for which he was tried are still strong in my recollection as it occurred in my own neighbourhood . . . .

> Refused–. This man seems a most improper man for the police; but being in it, the opportunity may be afforded him to prove that he is a reformed character . . . .

> *(signed)* G.A.

Both passages are woven into the discussion which follows after Fubster has detailed Cole's record. Arthur asks:

"Who signs?"

"Muster-Master Mason."

"And your recommendation is—?"

"I regret, your Excellency, that this man has been allowed to join the police. The circumstances attending the assault on the woman for which he was tried are still strong in my recollection, as it occurred in my own neighbourhood."

As Cole has been acquitted, Arthur chastises Fubster for making the charge the basis of his recommendation. The application, nevertheless, is refused:

"Apart from that altogether though, Mr. Comptroller," the Governor went on, as Fubster remained silent, "the applicant must be refused. The man seems a most improper subject for the police; but, being in it, the opportunity may be afforded him to prove that he is a reformed character."

"Yes, your Excellency. Shall I minute that observation?"

"Certainly. Now the next."

The "next" are convicts Henfrey and Porter, whose applications are summarily dismissed before the officials discuss in some detail the case of convict Longden, who has smuggled out of the colony the letter which is read out by Fubster. What Fubster does *not* read out is a summary of Longden's record, which suggests that Longden's career is not modelled on the career of any convict in the 1832 return of applications for tickets of leave. Instead, Astley invented him so that he could reproduce the letter, the text of which derived from a convict's letter which Astley was shown by Thomas Whitley in Blackheath in April 1891. What happened after this is not altogether clear, but it is likely that Astley took a typescript copy of the letter with him when he returned to Sydney, paraphrased it, and then, much to Whitley's delight, worked parts of the paraphrase into the story he was in the process of writing.[37]

It would seem, then, that "A Day with Governor Arthur" is based on a parliamentary paper supplemented by personal testimony and the Whitley curio. But we are not finished yet. Astley's own observation or imagination was needed once (in that he wrote that the clock in Arthur's office was "by Dent, London; you can see it, if not hear it, today in a Hobart public office"), and there is evidence that he consulted or at least remembered his gleanings from a further

half-dozen sources. The most important of these was Arthur
Griffith's *Chronicles of Newgate*, first published in 1884, which may
or may not have corroborated the wording of the executioner's oath
but certainly gave Astley the idea to end the oath, and the story, in
such a dramatic way. The clue to Astley's use of the *Chronicles of
Newgate* is the last sentence in his introductory note: " 'The
Sheriff's bidding', which concludes the administration of the oath,
was uttered, it is asserted, on as recent an occasion in England as
the appointment of that late honoured servant of the State, Calcraft." To have written so, Astley must have read a report of
Calcraft's ordination. The following extract from the *Chronicles of
Newgate*, one of only two books I have found which discusses the
ordination, fits admirably:

> I cannot find that Calcraft was sworn in when appointed, or any exact
> information when the old forbidding ceremony ceased to be practised. It
> was customary to make the executioner take the Bible in his hand, and
> swear solemnly that he would despatch every criminal condemned to die,
> without favouring father or mother or any other relation or friend. When he
> had taken the oath he was dismissed with the words, "Get thee hence,
> wretch!"[38]

Griffith is suitably uncertain (note Astley says "it is asserted"), he
uses phrases similar to those used by Astley, and the extract comes
from precisely the kind of book Astley was interested in reading
between 1884 and 1891.

Perhaps now we are closer to the workroom. Astley's claim that
no story *he* had written had "not been suggested by, or based on,
fact" may still be valid, and the *Daily Telegraph* may still have been
correct in not questioning whether the tales were founded on fact.
But there can be no doubt that Astley protests his innocence too
much. His convict world was not hewn from "rough blocks of black
granite";[39] the phrase is H. M. Green's, a representative critic
accepting at face value that Astley built his stories from great slabs of
documentation though this sometimes meant compromising his art.
Astley's documentation was extensive but his convict world was of
more subtle construction than Green imagined; it was a series of
tapestries, the fabric of which was worked from threads that were
often disparate. And however well concealed by Astley, the
technique *was* recognized by those who ventured nearest the loom.
It was recognized by Whitley, who congratulated Astley for having

"admirably worked" the convict letter into "A Day with Governor Arthur," by Charles White, who felt guilty wherever he had to interrupt Astley's "splendid story weaving work" in order to ask for political leaders, and finally by Archibald, who stressed how the "material circumstances interwoven" with the tales were authenticated by "official testimony of one sort or another."[40]

III   *The Effects of the Technique*

In his own way Archibald was not all that far from the truth, but, strictly speaking, Astley was haphazard, perhaps even cavalier, in his approach as an historian. In that he turned as much toward his interview notes as toward his gleanings from the written record, his methodology is suspect, certainly not scholarly; and although his collating technique sometimes meant that he corroborated information which needed to be corroborated, it also meant that there were times when the historical truth conflicted with other considerations, artistic, polemical, antiquarian, occasionally all three. When the conflict arose, the historical truth was seldom revered in any scrupulous or rigorous way but more often rearranged, or manipulated, or even, at times, jettisoned. In sum, Astley's methods were promiscuous enough to convict him of a number of historical sins in addition to his sin of bias.

For example, *Bulletin* readers comforted by the appearance of historical identities probably did not guess that Astley habitually located them in surroundings in which they were not familiar, which means that Scragge appears as a barrack-master in Sydney even though Joseph Childs spent little time on the mainland before or after his appointment to Norfolk Island. Or to reverse the error, Parson Ford appears in several Norfolk Island stories even though William Bedford never visited the island. (On one occasion Astley depended on the wonders of aviation to transport a penal official from a Norfolk Island story to a Bathurst one set in the same year; on another he depended on the mercy of the gods to resurrect a penal official killed in a Macquarie Harbour story of the 1830's so that he could take his place in a Norfolk Island story of the 1850's.)[41] Similarly, *Bulletin* readers comforted by the mass of detail packed around the stories probably did not know that some of it was flecked with bogus ore. All the stories are riddled with minor anachronisms and inaccuracies, inconsequential perhaps but clearly a result of Astley's collations. And again "A Day with Governor Arthur" is a

useful story to study, because of the errors in the minor details
Astley supplies. Arthur, to repeat, did not start work punctually at
ten; he approved not one in ten applications for tickets of leave, but
one in three; Fubster was never a penal official; a Comptroller-
General of Convicts was not appointed until 1853; and the *Fairlie*
did not arrive during the regime of Governor Sorell (1817–1824), as
Astley states, but in 1837 and 1853.[42] The *Fairlie* is referred to by
Arthur as "Double-Classer," which Astley glosses as a "ship containing male and female convicts." This is pure invention, as much of
the flash language so carefully explained in footnotes to other stories
also seems to be. Phrases like "Cracking a whid in prime twig" and
"the nubbling cheat trick" contain authentic catchwords which have
been accurately translated, but other phrases which Astley uses and
glosses ("Bible," "Dyed rags," "swinger," and so on) he seems to
have invented himself.[43]

Thirdly, the documentary record which the subservient Astley
could not bring himself to expunge from the text is not always
convincing. Some of it is authentic (most of the newspaper quotations, for example, and the reproductions of convict pardons and
assignment passes) but more of it is not: the citation of obscure
records is suspect and Astley's statements about the methods he
used to trace a convict though the records ring counterfeit.[44] Clearly
fact is leavened with fiction, and furthest removed from fact are the
identification marks of the convicts themselves. Astley admitted that
the names he had given them were fictitious; what he did not admit
was that the additional details he usually supplied were also
fictitious. Thus in "Absalom Day's Promotion," a story set in
Tasmania in 1836, he supplies a number and the name of a ship for
each of the nine convicts who are hanged by Absalom Day,
"promoted" from condemned prisoner to executioner when
hangman Richard Johnson refused to "turn off" so many at the one
sitting. Yet of those nine convicts, three are supposed to have arrived on ships that did not reach Tasmania until 1838, 1839 and
1847,[45] and they, with three more, have a convict number only
possible under the probation system, which did not begin until
1840.[46] Of the remaining three, no convict who arrived on the *Asia*
in 1824 was given the convict number 440, the number given to
"John Bond, per *Asia*" in Astley's story, no convict who arrived on
the *Arab* (second trip) in 1834 was given the convict number 687,
the number given to "Charles Argyle, *Arab* (2)," and no convict who

arrived on the *Norfolk* in 1835 was given the convict number 2320, the number given to "James Travis, *Norfolk*."[47] Finally, none of the six convicts whose probation system number was borrowed by Astley ended his career on the gallows, for each was granted a ticket of leave or a pardon before the expiration of his sentence. The convict 8764, to take just one example, "John MacKenzie, per *Elphinstone*" in Astley's story, was in reality William Longden, who arrived on the *Duchess of Northumberland* in 1843, was granted a ticket of leave in 1852, and was drowned in the River Mersey a year later.[48]

Much of the documentation which Astley provides cannot be checked as thoroughly as this. Nor need it be, if a check of the rest only reveals that Astley gave his convicts fictitious names and chose at random their numbers and the names of their ships. But such a check tells us more than this. It tells us that although stories like "A Day with Governor Arthur" were based on documentary material when they appeared to be based on less reliable sources, the reverse applies more often: a story like "The Evolution of Convict Hendy," which appears to be based on the convict records, was inspired by a shipping notice, a column of advertisements, and a news story in one issue of the *Hobart Town Courier*. In short, despite Astley's flamboyant displays of scholarly evidence, his methods were such that the documentation of the convict stories, like the incidental detail provided, is a mixture of fact, half-fact, and fiction. And when we consider the trouble that Astley went to to suggest otherwise, the conclusion cannot be avoided that he was not merely biased as a historian, but also something of a confidence trickster.

CHAPTER 7

The Truth of the Fiction

I   The Dilemma of Historical Fiction

B IASED in the picture he presents, unscholarly in his use of evidence, at best an unreliable and misleading witness and at worst downright mendacious, these are unflattering conclusions to reach about Astley, the historian. But the implications for a judgment of Astley, the artist, are not necessarily all that serious. Most of Astley's English predecessors surrounded their historical fiction with scholarly paraphernalia to give it at least an appearance of authenticity, but the accuracy—or otherwise—of this documentation has not been influential in the critical decline of such writers as Edward Bulwer Lytton, Harriet Martineau, William Harrison Ainsworth, and G. P. R. James.[1] Nor, to bring the comparisons closer to Astley, has the literary merit of other novels been indicted merely because their authors feigned to write from personal papers (as Defoe did in *Moll Flanders*) or because they rearranged established fact (as Conrad did in *Heart of Darkness*).[2] With a writer like Shakespeare, it is accepted that by manipulating the information he culled from the historians Holinshed and Hall he *improved* the structure, the artistic balance, of plays like *Henry IV* and *Henry VI*.

Henry IV and *Henry VI*, however, earn the title of "history" plays, just as Astley's convict stories are seen as samples of "historical" fiction. Like Scott in *Redgauntlet*, like Dickens in *A Tale of Two Cities*, like Thackeray in *Henry Esmond*, Astley has recreated and interpreted a society which for him was historical, a society from which he was at least two generations removed, to accept the criterion of one recent theorist, Avrom Fleishman.[3] (This means the exclusion of novels like *Hard Times* and *Vanity Fair*, which have become source materials for social historians of a later generation.)

And the writer of historical fiction sometimes finds himself in a dilemma as he tries to fulfill his responsibilities both as historian and as artist. For Manning Clark, perhaps the greatest Australian practitioner of the art of history, the division is not all that great, since history should aim to be great as literature.[4] But in practise the historian has certain limitations imposed upon him. He and the artist approach truth from directions that *may* be different. The historian is "scientist" as well as "artist," limited by evidence, the known data provided mainly by the documentary record. Fact is his raw material and although he may become myopic as he burrows into the thickets of facts, the further he strays from these the less his truth is historical truth. In trying to tell what did happen he is only entitled to reconstruct what *must* have happened.

This kind of restriction creates problems for the writer of historical fiction. *A Tale of Two Cities* and *Redgauntlet* are regarded as successful historical novels because of the way they enliven a period, or "express" history, but it is significant that Dickens and Scott were careful not to disturb too much of the undergrowth: *A Tale of Two Cities* has no historical characters (which may well disqualify it as an historical novel)[5] and in *Redgauntlet*, as in most of Scott's Waverley novels, historical personages hug the corner of the stage. Astley proceeds much less cautiously: historical identities like Arthur and Maconochie are active participants in his stories, and he makes so little effort to conceal his documentation that he is exposed by it. There is enough evidence to reach the conclusion that he is a writer of "bad" history.

The paradox is that sometimes the writer of historical fiction must write bad history in order to write good literature. Many historians would agree with Henry James that "life is so untidy,"[6] that sometimes the evidence is difficult to manage and that sometimes the facts can cut across the purpose of the historian thinking of his art. But whereas the historian's art, his pattern of interpretation, must be modified according to the demands of the evidence, the writer of historical fiction may be called upon to modify the historical evidence to serve a higher order of truth. The "peculiar energy" of historical fiction, suggests Fleishman, is that it "retells history in order to make a truer story than has been written by historians, prophets or other artists"; the story is not "truer to the facts," but is "intellectually more acceptable."[7] It is just this issue that Alan Marshall takes up in his preface to *I Can Jump Puddles. I Can Jump*

Puddles is an autobiographical rather than a historical novel, but it does purport "to give a picture of a period that has passed." To do this, Marshall found it necessary to "go beyond the facts to get at the truth."[8]

There must therefore be an area of compromise for the writer of historical fiction. Astley's fiction can fairly be judged as historical fiction only if he is permitted to inhabit the twilight world where the truth of history shades into the truth of literature. He can be permitted his bias and he *must* be permitted some license to fill in the gaps, to extend the historical fact to half fact (legend or manipulated fact) and even to fiction (invented fact); to extend the question "what happened?" to ask, "what *could* have happened?" Again to quote Fleishman, Astley as a writer of historical fiction can usefully be compared with "the restorer of a damaged tapestry, who weaves in whole scenes or figures to fill the empty places which a more austere museum curator might leave bare. But if the insertion is made on the basis of sympathy, experience and esthetic propriety, it can lend revived expressiveness to the tapestry."[9]

If Astley is allowed this freedom, then Douglas Stewart's separating emphasis is wrong—"what 'Price Warung' really needs, especially as so much of his appeal depends upon his air of authenticity, is a more scholarly edition showing, where possible, how much is fact and how much is fiction."[10] Such a scholarly edition is an interesting project, a necessary one if the claims about the factual accuracy of his work which Astley went to so much trouble to make are to be evaluated. But Stewart surely implies too much mere checking of the facts. Certainly our knowledge of Astley's deceits threatens the verisimilitude of his historical fiction, for the genre obviously demands some correspondence with the established evidence. (The contemporary novelist, Mary Renault, goes so far as to claim[11] that there are *no* grounds on which the facts can be falsified.) But Astley's success still depends, as Stewart himself states, on how authentic his stories *seem* to the reader, who cannot be expected to grub around among the records. Ultimately there are more important questions to answer than, what changes did Astley make? For example, why did he make the changes he did—for reasons of esthetic propriety, or for something else? And perhaps more important, what effect do the changes have? Can they be noticed? Do they ever improve the stories without destroying the truth of Astley's picture of convict life?

II *Astley and the Twilight World*

Before answering these questions, the point should be made that if Astley had been a more austere curator part of his tapestry must have been left blank, as can be shown by the way "A Day with Governor Arthur" and "The Evolution of Convict Hendy" were put together. Given that, it can then be argued that if Astley had not woven his narrative pattern from separate threads of evidence, he might have produced a different—and better—kind of story. The profit of such speculation is much the same as that which accrues to a reader who wonders whether Marston would have been a better dramatist had he written more like Shakespeare. What can be demonstrated is that Astley's decision to take advantage of the freedom to fill in the gaps, to extend his enquiry past "what happened," is largely responsible for the success of stories like "The Pure Merinoes' Ball," its sequel "Marie Antoinette's Fandango," "Secret Society of the Ring," and "The Bullet of the Fated Ten."

In the first pair of stories he extends known historical fact, the rivalry between the emancipists and the colonial aristocrats (the "Exclusives" or "Pure Merinoes") in the Sydney society of the 1820's, to a fictitious conclusion: there never was a ball at which a female convict disguised as Marie Antoinette danced with Sir Charles Darling, the Governor's nephew and secretary.[12] Yet the incident is a hilarious example of what *could* have happened, given that emancipists felt bitter about their exclusion from the social gatherings of the free colonists.

The conflict between the two classes is emphasized right at the start of "The Pure Merinoes' Ball," when it is reported that Colonel and Mrs. Chester of Chesterdale have organized a masked ball to celebrate the return from England of their son and his "home"-born bride, and that Mrs. Chester has added a note to the invitations declining to receive "any member of the Emancipist Families." This is not the first time that Mrs. Chester has insulted the emancipists (having once in a stage whisper asked her husband at church whether the wording of the prayer for prisoners shouldn't be "prisoners, captives and Emancipists"), but "the sensation she had created then," Astley tells us with a straight face that he retains throughout both stories, "was nothing to that occasioned by her card." The conflict erupts when Miss Harrington, one of those favored by an invitation, goes to "console" her unfortunate friend

Miss Kent, the daughter of an emancipist. Kent, who has "risen to wealth rapidly on rum," is enraged by this additional insult and sets about organizing a fund to wreck the ball. The money contributed by the wealthy emancipists is used mainly to buy up the promissory notes which Harrington, a spendthrift like most of the Exclusives, has scattered about the town. Kent now is in a position to blackmail Harrington, and to the chagrin of his family Harrington is forced to escort to the ball the convict Ruth Fenwick, disguised as Marie Antoinette.

The ball, the centerpiece of Astley's tableau, is a glittering occasion, attended by most of the notables of Sydney society. The Governor is sitting with the unmasked hostess, "an Imperial Elizabeth in black velvet," the Chief Justice is a Judge of Assize, our old friend Scragge is there as a Greek pirate, and Harrington is in the "not altogether inappropriate disguise of a Bandit of the Apennines."

The focus of attention, however, is on Marie Antoinette, the belle of the ball. With Lieutenant Charles Darling, the Governor's nephew, she forms the bottom couple in the first set of the state quadrilles: "In *Le Pantalon,* her partner thought her pretty: in *L'Eté,* beautiful; in *La Poule,* fascinating; in *La Trenise,* entrancing; and in the *grand rond* of *La Finale,* a goddess! Marie Antoinette had not mixed with the best West End Society for nothing. Her conduct and her speech were unexceptionable. As yet she had not tasted a mouthful of champagne." The last sentence is a warning of the effect of the champagne offered by Sir Charles at supper. And when the toast to the King is announced, she recollects aloud that she once danced the fandango with the King at Brighton, demonstrates how by dancing on the tables (Sir Charles "declined the invitation" to be her partner, Astley reports), and unmasks. The discovery wrecks the celebrations and shocks Harrington most of all, for he has been tricked into thinking he has escorted Kent's daughter. Nor has he any way of explaining himself out of his embarrassment after Kent arrives, most apologetically, to say that he has just heard that his assigned convict had been induced to come to the ball to make a scene. "As we happen to know that the Pure Merinoes' Smash-up Fund had been originated by Mr. Kent," Astley concludes, "we take the liberty of doubting his veracity."

"The Pure Merinoes' Ball" and "Marie Antoinette's Fandango" are light-hearted pieces in which Astley displays his comic skills; in keeping with the occasion he is content to remain behind his satiric mask. The two Ring stories are much more somber in tone, dramatic re-creations of the legendary secret society which was supposed to have flourished on Norfolk Island in the 1830's and 1840's. But again Astley has extended the evidence to a conclusion which is probably fictitious: little was known of the Ring, even by Astley,[13] other than the fact of its existence, and it is highly questionable whether it had the complicated liturgy described in "Secret Society of the Ring" or conducted ballots like the one in "The Bullet of the Fated Ten." Yet both stories, at least the relevant Ring scenes, are successful re-creations of what could have happened, much more vivid than the Ring scenes in *For the Term of his Natural Life*, where Clarke relied almost entirely on the limited historical evidence.[14] The powerful ballot scene in "The Bullet of the Fated Ten" is one of the best things Astley wrote; and whereas in the Marie Antoinette stories he has plenty to say, albeit from behind the mask, here is one of the few occasions when he is content simply to tell the story, to balance documentary verisimilitude with an economy of narration that works to sustain the tension. Significantly, it was a practicing dramatist, Alan Seymour, who thought "The Bullet of the Fated Ten" would have made "wonderful television":[15]

Once more had St. Philip's clock struck, and once more had the patrolling watchmen exchanged "All's well!" with the sentries of the gaol. And the Ten, with faculties tense and alert, moved involuntarily as they identified the sounds. The hour of ordeal had arrived. Those of them who were doomed to die would face death lightly, perhaps flippantly, but here was the balancing of Fates—death or freedom. They would have been less even than the human animals they were if they could have prepared for the ballot with lightness of heart.

The first dispute arose over the order of their going to the door. Only the "Fiver"—the "Outsider"—knew to which man in order of procession would he give the bullet. It might, so far as the Ten knew, be to the first—it might be to the last. Really, the odds were against the first as much as against the tenth, and as much for the sixth or seventh as for any other. Still, the dullest convict had his superstitions. They would all have gone third if they could.

"Go," at last, after confused whisperings that merged into anger, declared Pedder, "in order of age. You are the oldest, Drummer; go 'long. Name your ages; no lyin' now."

No one lied.

Drummer said he was fifty-five.

Short answered next, "Nineteen!" Lewis said he was thirty-six, just over; he had spent his birthday in gaol. Hanley was forty.

"I'm in my twenty-fifth year," whispered McCarthy, "and it's likely I'll not see the end of it." It was a poor jest, but it told for the instant.

Pedder gave his age thirty-two. "That's mine too," said Donnell, "what month?"

Pedder didn't know, and said so. "When was Donnell born?"

"The first of April!" Another low chuckle.

How was that point to be settled? It took but a second to decide. In that instant Blake had pulled off three buttons from his jacket. (It was contract thread, and parted with readiness.) "Here," he said, "I have two buttons in one fist and one in the other? Who chooses? Odd or even?"

"I'll take first," said Pedder, and he felt for Blake's left hand. "Odd!"

" 'Tis even," whispered Blake.

"Then I'll be younger 'n you, Mike," said Donnell, "you can go first." And so that point was got over.

Blake was twenty-five, Clyde was twenty-four, and Entworth forty-one. So this was the order: Drummer, Entworth, Hanley, Lewis, Pedder, Donnell, Blake, Clyde, McCarthy (a month younger he was than Clyde), and Short. Short was the "baby."

They drew deep breaths as this first stage was over. Then—

"No cockumin'," said Pedder impressively, "who is given the bullet keeps it to himself. He is not to say without orders. An' them who do not get the bullet, well, they should die game, 'Ringers' or no 'Ringers'. They'll have had their chance. Fall in!"

They fell into line, stooping, every man of them, so as to hold their irons up and save clanking. Noise would have robbed the ceremony of something of its awesomeness. And they filed up slowly—so slowly.

Tremblingly, the old man put his hand through the spy-hole—which should have been closed, but was open. Open by the "Ring's" orders!

A finger-tip touched his open palm, but—no bullet. And he knew the bullet was not for him.

Entworth followed, and murmured as the warm finger touched his icy palm. He thought for the moment that he was the fortunate one. For the moment only.

Hanley and Lewis went forward, and slunk back into silence. Not one of the four knew aught as to the others' luck or ill-luck. All he knew was he was not the successful one.

Something had told the gang that Pedder would win the bullet, and, indeed, though they could not guess how it would be possible for the "Outsider" to discern Pedder, yet they feared in a vague manner that "The One" might have some occult means of intimating to the other. But there was no sign from Pedder to indicate success or failure as he withdrew his hand.

So they went on—Donnell, Blake, Clyde, McCarthy, Short. Each put his hand through and each withdrew it.

And one alone held the silver bullet, and he was the last to protrude his hand. Short had not prayed, and he had won the bullet!

In these four stories, then, Astley has ventured into areas where the historian cannot safely go. His imagination has allowed him to add to his information, to explore the artistic potential of the established facts while remaining within the confines of historical possibility, to lend revived expressiveness to these parts of the tapestry. And perhaps the best witnesses to his success are historians like Barry and Ward. Aware of his limitations as a scholar, they have continued to cite his fiction as evidence of one side of the story. They have been happy to let him inhabit his twilight world and have approved his recovery of "what could have happened."

But if "The Bullet of the Fated Ten" and "Marie Antoinette's Fandango," in particular, are imaginative answers to this question, other stories are imaginative reconstructions of what *did* happen. "Parson Ford's Confessional," "The Ross Gang 'Yarner'-ship," and "Captain Maconochie's 'Bounty for Crime' " are three stories more firmly grounded in fact than the four we have just considered: each is either based on a specific incident in convict history or can be linked with a specific source. So in these stories Astley's success stems not from the way he has added to the evidence, but from the way he has *adapted* it.

In 1839 William Bedford, Astley's model[16] for the protagonist of "Parson Ford's Confessional," was involved in an incident on which the story was obviously based. Accompanied by Lady Jane Franklin, wife of the Governor, he went to preach a sermon at the Female Factory, where his sanctimoniousness so enraged the prisoners that they refused to let him finish. According to one account, he was physically attacked and both his masculinity and his life threatened. According to another, the prisoners first tried to cough him down and when the warders proclaimed silence, "they all with one impulse turned around, raised their clothes, and smacked their posteriors with a loud report."[17] Both these versions of the incident are funny enough, but Astley has ingeniously rearranged things and the result is a tighter and still funnier story. By moving the date of the story forward so that it corresponds to Davey's administration he is able to score off Davey's known profligacy and lax control ("He had all the virtues of a good governor," writes Astley, "except dignity, firmness, purity, honour, sobriety and magnanimity"). At the same time Astley establishes an ironic contrast between Davey, who is hearty and genial as well as lax and profligate, and the holy-roller Ford, who is pompous and mercenary as well as respectable. This contrast, so well balanced by Astley's sardonic jibes at *both* men, makes for much of the humor in the story, which is climaxed in the scene at the Female Factory. Presumably Astley had two versions of what had happened, either of which he could have used to close his story with a scene of high farce. Instead, he chose to have the female prisoners suggest that Ford himself is a profligate. The ending is still farcical, perhaps, but it is not a conventional twist of the plot. Since Astley has suggested elsewhere what might be going to happen, the surprise is not for the reader but for the characters; *our* enjoyment comes from our anticipation of Ford's discomfort. (And the point is not labored: the scene is a short one, less than two pages.) The ironic tone has been sustained throughout the story, even, incidentally, in the short denouement where Astley ties up the loose ends of the plot and concludes on a characteristically mocking note:

Not for many years was Ford allowed to forget this episode. Governor Arthur, fifteen years afterwards, referred, at a birthday dinner, to Parson Ford as one of the "fathers of the colony," and was immensely surprised at the uproarious laughter his compliment elicited from all colonists present—save Ford.

In the second example, "The Ross Gang 'Yarner'-ship," Astley takes us to Ross in the Tasmanian midlands, where Arthur Athroyd escapes the usual initiation into the brutal probation gang because he is able to recite "A Convict's Tour to Hell," a famous piece allegedly written by Frank Goddard, otherwise known as Frank McNamara and "Frank the Poet," in which the writer dreams that he tours both heaven and hell, finding notorious penal administrators like Logan and harsh colonists like Mudie to be inhabitants of the latter. The eight segments of the poem which are quoted in Astley's story come from a text supplied by Thomas Whitley, who had already helped out with "A Day with Governor Arthur." But it is not Astley's incorporation of the eight segments into the story which attests to his inventiveness as much as his development of the character Athroyd and the situation whereby he can escape the initiation by becoming the gang's storyteller. (The previous "yarner," about to depart on a ticket of leave, teaches Athroyd the poem in exchange for a fig of tobacco.) The first scene, for example, is a dramatic set-piece reminiscent of the opening to "Lieutenant Darrell's Predicament," a powerful piece of theater in which Astley captures better than anywhere else in his fiction the low slang of the convicts:

"Chummy, yer'll have to pitch us somethink!"
" 'Ear, 'ear!" came in a strident, ironical chorus from the bed-places.
"Hi, parson, stir yer pins!"
"Hooray for parson! Give us some preachin', old Devildodger!"
"No, tip us a yarn, but sarmints be blowed!"
"Aye, aye, Chummy, no sermon, but give us a song."
"Vy, 'e can't sing nothink but 'Hold Hunderd,' and 'Vake my soul an' with the sun."
"Well, old White Choker, yer'll have to give us something, quick, or we'll make you run the ranks! You got to do something to pay your footin', if you won't give us 'Franky' "
"Verily, dear Brother Snufflebuster, unless thou art moved to speak quickly these thy brethren in the System will be obliged to admonish thee, and to inflict upon that mass of corruption, thy sinful flesh, the chastening hand of affliction!"
"What, no answer? The right reverend refuses to speak, pals! What shall we do to him?"
" 'It 'im hon 'is 'ead!"
"Stand him on his head!"
"Douse him!"
"Make him dance the bayonets! You've only been out three months, and must have brought the latest dance with you, parson, of course, from home—home, sweet home!"
"Sling him to the rafters!"
"Rank him!"
" 'Ear, 'ear! Rank him, aye, rank him!"
And "Rank him!" had it.

After this come the asterisks and an invitation to the reader ("Let us go back three months—to the time of the Rev. Mr. Athroyd's arrival") which reestablishes a normal chronological sequence; in the rest of the story Astley tells what happens between Athroyd's arrival and his "ranking," or running the gauntlet. The disadvantage of this

opening is that it gives away the ending. Its value is to emphasize
the nastiness of the gang and the unpleasantness of their initiation
ceremonies.

Such emphasis has more point because Astley made Athroyd a
special kind of convict, not an illiterate but an Oxford graduate. It
would seem that Astley wanted him to be educated so that he could
explain the polished text of "A Convict's Tour to Hell": Athroyd has
sufficient scholarship to be able to restore a text mangled by
memorial reconstruction, thereby saving the poem and making
himself even more popular with the gang. But at the same time as
Astley made Athroyd an Oxford man he also made him an ex-
minister, a more important decision because of the ironic conflict
which results. "A Convict's Tour to Hell" is, to Athroyd, an of-
fensively anti-authoritarian, sacrilegious piece.[18] The better the
text, the greater the offense; but also, the greater Athroyd's popularity with the gang, which understands the barbs more clearly. For
a time Athroyd accepts his good luck and reconciles himself to his
moral predicament by not quoting the most irreverent lines. But
finally, as the opening scene makes clear, he refuses to recite the
poem altogether and is forced to face the consequences.

So in "Parson Ford's Confessional" and "The Ross Gang 'Yarner'-
ship," Astley's manipulation of the evidence seems to work. The
problem with both stories is that it is uncertain how much evidence
he had in his possession and difficult to know to what extent his
transforming skills have been brought to bear. Bedford was known
as "Holy Willie"[19] in his own day, and the incident at the Female
Factory is precisely the kind of story which would have been recalled with relish whenever Astley asked for information about him.
If Astley got the story from personal testimony and not from a
written account, it is conceivable that the version of the facts that we
get in "Parson Ford's Confessional" was the only one in his possession. Similarly, it is conceivable that "A Convict's Tour to Hell"
was Astley's only source for "The Ross Gang 'Yarner'-ship," and that
both Athroyd and the office of storyteller in probation gangs are his
invention.[20] If this is so, then "The Ross Gang 'Yarner'-ship,"
however credible, is not a reconstruction of what happened and can
only be considered along with "Marie Antoinette's Fandango" and
"The Bullet of the Fated Ten."

With "Captain Maconochie's 'Bounty for Crime' " we are on surer
ground in trying to assess Astley's adaptations. The story derives

solely from the first annual report submitted by Alexander Maconochie to his superior, Governor Gipps, in 1841,[21] in which Maconochie gave a résumé of his first year on Norfolk Island. He claimed that his humane methods, in particular his "mark" system of rewarding good conduct, had led to improved standards of behavior which were confirmed by the appended statistics. Maconochie's prize convict was Thomas Stacey, a recalcitrant whose conduct had so dramatically improved that a transcript of his punishments under previous commandants was included so that it could be contrasted with the record of his reform under Maconochie's administration.

Thomas Stacey is the "Tobias Tracey" of Astley's story, a convict who defies Maconochie when they meet and who is won over when Maconochie agrees to leave his office while his unescorted wife stays in the room with Tracey.[22] In order to show how much of a risk Maconochie is taking, Astley documents Tracey's record up to the Commandant's arrival on the island, using, of course, the statistics Maconochie had supplied to Gipps about Stacey. Although Astley is mostly content to summarize these statistics he transcribes fully one part of them when concluding his discussion of Tracey's earlier career.

So far, Astley has transcribed the records in much the same way as in many other stories, "A Day with Governor Arthur," for example. But the climax to the story is the dramatic bounty scene, and it is here rather than in the preliminary documentation of Tracey's career that we see Astley getting the best out of his source. In the original, Maconochie told how he planned to have Stacey removed from the main settlement and sent to a timber gang, "and thereby, it may be said . . . 'offer a Bounty upon Crime'; but I am confident that I shall gain more than I shall lose by such proceedings." Astley has taken the phrase "Bounty upon Crime" (which is used by one of his minor officials) and made it part of the title of a story where Maconochie does indeed gamble on gaining more than he loses by his treatment of a particular convict. But if Astley got his *idea* for the scene from Maconochie's comment, he also made that scene much more forceful by introducing Maconochie's wife—the pressure on Maconochie is strengthened, and the gains and losses that Maconochie weighed for Gipps have been made more personal. But even this results from Astley's eye for the dramatic possibilities of his source. "Throughout my first year on the Island," Maconochie had written elsewhere in his report to Gipps, "I showed the greatest

Confidence in all; walking familiarly among them; taking my wife
and family to every Corner of the Island; without Protection."

Finally, the effect of the bounty scene is reinforced when Tracey
recapitulates at the end of the story. To help him, Astley had the
record of Thomas Stacey's improvement after Maconochie's arrival
in 1840, which showed that in February he was convicted of fighting
and insolence, and in October of "Attempting to break into Mrs.
Wholegan's Shop with a crowbar." (His third offense, in March
1841, led Maconochie to decide to remove him to the timber gang.)
Because Astley's bounty scene takes place in February 1840, the day
after Maconochie's arrival, there was no need to mention Stacey's
first and third offenses. The Wholegan incident, however, was used
to conclude the story. After Tracey's defenses have been broken
down by Maconochie's trust, Astley takes up the narrative:

> Not all at once did Tracey, after that supreme instance of trust, come back
> to the path of well-doing. His fight, however, against his past was strenu-
> ous.

> It was in February that Captain Maconochie trusted him. And till the
> 23rd October of the year following, he kept almost a clear record. "View"
> sentences had ceased entirely, and to the extreme disgust of the gentlemen
> possessing a more extensive acquaintance with the System than Captain
> Maconochie, Mr. Tobias Tracey declined to preserve by frequent atten-
> dances at court his average of "offences needing formal trial".

> Mr. D.A.C.G. Shanks, on 23rd October, applied to the Superintendent
> for a trust man to handle some stores. And Mr. D.A.C.G. Shanks, being in
> an unbending, not to say affable mood, condescended to pass a pleasant
> word with the trusty man commissioned by the Super. to wait upon his
> Commissaryship.
> "You're Tracey?"
> "Yes, Sir!" with a salute.
> Mr. Shanks laughed. "You're the man the Super. trusted the day after he
> took charge—trusted his wife with?"

> There was conscious pride in Tracey's voice as he replied,
> "He did, Sir!"
> "Why, you donkey, he held a cocked musket in his hands all the time!
> Fine lot of trust in that, wasn't there?"
> Convict Tracey was stunned. "Are yer a-speakin' of th' truth, sir?"

With a brutal oath Mr. Deputy-Assistant-Commissary-General Shanks affirmed that he was.

* * * * *

That same evening Tracey broke into Mrs. Wholegan's store with a crowbar.

This short denouement is a fitting ending to the story: tonally, because it balances the preceding scene, the emotionally-charged confrontation between Tracey and Maconochie; thematically, because it is an officious man of the System, the four-initialled terror Shanks, who really betrays Maconochie's trust. As for the final sentence, Astley only needs to suggest Tracey's future career; to have written more would have weakened the impact of the story. Probably Astley was influenced at this point by not knowing what had happened to Stacey, who was never mentioned in later reports by Maconochie. But what is more important is his control over Maconochie's *first* report, even to the point in this instance of making minor changes in chronology. By selecting the most suitable of Stacey's three offenses and by placing it in October 1841 instead of October 1840, Astley has strengthened the contrast between Tracey's career after the bounty scene and his career after Shanks's betrayal.

To return, then, to the questions posed earlier in this chapter. The last two are easiest to answer: Astley's manipulation of the historical evidence cannot often be noticed, and his changes improve some stories (not only those discussed, but others like "Mr. Slyde's Auction," "The Felicitous Reminiscences of Scourger James," and "Absalom Day's Promotion")[23] without destroying their credibility, or "truth." As to why Astley made the changes he did to the record there are several explanations, but it must surely be clear that sometimes his additions and subtractions were based on esthetic considerations, in particular his awareness of the need to exploit the dramatic potential of the material that his antiquarian's net had gathered in. Sometimes, then, his creative skills allowed him to harness the power which lay in the records. To be sure, the effect is usually intended to be powerful, for the world Astley creates is always a world of suspense, excitement, violence, and tension; even his most subtle scenes are melodramatic period pieces, with their serial-like trappings and their dramatic dashes, asterisks, and exclamations, and even in his lighter pieces there is the inevitable climactic big bang. But as John Barnes has said of the scenes in *For the Term of his Natural Life*, at their best they are first-rate melodrama;[24] they have an atavistic, atmospheric power that can still make our flesh creep. And if it is accepted that Astley's stories are melodramatic, even Gothic, that their creator is using staple nineteenth-century conventions, then perhaps it is easier to accept that he is so obviously overstating his indictment, that his reconstruction and interpretation of the past are only one side of the story.

III   *"The Historical Concreteness of the Atmosphere"*

Our acceptance of the extreme situations in which Astley's characters find themselves is made even easier by his second great skill, his ability to create a credible external world. Despite the bond of confidence between reader and author being stretched thin by our knowledge of Astley's idiosyncrasies as a scholar, it is doubtful that the bond is ever broken just for that reason. It is important to remember here not that Astley mixed fact with fiction but that there is enough fact for readers not to notice the sins of commission and omission. (So if we point out the incidental details that Astley got wrong in "A Day with Governor Arthur", those he got right must also be cited: the population figures, the physical description of Arthur, and so on.)[25] It is not enough to say, then, that Astley introduced great slabs of "evidence" under false pretences; it also must be admitted that the blending and the arrangement are convincing. The acceptance by Nettie Palmer, Morris Miller, and others that Astley merely "wrote up the records" is a useful reminder not merely that he perpetrated a confidence trick, but of *how well* he perpetrated it.

How could they—or we—think otherwise, given Astley's attention to detail: his authoritative statistics, his accumulation of corroborative documentation, his use of familiar names and places, his selection of significant fact (some of it seemingly quite inconsequential), the way he moves through the records almost as a contemporary? Even more important is the way he organized this detail to create a "historical concreteness of atmosphere," of the kind George Lukacs found[26] in Sir Walter Scott's work. Astley's feigned propriety in "The Felicitous Reminiscences of Scourger James" has already been mentioned, but this was just one of several editorial techniques he employed to persuade readers to suspend their disbelief. A more common tactic was for Astley to appear ingenuous and confident, punctuating his narratives with the kind of parenthetical comment which still brings the System alive, as in the opening of "The Amour of Constable Crake": "Hyde Park Barracks, Sydney, in the Early Twenties. The buildings stood then just as they do today, where they form Chancery Square." Or to take another story where he intrudes just enough to confirm the realism of his setting, this paragraph opens the narrative of "Mr Pounce's Reprieve":

One day Mr. Pounce, having taken a morning constitutional on the racecourse, was returning home to his bower of domesticity—he lived in a little cottage in Macquarie Street built on the site occupied at a later date by that particular house in Lyons' Terrace which was tenanted for some years by Judge Alfred Stephen (you can see "Stephen" scratched in half-a-dozen places on the window-panes now) when he chanced to espy a military-looking figure standing just where William Street takes the sudden dip to Woolloomooloo.

A convoluted sentence, to be sure, but Astley has retained control over his material. It seems to be authentic because Astley is confident and loquacious. There are precise details (Macquarie Street, Lyons' Terrace); an invitation to check the facts ("You can see. . . ."); extra information. It seems as if Astley has walked the ground where Pounce once stood, or rather, *could have* stood. We might wonder whether Astley needs this much detail and why it has been introduced. What is not at issue is the apparent authenticity of the scene.

Similarly, the effectiveness of "In the Granary," to take one last example of Astley's use of detail, depends on the credibility of his decision to situate two convicts in an unlikely location, a disused underground grain-store on Norfolk Island, where they are kept in darkness in chains. For a time at least any doubts about the setting are assuaged by the accumulation of circumstantial evidence at the entrance to the story. Astley begins:

There is no doubt that the place was originally devoted to the purpose implied by the name. . . . Captain Piper designed it—Captain Piper, the genial officer of the New South Wales Corps who was so beloved of John Macarthur; afterwards the Naval Officer whose accounts refused to balance because he had been so obliging as to allow duties to "stand over" indefinitely; and later still, the free-handed squire of a Bathurst estate. He was Commandant of Norfolk Island in the years immediately preceding the removal of the Island settlers to their new and poorer homes in Van Demonia. It was his invention.

A rapid check with the historians, which Astley invites us to make by refusing to name specific dates, reveals that his information about Piper is accurate.[27] More important, however, it has allowed him to do something about the improbability of the setting. (Piper obviously must have existed; therefore, the grainstore, his "invention," obviously existed as well!) And having established an identity for Piper, having, that is, grounded the story in what *seems to be* precise fact, Astley now proceeds to establish a more precise identity for "the place": "Eight by six by ten in dimensions; four hundred and eighty cubic feet in capacity. How many bushels of wheat and maize would that contain?" The answer? The characteristic and tactically useful admission, "We do not know: all that we can assert," says Astley, developing a beguiling confidence which is reflected in the rhetorical crescendo of his prose, "is that twenty-two years after Captain Piper had departed from the Island, this eight by six by ten excavated chamber, with the stone floor, and stone walls, and stone ceiling—this windowless room with but one solitary aperture, and that in the roof—was occupied by . . . two convicts."
     The presentations of detail are not always as successful as in these three examples. Astley can be loquacious, as we shall see, not because he wants to convince his readers but because he wants to parade his antiquarian's skills, because he has become vindictive, or simply because his prose makes him seem long-winded; even in "In the Granary" his talkativeness finally undoes him. Yet the irony remains that when we are convinced of the truth of Astley's historical fiction it is chiefly because he *is* so talkative, so ready to be involved with the stories he is sharing with his readers. Although obviously a subjective narrator, and a moody one at that, his confidence and ingenuousness are infectious; they disarm our suspicions. At times Astley's confidence is such that he seems quite happy to appear the prattling gossip who has lost track of his story, or to defy his readers to disbelieve him. In "Lieutenant Darrell's Predicament" he gets *himself* into a predicament by allowing con-

vict Robbins to issue the instructions about the revenge to be meted out to the Lieutenant. Astley suddenly remembers that Robbins has just had his mouth distended by the tube gag torture, but so sure is he of his audience that he candidly admits, "For a man with festering lips, Robbins did a surprising amount of talking that day!"

In his best moments, then, Astley's indictment works: the world he fabricates, though stark and violent, is credible, and this is the basis on which his effective re-creation of man's inhumanity to man is built. The question still to be answered is, how many good moments are there? There are obviously times, as in the Jane Applegarth stories, when we are not taken in or not moved. But how many failures are there, and by how much do they limit Astley's achievement? Or alternatively, are the successes a fair return from the large number of stories Astley had published? The simple answer is that there are a significant number of failures, but it must also be said that, even when the obvious failures are discarded, problems remain with Astley's fiction, and these problems are artistic rather than historiographical in origin.

CHAPTER 8

"No Neutral Tints"

I "Constructive Power"

THE first problem with Astley's fiction is that he persistently strove for the powerful effect. The kind of impact he sought often lay close to the surface of the material he was shaping; if not, he imposed it on the convict stories just as he imposed a sensational climax on Riverine tales like " 'Dictionary Ned' " and "The Idyl of Melool Wood-pile." The lack of "constructive power," it will be recalled, made him dismiss some of Lawson's stories as anticlimactic and inconsequential, but many of his own are too *well* constructed, too ingeniously planned, too climactic, particularly when it is considered that when writing about the convicts he was inevitably writing about the extremes of human behavior. So not only did he plan each convict story to expose a particular evil of the System (just as he planned each Riverine tale to explore a similar "tragic" theme): in many he wrote lengthy introductions in which his intentions were unashamedly revealed. "Convict Jerrick's Death-Mask," for example, begins with a long-winded survey of the "bad" penal institutions at the end of which Astley concludes that the worst was Port Arthur in the 1820's and 1830's. Why? Because that was when penal officials succeeded best in having each convict put to "the work for which he was least fitted in excess or capacity." Having labored to make his point, Astley seems suddenly to remember his story. "This much by way of introduction," he comments, and then forges a tenuous link: "The before-referred-to invention of the Régime never received a happier illustration of its utility than when it broke the refractory and stubborn spirit of convict Benjamin Jerricks, aged 23 years, per ship *Marquess Wellesley*."

Not every story is affected by this blatant signalling of theme, but the wandering preambles are symptomatic of the artificiality endemic in Astley's fiction. "Convict Jerrick's Death-Mask" seems to be a manufactured illustration of a thesis which Astley is arguing. As A. G. Stephens put it, Astley "seems to vision clearly the result he wishes to obtain;"[1] that is, the stories are sometimes so carefully plotted to bring out a particular effect that the result is a literary fabrication and not a mercilessly realistic re-creation. Douglas Stewart makes just such a judgment of "The Liberation of the First Three" and "The Liberation of the Other Three," suggesting that the final impression is that Astley, "a lover of the dark and the bizarre, has contrived all this merely so that he can present his macabre scenes of the dead men propped up with candles in their hands to be shown present at roll-call."[2] The coal-mine scenes are successful despite Astley's contrivance, and other stories are successful *because* of it, but sometimes we are forced to conclude that Astley is not a scene-painter but a scene-arranger who uses gimmicks to achieve his effects. Two stories included in standard Australian anthologies, "John Price's Bar of Steel" and "Lieutenant Darrell's Predicament," suffer in this way. In the first Astley's gimmick is the knitting needle secreted by Price in the clothing of the convict Danny Duncan. In the second Darrell is faced with a "Lady or the Tiger" predicament, obviously derived from the short story by Frank Stockton published eight years before.[3]

Elsewhere Astley makes abundant use of ironic reversals of fortune intended to show how pervasive the System can be but often unconvincing. In "Convict Jerrick's Death-Mask," to continue with that story, the refractory and stubborn spirit of Jerricks is broken by Dr. Rossell, who *happens* to be his father, though Rossell does not learn that until it is too late to save the convict. In "Toulmin of Toulmin," a prisoner transported under a pseudonym is rostered to act as signalman on Phillip Island and *happens* narrowly to miss the arrival on nearby Norfolk Island of his mother, who has been scouring the world to tell him of his pardon. In "For His Child's Pleasure" the convict summarily tried and hanged for interrupting Governor Foveaux's afternoon nap is executed in sight of his wife and child, whom he *happens* to have brought with him. Or finally, there is the last ironic turn of the screw in "The Felicitous Reminiscences of Scourger James," where the ex-scourger interviewed by Astley is flogged by his fellow inmates, who make use of the whip which *happens* to be left behind when Astley leaves. The problem with stories like these is not whether historical fact has been distorted—

Price, after all, did convict a man for an offense very like Duncan's. Rather, they are distorted and unconvincing because Astley has resorted to literary convention. The power of his indictment is debilitated by what seems to be contrivance, and also, when the range of stories is considered, by repetition.[4]

II *Astley's Characters*

The second problem with Astley's convict fiction, his characters, is clearly illustrated in "A Day with Governor Arthur." Astley is anxious to expose Arthur's severity, so portrays him as a "spare-framed, thin-faced, medium-sized man . . . clean-shaven, save for a tinge of greyish whisker; with steely-grey eyes that look with a critical disbelief in everything except the System; with a rasp in the voice. The lines at the corners of the drawn-down lips spell 'Martinet'; the wrinkles of the brow and the crevices between the eyebrows tell that he is a precisian." This "phrenological" characterization is certainly exaggerated but not, to judge from a surviving portrait,[5] all that inaccurate. Yet there are some modifications, for in order to be consistent, in order to show that Arthur, the archetypal official of the System, not only *looks* severe but is severe in his conduct, Astley has him start work punctually at ten and has him approve only one application in ten for tickets of leave.

Astley has made these changes to be consistent in his characterization. The *effect*, however, is that we notice not Arthur's consistency but his flatness: he is too severe, too one-sided. He emerges as a stereotype hardly distinguishable from those other "Men of the System," Banks, Darrell, Scragge, and Rossell. And so it is with the other groups of characters who inhabit Astley's dark world, wearing conventional costumes which are appropriate to the conventional dialogue they exchange. The upper-class degenerate Bob Warphy, like his soul-mate Frederick Dutton in the political serial, "The Strike of '95," is "tall, florid-faced and portly-framed";[6] the convict cannibals in "The Liberation of the First Three" and "The Liberation of the Other Three" have "slavering mouths" and "twitching lips"; the aristocratic convict Edgar Mann in "The Pegging-out of Overseer Franke" has "fine lips," "delicate nostrils," and "straightforward lucid eyes"; the spirited station heiress, Kate Latchford, has an "exquisitely-shaped upper-lip, and an under-one that expressed decision no less emphatically than beauty."[7] Even more a reflection of popular attitudes are the bit players, the children with their pretty lisps,[8] the visitors to the "cawlonies"[9] with their affected "bai jove" accents, and the minority groups with their odd idioms. Thus Astley's Irish characters ("this is his dodge to take up our toime, me men"), his aboriginals ("a chorus of gutterals"), and his Jews (" 'I'm afraid he vent 'vay'—them vas his very verds, Dicky")[10] speak just as they do in the contemporary cartoons of "Hop" and Phil May.

That Astley is more successful with the convicts is evinced by the pungent language at the opening of "The Ross Gang 'Yarner'-ship" and by the laconic, periphrastic reminiscences of scourger James. But it is doubtful whether Russel Ward is correct[11] in suggesting that the flow of convict speech is always convincing. Sometimes the speech of Astley's convicts, although ungrammatical or mispronounced and therefore "slangy," is unidiomatic: "I 'udn't do it," "Good for yer," "Yer did—th' kin'st thin'—pos'ble"; and neither "The Felicitous Reminiscences of Scourger James" nor "The Ross Gang 'Yarner'-ship" is free of the problem. Elsewhere, convict speech which *is* idiomatic still seems forced because Astley's habit of notating colloquialisms means that phrases are brought out of context and made to seem decorative: "Come on an' flog me—or p'r'aps ye'd like me to do the nubbling cheat trick?*"; "that's old Pounce, I'll swear, who was lagged for doing some dummy 'old ooman's tickets'.*"[12]

Several critics have argued that the compression demanded by the *Bulletin* gave Astley so little room to develop his characters that he was forced to make them this one-sided. Vance Palmer, expanding this argument, suggested that "Secret Society of the Ring," Astley's longest story and originally published in four parts, showed what he could do with his characters when not confined by so narrow a space.[13] But the merit of the story comes not from the life of the characters. Its power is sustained only in individual scenes and only, with one exception, in those impersonal group scenes where the central personal conflict of the story—Maconochie's battle with the Ring to retain the allegiance of the convict Reynell—is not significant. The same comment can be made about all the characters whom we meet at some length—Reynell, Maconochie, Johnson, Dutton and Warner in "The Strike of '95," the convicts in "The Bullet of the Fated Ten," the characters who appear in a number of stories. None of these characters shows much development: they have little complexity, even when they face complex decisions.

They have the same lack of substance as the gallery of figures appearing in only one or two stories.

It cannot be denied that Astley often hits the mark with his characters, particularly when dealing with the pretentious ones. In "Marie Antoinette's Fandango" the society girl, Nell Harrington, is told she cannot go to the prestigious Chester ball: " 'Pa! ma! Oh!—oh!' (Preliminaries to hysterics)," writes Astley. Her mother demands an explanation from the embattled husband—"Will you, if you haven't quite lost your senses, be good enough to explain, sir"—and is as nicely dismissed by the parenthetical comment, "Never before had Mrs. Harrington felt the necessity to play with severity the combined rôle of the Injured Mother and the Outraged Wife." Similarly, in "Convict Smith the Second" Smith is sent on an assignment because "The Surveyor being, of course, a big man, and entitled to move in the best circles—had not the Lord Lieutenant himself extended him one finger at a county festival three years ago?—did not propose to do the work himself." The problem, however, is that every character, not only those who make limited appearances, is as summarily dismissed. There are the Men of the Regime, cataloged in three stories;[14] the chorus of convicts, grouped at levels on the degenerative scale; the humanitarians, also cataloged; the licentious and corrupt free settlers; the minor figures. Given their identities, their actions—or rather, gestures—are predictable. It is inevitable that the administrators are either thoroughly evil or at best unthinking and unsympathetic, it is inevitable that the convicts degenerate, it is inevitable that the humanitarians wring their hands in anguish at their impotence. Even then Astley takes no chances and proceeds to tell us everything. He explains the emotions of his characters (" 'Go back—to be flogged for a whim! *Thank you*, Madam!' He tried to speak with an ironical politeness");[15] he lays bare their motives (the description of Governor Arthur's severe appearance concludes with the comment that a man with a heart would have been out of place in Arthur's chair); he prepares us for their suffering with morbid enthusiasm. ("Thus the scene; now for the action . . . And wait for what came next!")[16] With such editorial directives, reading an Astley story is like watching a production of Eugene O'Neill where an actor has been placed at the side of the stage to interpolate O'Neill's comments on the characters.

It can also be argued that Astley's characters should not have been too complex, given that he *was* restricted by the *Bulletin*. But by allowing them to be only puppets who could be manipulated to represent shadings of good or evil, Astley endangered the realism that he was so anxious to establish in his fiction. It is not the verisimilitude of the situation in which his characters find themselves which is at issue now, simply that his characters are not credible. The same can be said of him as has been said of Bernard O'Dowd, that for "real things he substituted political abstractions, abstracted emotions, generalisations which his imagination never made concrete."[17] For the most part Astley's characters, grouped and juxtaposed in almost allegorical terms, have only this kind of identity. And in this regard William Fitchett's jingoism may well have made him prejudiced toward Astley but it also enabled him to see more clearly Astley's own prejudices: "Price Warung's literary methods," Fitchett wrote in a review of *Tales of the Convict System*, "are of delicious simplicity. He knows no neutral tints. Every convict, according to him, was an odd compound of Uncle Tom and Dick Turpin, while every prison official is a distillation of Legree, Torquemada, and Charles Reade's Mr. Hawes!"[18]

III *Problems of Narrative Technique*

The third major problem with Astley's fiction concerns his use of detail and documentation, and again a useful starting point is A. G. Stephens, who felt that "introduction," "scenery," and the like were justified only when they aided the short story: "whatever helps it is an advantage; anything more is a disadvantage."[19] What Stephens was suggesting is that too much exposition and editorial discussion can interfere with the narrative progression which is important even in Astley's scenic fiction. And although Stephens begs the critical question it is all too obvious when Astley has not allowed himself enough room in which to tell his story. The lengthy thematic prefaces and the early paragraphs of recapitulation are bad enough: they surround and harass the stories, stifling some of them. But the problem extends past the sprawling introductions to Astley's stories to the narrative sections, which continue to be cluttered up by redundant information, by corroborative evidence, and by Astley's editorial tactlessness.

Too often, in short, the documentation and commentary which Astley supplies, however well intentioned, are harmful to his stories because they bulk so large as to have an unbalancing effect. So in relatively successful stories like "Absalom Day's Promotion" and "A Day with Governor Arthur" the quotations and the reproduction of what purports to be scripture are sometimes superfluous; in a less convincing one like "Captain Maconochie's 'Bounty for Crime' " they are downright extravagant. Nor do the footnotes always help the stories by confirming Astley's control over his material. Just as often they confirm his *lack* of control because they are used to explain self-explanatory terms or to score off fellow historians. This problem occurs even in "Parson Ford's Confessional": in one scene Davey is talking with his mistresses, one of whom simpers a reply during which the irrelevant fact is interpolated that she was "the identical pretty piece of frailty respecting whom Captain Colnett, of H.M.S. *Glatton*, had quarrelled with Governor King." Still not content, Astley adds a gossipy footnote: "Considering that, as a rule, Rusden, the historian, damns the cause he advocates, it is an unfortunate thing for Governor King's fame that Rusden defends his conduct in the Colnett case. King's action appears, however, eminently creditable to him, even in the light of the superior morality of this generation. Tested by contemporary canons, it reflected infinite honour upon him."

"Parson Ford's Confessional" survives such historiographical gymnastics, but the dangers of Astley's interference are clear. How destructive his comments become can be seen by returning to "In the Granary." The introduction discussed earlier is useful by Stephens's criteria. The plausibility of the "scenery" has been established and, by stating that some years after Piper had left Norfolk Island the grainstore was occupied by two convicts, Astley has got to the point where he can depart on the central narrative. Instead, he departs along another track:

Piper had designed the chamber to store surplus grain. Again and again had Government barns and store-buildings been broken open by prisoners who insubordinately declined to starve while the stores held stocks of foodstuff, and who preferred a short shrift and a long rope to an empty stomach. And, therefore, Captain Piper resolved to defeat the mutinous and starving rascals. He had this chamber dug out—built in with stone—closed with an iron door in the roof, which door turned upon a pivot and was fastened by padlocked clamps. When he had filled the granary with grain, he favoured it with additional protection by sentries. And, upon the whole, the Captain's plan was successful. Not more than one prisoner died from actual starvation during the period the granary was full of a reserve stock in case the store-ship with supplies from the Old Town failed to make the Island in due course. And he, it is believed, died because he was forgotten. They locked him up in the old gaol cell and quietly overlooked him for ten days. And when they remembered him he had gone to report himself to the authorities of a Higher System.

The incident, Astley admits, is "by the way," and he returns to the thread of the story:

Wright was Commandant. And when he took charge he found, in the course of an examination one day, an iron door level with the earth and rusted in its socket of stone. He wondered what it could be for just so long as it took to send a soldier for the blacksmith, and for the time the blacksmith was engaged in forcing the clamps. When the iron plate was made to revolve upon its pin, Captain Wright—a Ghoorka, in after years, let the life out of his body in a vain attempt to find the ex-Commandant's heart—looked down into the cavity, smelt its exhumed mustiness, and, gleefully, smote his thigh with his gloved hand.

Apart from the aside about the ghurka the paragraph is directly relevant. But Wright decides the granary is just right for two incorrigible convicts, and Cook's reaction to this leads Astley to make further comment:

Not being an officer and gentleman, and not, therefore, wholly intoxicated with the absolutism of power, Overseer Cook shuddered. He was an instance of the square peg in the round hole. Transported for some aimless ranting in a London street over the Peterloo massacre, he was tried under one of the Six Acts, and awarded, in recognition of his patriotism, seven years' residence across the seas. On securing his certificate of freedom, he became a clerk attached to Sydney Police Office, and on the re-settlement of Norfolk Island as a penal establishment, was appointed an overseer. He was at once an exception to one rule and an illustration of another. An ex-convict who became an overseer generally so acted that, between himself and an average "officer and gentleman" acting as commandant, there was little to choose in respect of brutality. Cook was an exception to this rule. But the rule that a man transported for seditious utterances—for permitting scorching words to pour forth from the volcano of a heart which burnt with a fiery pity for the poor, and a fiery contempt for the social conditions which held the poor in bondage—proved a genial taskmaster to prisoners when clothed with authority, this he illustrated daily. Cook, with every temptation to be otherwise, remained kindhearted.

He shuddered, and ventured to hint a remonstrance.

By the end of the story there have been, if we include the five footnotes, a dozen more interpolations, and both the credibility and the effectiveness of the granary scene have long succumbed to Astley's editorial gyrations. It does not matter, perhaps, that so slight a story as "In the Granary" has been lost within a narrative that flags or at best stutters along in low gear, but elsewhere Astley's intrusions have unhappy consequences. In particular, the dramatic potential of many stories is not realized because Astley cannot avoid telling—and retelling—all that is happening. For example, the constant reminders that the three convict cannibals *are* cannibals weakens the impact of the "In Shoes of Death" stories because the ending is predictable. Conversely, where the ending is deliberately predictable (in the sense that Astley has suggested what it *might be* so that we can enjoy knowing more than the protagonists), the technique is not always sustained. It is in "Parson Ford's Confessional," but in "Marie Antoinette's Fandango" we are prepared for the climax in no fewer than three parentheses. The damage is not irreparable and "Marie Antoinette's Fandango" remains one of Astley's best stories. But in "The Liberation of the First Three" and "The Liberation of the Other Three" where Astley also gives away the ending three times, he greatly weakens the bitter irony whereby the coal-mine cannibals kill the three convicts with whom they have sworn allegiance and then kill each other.

It should be clear from a discussion of these problems that just as some of the generalizations made about Astley's methods of construction need to be modified, so do some of the generalizations made about his achievement: for example, such comments as that he has "a superb feel for incident, for the deceptively casual building-up scene by scene . . . to a state of tension"; or, "He has the capacity to hold interest, to awaken and sustain suspense—to tell, that is, an exciting tale"; or, "No one would deny that he tells a rattling good yarn."[20] To suggest that Astley never develops tension, that he never holds the interest or excitement of his readers, that he never tells a rattling good yarn, obviously does him less than justice. But all too often when he creates a promising situation, a credible reconstruction of what happened or an imaginative guess at what could have happened, the promise is not fulfilled. We are left to emphasize his capacity rather than his achievement, we are left to regret what "could have been."

Part of the explanation, quite simply, is that Astley's creative talent was limited. When forced on his own resources he lacked the imagination or the sensibility (and given recurring ill-health and the need to write quickly, perhaps also the energy) to avoid the traps of literary convention. The novelese in "The Strike of '95" and the banal absurdities in "The Idyl of Melool Wood-pile" provide ample evidence of how little originality he possessed, and even his convict fiction, where he had the oral evidence and the written record to sustain and divert him, is also partly shaped by his sentimental belief in the reality of romance. But only partly shaped: even when the limits of his originality are set, even when it is accepted that he wrote period fiction, it is not the obvious failures which are to be regretted as much as the significant number of stories ("The Liberation of the Other Three," "John Price's Bar of Steel," "Captain Maconochie's 'Bounty for Crime'," and so on) which have a potential that is not fully realized. There remains Astley's inability always to make the best use of the talents he *did* possess. The explanation for this lies in the paradoxes inherent in those talents.

IV   *The Defects of Astley's Qualities*

Astley's chief talent, apart from his entrepreneurial eye for the possibilities in his sources, is his ability to convince his readers to believe and be moved (or in lighter moments entertained) by the stories he tells them. It is very much *Astley's* show, as I have suggested; he is a participating author, both authoritarian and authoritative. He succeeds when he convinces us that, however garrulous he becomes and however involved he might appear as narrator, editor, commentator, or pageant-master, he has nonetheless managed to preserve his artistic detachment. The essential problem is that he is not always able to control the extent of his involvement. When this happens, his presence does not enrich, but impoverishes, his fiction.

The most obvious manifestation of the problem is the way in which he loses control over the detail he has introduced to buttress and support the stories. Although critics like Morris Miller and Nettie Palmer are wrong in suggesting that he was subservient to the facts (to repeat, he was subservient only to what *appears to be* the facts), their critical extension remains sound. The unrestrained accumulation of documents is evidence that in attending to detail Astley does lose sight of his responsibilities as a *raconteur*. And the same conclusion can be reached about the other kinds of evidence he supplies—the footnotes, the scholarly asides and interpolations, the inconsequential information. Too often, then, Astley gets himself entangled in the net of substantive evidence that he has placed to trap and suspend our disbelief; or to put it another way, too often Astley is garrulous not because he wants his stories to be credible but because he wants to demonstrate his intimate acquaintance with the history of transportation.

If this was all, then it could be concluded that Astley is self-indulgent, that sometimes his control as an artist succumbs to his passion, basically that of an antiquarian, for unearthing information and passing it on. He is like those modern historians who ferret out the evidence in such quantities that they have trouble in deciding what to leave out.[21]

But Astley is possessed of a second great passion which he indulges: his vehement desire to show that the convict system was an unmitigated evil which blighted the growth of the colonies and went a long way toward explaining the problems of pre-Federation days. There can be no denying the strength of this conviction, or that Astley's stories are intended to be an indictment of the evils he saw in the convict past; they are informed by a sincerity as deep as that of the humanitarians and reforming pamphleteers who campaigned during the transportation era itself. And just as some of what *they* had said was true, so some of Astley's stories retain truths about man's inhumanity to man. Astley's sincerity, then, is the source of much of the power in his fiction, and it was to this sincerity that Nettie Palmer responded when she suggested that one of the chief qualities Astley brought to his tales was an "intensity, almost a gusto, of moral indignation."[22]

Yet such was Astley's indignation, such was his anxiety to reveal these truths, that he lost his sense of perspective and with it his sense of the need to remain detached. Too often in his fiction he becomes vindictive and bitter, even enraged, determined that no reader possibly fails to see the ramifications of his indictment. The inevitable result is that the control of the artist succumbs not only to the enthusiasms of the antiquarian but also to the prejudices of the polemicist. In Avrom Fleishman's terms, Astley has the sympathy and the experience to write successfully about the convicts, but not always the esthetic propriety. His lens, always narrow, is so narrow at times as to be *obviously* distorted by his prejudices and this in turn imperils the verisimilitude of his work. William Fitchett directed attention to one effect of Astley's prejudice when he suggested that Astley's characters were oversimplified, that they had no neutral tints. A. G. Stephens directed attention to another when he suggested that Astley's stories were contrived, that he seemed to vision clearly the results of his work. But these are not the only expressions of his lack of detachment. As the quotations from "In the Granary" must surely make clear, Astley's editorial prodigality (the main reason why his stories don't realize their *dramatic* potential) stems also from this desire to emphasize how evil the convict system had been and to extract the maximum amount of sympathy for the convict forefathers. More often we remember not the way Astley's vehemence is controlled but the ways it is indulged: the transparent directives about what to think, the sneering asides, the derisive rhetoric. These excesses are reminiscent of the excesses in the political journalism so perhaps it is fitting that the Sydney *Worker*, in attempting to summarize the problem with the journalism, should also provide an appropriate summary of the most significant problem with the fiction. "A writer should never allow his feelings to run away with his pen. When a man writes during a fit of rage . . . he has a tendency to hit and kick at anything under the sun, and the consequence is that he falls over himself in his anxiety to hurt."[23]

V *Style*

There remains Astley's style to be considered. If some critics have erred in describing Astley as objective and scientific in his historiography, they are just as far from the truth in suggesting that his prose was objective and scientific, that in his hands "unnecessary words are ruthlessly scored out," to quote Morris Miller.[24] H. M. Green agreed: Astley has "a simple, direct style," developed when "the *Bulletin* taught him conciseness."[25] Astley, however, rarely followed Archibald's famous directives to stick to the sturdy nouns, and if he was unlike Lawson in this aspect of his work he was like more *Bulletin* writers, perhaps, than is generally acknowledged. His style is "literary," his diction, acquired from his reading of English authors, full of archaic and euphemistic alternatives for simple words and phrases: "inveracity," "purblind," "pachydermatous," "deponeth," "contiguous," "opprobrium," "tonsure," "rubicund," and best of all, "hebdomadal incursion" for "weekly inspection" in "Toulmin of Toulmin." There is no doubt that Astley consciously

preferred the verbose euphemism to the short, precise word: he
ransacked the dictionary for suitable phrases, revising his manuscripts in the light of his discoveries. (There were limits to his
vocabulary, nonetheless; phrases like "pretty frequently" and
"whitey-brown" recur repeatedly in his writing.) How much he was
further affected by the verbiage in transportation literature is not so
clear, but even by comparison with these sources Astley's diction
seems antiquated and needlessly indirect.

The description of Bishop Willson, to return to "The Consequence of Cunliffe's Crime," suffers by comparison with the
undistinguished writing in the source, W. B. Ullathorne's *Memoir
of Bishop Willson*. Ullathorne has Willson "of middle stature and
somewhat portly," with a mouth that "was firm and gentle in its
lines"; Astley has Willson "somewhat slightly over middle height"
with a "certain dignified portliness of presence," and suggests that
"firmness characterized the mouth, yet softness and gentleness
reposed in its curves." The extra inches, the added dignity, and the
sharper contrast between Willson's firmness and gentleness are
intended to delineate Willson in a way important to Astley's story,
but the impact is weakened by the prolixity of the prose.

And the impact of the stories is weakened not just by the words
Astley chooses, for his diction is but part of the fabric of his prose.
Moreover, what is important about Astley's undisciplined prose is
not its intrinsic lack of felicity, but the way in which it magnifies
some of the other flaws in his fiction. Surely one of the reasons why
Astley's characters are so conventional is that what Astley writes
about them or has them say is conventional: they are dressed, or
made to talk, in the appropriate clichés of their class. Again, not
only are there irritating digressions, the sidepaths are littered in
such a fashion that the going is made even more tortuous, and
readers are forced to pick their way through such sentences as: "You
will remember we told you a chapter or two back something about
Mrs. Taylor's 'letter-day', and then interposed with an account of
the evolution of Convict Hendy (original No. 1001–28, per *Roslyn
Castle*, island No. 42–116), the why and the wherefore of the thus
linking of the incidents being the circumstance that Philip Hendy
was one of those favoured by Mrs. Taylor acting as his amanuen-
sis."[26] There is some excuse for Astley with this sentence, which
emerged while he was dictating to a typist hurriedly preparing the
stories for serialization in *Truth*. But even in the *Bulletin*, where

supposedly Archibald was on hand to effect the repairs, countless clumsy and inelegant constructions occur ("before-referred-to," "the particulars of the break-out above related are necessary for an understanding of the sequel")[27] and much haphazard punctuation: "We were going to tell you to-day of the loss of the *George III*, but, on second thoughts, instead, will narrate a story which in itself is a not uncharacteristic expression of the ways of the Old Régime, though, in point of grimness, compared with the going-down of the *George III*, it is a glimpse of sunshine in Cimmerian darkness."[28] From the *Bulletin*, too, comes perhaps the worst sentence in Astley's fiction, this one from "Gowrie's Last Joke": "A stupid, dazed blundering forward of horse and man, and the gulp-gulp of the maelstrom of mud sucked instantly (so it seemed) the poor animal down to the girths." It is not only Astley's horses which are sometimes hopelessly bogged.

Thirdly, Astley's style contributes to the ineffectiveness of his descriptive writing, even though his abiding interest in the visual evidence of transportation and his itinerant occupation meant that he visited the locations of his stories. There are successes, it must be admitted: the early descriptive paragraphs in "Mr. Pounce's Reprieve" and "In the Granary," where Astley is chatty and expansive for a particular purpose; or in contrast, the opening to "How Muster-Master Stoneman Earned His Breakfast," where perhaps uncertain about his role as narrator (this is the first time he has been published in the *Bulletin*, remember), he is severely documentary in his style:

An unpretentious building of rough-hewn stone standing in the middle of a small, stockaded enclosure. A doorway in the wall of the building facing the entrance-gate to the yard. To the left of the doorway, a glazed window of the ordinary size. To its right a paneless aperture, so low and narrow that were the four upright and two transverse bars which grate it doubled in thickness no interstice would be left for the admission of light or air to the interior. Behind the bars—a face.

In similar vein, though the syntax is less choppy, is the description of Macquarie Harbour in "Lieutenant Darrell's Predicament":

The pine forest was situated in the delta formed by the junction of the Franklin and the Gordon, some twenty-five miles distant from the debouchement of the latter splendid river into Macquarie Harbour. Of an area and a density to occupy at least twenty convicts for a twelve-month, the timber was too far away from the main settlement for the workers and their guards to traverse the distance daily, and hence it became necessary to erect barracks on the spot. This had been done, and the rude structure—a prisoners' dormitory and meal room, 40 ft. by 20 ft., a guard-room of half the dimensions for the soldiers, and two small rooms for the officer in charge—had been tenanted by Lieutenant Darrell and his *entourage* some weeks before the day of the revolt.

Both these extracts, despite some evidence of verbosity ("paneless aperture," "interstice," "debouchment," and so on) are convincingly grounded in the kind of detail which is a useful part of a historical narrative, the kind of unpretentious detail which is present also in "Mr. Pounce's Reprieve" and "In the Granary," balancing and giving point to Astley's loquaciousness. In all four stories the description is part of an ongoing narrative, and Astley has painted sparingly, using simple blacks and whites. The problem is he seldom contained himself in this way, preferring to introduce atmospheric color to his landscapes which, given the artificiality of his vocabulary and the elaboration of his syntax, rendered ineffectual his intimate knowledge of topography and setting. So although Astley lived and worked in Bathurst and studied the convict remains at some length, his description of them in " 'In Floggers' Corner' " is disappointingly imprecise and exaggerated:

On this August morning the first blush of an early spring had fallen upon the enclosure. A petulant rain had ushered in the day and with it had come the beautiful new year. An elm in the angle next the super [intendent]'s house that, yesterday, was rude and sharp against the western sky, now sent forth countless tiny shoots, and upon every diminutive point glistened a trembling diamond. From the luminous wet of the grass walk peeped specks of colour, the vanguard bannerets of the coming host of wild flowers. In a box on the sill of the Superintendent's window the miniature volcano-cups of the crocus were bursting into bright gold. And above all, the delicious warm air hung with a rapturous buoyancy that lifted up the soul as does the "sightless song" of the lark. Even into the floggers' hearts penetrated some of the priceless beauty of the new-born Spring.

Even this poor stuff does not mark the bottom of the pit: Norfolk Island, 850 miles from the mainland, was the one convict settlement which Astley did not visit,[29] so his "topographical" research could only come from books or from etchings and paintings. The contrast inevitably pointed by writers and artists, that Norfolk Island was a natural paradise transformed into a man-made Hell, became a thematic temptation he could not resist. He habitually evokes the romance of Norfolk Island as a way of emphasizing the horrors which his evil men have produced. "John Price's Bar of Steel," to take one characteristic story, opens with Price taking the evening air:

> The sea-breeze fanned the symmetrical stems of the giant Araucaria transplanted by Colonel Foveaux to the front of a Government Cottage, and swept from its fronds a chord or two of the music which the undisturbed centuries had there garnered. The nearer face of Mount Pitt, alpine in its solitude, was dazzling in the pallor of a South Sea moon; the blue of the ocean lay intersected with broad, fan-like beams of pearly radiance. It was such a night as poets dream of and delight in, and, in other climes, as the nightingale sings to the listening rose; such a night as, in this newest clime, John Price enjoyed to the utmost.

That the information which Astley supplies about fauna and geography is accurate can hardly be noticed amid the profusion of clichés and the rampant hyperbole. Astley obviously intended his description to have thematic significance, to be the lyrical prelude to a story which reveals the cruelty and inhumanity of Price. But the fact that the description is so artificial helps to destroy the credibility of the rest of the narrative.

VI *The Illusion of Control*

For all the criticisms that can be levelled against Astley's style, it should not be assumed that his writing was always affected. There were times when he obviously realized that if he infused too much color into his writing then the dramatic tension of his scenes would evaporate, and on such occasions his prose is simple and unassuming: when the ballot is being conducted in "The Bullet of the Fated Ten," or when the Ring is chanting its liturgy in "Secret Society of the Ring." Nor should it be assumed that no good ever came out of the pomposity and pretension which normally characterize his use of language. Several times his indirect and inflated style transforms direct statement into effective ironic understatement, a technique later mastered by Furphy. Astley's best moment is when Harrington arrives at the Chester ball in the "not altogether inappropriate" disguise of a bandit, but Tom Collins would have been nearly as proud to report that a character in "The

Skeleton Banquet" was of "litigious disposition—as tenant of a farmhouse, he once carried on a suit-at-law against himself as trustee of the farm property"; or that an old bullocky had "pitched his shanty of casuarina slabs there 'cos he didn't go much on company, an' liked his own thought an (adjective) sight better than other folk's gab."[30] (But perhaps even Tom would have gagged at "the why and wherefore of the thus linking of the incidents being the circumstance that . . ." at the start of "The Whale-boat Plot"!) In each case Astley is having some fun, an indulgence he did not allow himself often enough. But even in more serious stories his style sometimes forced him to tone down the horrors which he accumulated. "The Pegging-out of Overseer Franke" provides a good example:

> On the Thursday night they bolted, under Mann's leadership, and seized a schooner which lay out in the mainstream. Overseer Franke, of course, raised a remonstrance as to their going, but they treated it as unpolitely as they did his complaint that they were hurting him, when they pegged him out—*alive*—with tent-pegs and lines on an ant-hill in the heavily-timbered gorge between two hills.

> Alive—with food just *outside* his reach—and a bullet-hole through his right hand, into which aperture the ants were directed by the ingenuity of one Mann, who made a sweet track of the Overseer's ration sugar from a hole in the hill to the hole in the hand.

Similarly, an illusion of control is usually preserved when Astley uses animal imagery to emphasize the assault on the natural order. Occasionally he is so outraged that he descends to rhetoric: "Henceforth he was to draw as a beast draws, and bear as a beast bears, and be whipped as a beast is whipped, and to have no vent for his agony save the inarticulate groan of the beast."[31] In contrast, however, is the report in "Convict Smith the Second" that "Bishop Willson once saved a convict's neck because he could break in a hitherto untameable colt. There was, by the way, no description of vicious brute, from a Norfolk Island Commandant and a Vandemonian Governor-General to a lunatic and a bushranger, that the Bishop did not tame." Or again, in "A Bathurst Field Day" it is alleged that Magistrate Snowlee carefully reads gazetted notices of missing stock so as to claim remarks "which, never less than £2 for a man, went sometimes as high as £50 for a horse." In similar vein is

Astley's comment in "The Evolution of Convict Hendy," after most of the free colonists who have gathered at the assignment office ridicule the assurances given by Anthony Kemp regarding the colts sired by his famous stallion "First Fleeter": "the animals were invariably guaranteed as of no vice," he writes (clearly implying that Kemp's assigned servants are the "colts"),[32] "and they inevitably killed a man when rising three years." As a final example there is the passage in "Janet Guilfoyle's Delusion" where he exposes the conditions on the infamous transport ships by writing as if he were referring to a studbook:

No employer, not belonging to the brute class, would have anything to do with a male convict *ex* the *Marquis of Huntley* (1), or *Lady Kennaway* (2). Every master wanted a *Medway* man. So with the women. To engage a female transport per *Hector* was to hire a she-devil; to obtain a *Morley* girl who had come out under good Dr. Reid and had *not* gone into the Parramatta factory, was to win a treasure.

The point is obvious in these quotations, and the fact that it is obvious means that it cannot be labored. Although Astley is in a position to do so (in each story he is, as usual, close to the action) he resists the temptation. In each he controls his indignation by remaining behind a satiric mask, projecting a straight face which his prose helps to maintain. With his authorial position securely established, Astley can afford the luxury of occasionally venturing forth. He seems uncertain in "A Bathurst Field Day" ("sometimes went"), mildly skeptical in "The Evolution of Convict Hendy" ("invariably killed"), digressive and not a little pompous in "Convict Smith the Second" ("by the way," "hitherto untameable"), and informative in "Janet Guilfoyle's Delusion" (in the catalog of "good" and "bad" ships). The same kind of detachment is evident also in "Mr. Slyde's Auction" where the central image of the cattle auction is beautifully sustained, in the climax of "Marie Antoinette's Fandango," and in "Parson Ford's Confessional."

It was probably stories like these that led Nettie Palmer to talk of Astley's indignation being "restrained" by his "ruefully humorous irony,"[33] and Colin Roderick to speculate that the characteristic "sardonic mood" of Astley's stories came from the convicts, "who expressed themselves ironically, concealing their resentment beneath mocking deference."[34] The trouble is, Astley could neither restrain himself nor conceal his resentment for long, which means

that (as in Riverine tales like " 'Half-Crown Bob' ") the illusion that
he has the ironist's control over his prose is more often lost than not,
and even some of his successes are made to seem unintentional. In
the extract from "The Pegging-out of Overseer Franke," for example, is his use of "aperture" and "raised a remonstrance" a conscious
attempt to distance himself from the horror of Franke's torture, or is
(as I believe) the understated effect accidental? In "Convict Jerrick's
Death-Mask," to take a second example, Jerrick's mother, in a
hysterical state, is wondering aloud whether her son is dead and is
stopped short by the gravedigger's answer, "They're mostly dead
when we buries 'em." A wonderfully laconic understatement; but is
Astley's description of the reply as "sententious" a feigned pomposity designed to give a even sharper edge to the exchange, or is he
indulging in the use of another long word? The result is what counts,
but against Astley's successes, accidental or otherwise, must be set
the scenes which are vulgarized by his way of expressing himself:
"Not all of Convict Jerrick went over to the Settlement side that
day. Some of him clung to the cat's tails, and some of him strewed
the ground at the foot of the triangles. For the flogger was in good
form, and the floggee was rather plump on the back, and tender
flesh rent easily." Or again: "Scourger Cracknecke worked his fancy
trick to admiration. He embellished the "surface" with three strips
of hanging cuticle, and by the deftest of wrist actions left one huge
drop of thick gore clinging to the top of every pendant of skin."[35]
    In both these extracts the diction ("floggee," "cuticle," "pendant")
and the rhetorical syntax detach Astley so much from the victim that
it is *he* who appears callous. In identical circumstances Marcus
Clarke stops short of sharing the sadism of his penal officials:

" 'Ten!' cried Troke, impassibly counting to the end of the first twenty.
    The lad's back, swollen into a lump, now resembled the appearance of a
ripe peach which a wilful child had scored with a pin. Dawes, turning away
from his bloody handwork, drew the cats through his fingers twice. They
were beginning to get clogged a little."[36]

    In his worst moments, Astley grips his Victorian quill with a
railer's zeal, and the unhappy result of this combination of self-
conscious overwriting and self-indulgent overstatement is self-
parody. The damage is most noticeable in stories like "Secret Society of the Ring" and "Captain Maconochie's 'Bounty for Crime',"
where Astley, clearly his own worst enemy, prevents himself

harnessing not only the power which lay in the sources but also the power which he had generated by his extension or adaptation of the sources. The actual Ring scenes in "Secret Society of the Ring" escape the debilitating effects of his writing, but the personal exchanges, between Maconochie and Reynell and between Maconochie and the massed convicts, bring him forth at his most vindictive. The gap between potential and performance is even wider in the climactic scene of "Captain Maconochie's 'Bounty for Crime'," where he cannot resist attempting to extract the last drop of pathos and pity. Maconochie extends his hand to Tracey:

"Poor man, poor man!" exclaimed Maconochie, and, pacing forward, he held out his hand. Tracey struck it aside passionately.

"Yer've left me nothin' but—oh, nothin', nothin' but hate—an' now yer give me your pity. To the devil who made yer an' th' Systum!" He leapt tigerishly on the Superintendent and was felled by a blow. There was nothing effeminate about Maconochie's muscles or his nerves, if there *was* just a suspicion of that quality attached to his judgment. No. 33–149 went down, and for a minute stayed down, dazed.

No word was spoken till Tracey, with eyeballs glaring redly instead of whitely, drew himself up to a sitting posture.

"Didn't I say as the nubblin' cheat 'ud end it soon? By th' Lord, sir, I thank yer!"

Maconochie had faced a mutiny from a quarter-deck; had, as a lad, confronted, with only a toy-dirk in hand, a howling circle of barbaric mountain tribesmen thirsty for his blood;—and yet, he was wont to say, never did human look appall him as that transport's glare of—gratitude.

"It's death—this—you know, my man?"

"Death—'tis—an' welcome!" It was a hyena shriek made articulate.

"My *friend*, let me help you up! Again Captain Maconochie stretched forth his hand.

Tracey looked up. "D'yer mean it?" The softening of the words passed in the next instant from his face and tone. "Mean it!" he continued, "o' course yer mean it! Be'n't it yer dooty to 'and me to th' gallows!"

Maconochie pressed down his hand—lower—lower still—till it touched Tracey's shoulder.

"Tracey!" he whispered, "Tracey! it is my duty to save you from—the gallows. That is why I am here. Tracey—let us be friends!"

VII *Astley and Archibald*

The contribution of Archibald to these excesses is not altogether clear, though from the limited evidence[37] available it appears he was on hand to make some of his famous repairs to Astley's manuscripts. At different times he tidied up Astley's constructions, corrected spelling, deflowered vocabulary, and even helped decipher Astley's handwriting, just about the worst, claimed W. H. East, that he received during nearly half a century as the *Bulletin*'s printer.[38] But Archibald made little effort to get Astley to write more succinctly,[39] and not all his tinkering (and it was *only* that) was beneficial. Many of the asterisks, dramatic dashes, and parentheses that he is known to have inserted have the effect of heightening an already heightened text. In other words, it is not simply a case of Archibald failing to save Astley from himself: in a small way he made a positive contribution to Astley's failures.

There are, perhaps, two reasons for this. One is implied in John Barnes's comment that Archibald, in encouraging writers to be original, overvalued the effect of sudden surprise and revelation.[40] This, combined with what A. G. Stephens considered to be Archibald's "instinct" for melodrama, produced a surprising amount of melodrama and contrivance in the *Bulletin* stories published in the 1890's, particularly in those published before Stephens became literary editor in 1896. In this way Astley's stories betray flaws common to most stories published in the *Bulletin* in the early 1890's. Where his stories differ is in their propagandist overstatement, and here we recognize the depth of Archibald's own hatred of the System, which he felt had originated a penal and judicial code the barbarity of which he had experienced at first hand in 1882. So extravagantly resentful was Archibald of the System that he allowed Astley almost a free hand in the way in which he wrote his stories, and allowed those stories to dominate the *Bulletin* until such time as Astley's erratic behavior and the emergence of other contributors caused him to call a stop. But until then Astley was, for Archibald, not so much a creative writer or, as he saw himself, a historian, but a maker of myths through whose pen the *Bulletin* could give vent to its Anglophobia. And so ingrained were Archibald's resentments in this particular direction that they affected his literary judgment, never as certain as Stephens's in the first place. Stephens would never have allowed Astley to expand himself as he did in "Captain Maconochie's 'Bounty for Crime'." Archibald did; and what I am suggesting is that without Stephens to guide his hand the editor in Archibald succumbed to the avenger.

VIII   *Conclusion*

Had not Archibald felt so strongly about the evils of the past, very probably Astley's stories would never have been published. Given that, a second irony is that the missionary zeal which abounds in Astley's fiction, which helped attract the attention first of Archibald and then of *Bulletin* readers, is one of the reasons why the stories seem so insular and dated today. (Lawson's poetry has not survived for precisely the same reasons.) So when Alan Seymour, reviewing *Convict Days*, asked, "What are these studies? Anthropology? Sociology? History? Penology? . . . Literature, then? 'Rattling good yarns?'":[41] he asked a question which is relevant in an assessment of Astley's fiction, but of little significance in an assessment of the convict novels of Clarke, Hay, Keneally, and Porter. These four novelists studied the history of transportation but all of them (including Clarke, despite his comments in the preface to *For the Term of his Natural Life*)[42] created out of their research a fictional world in which they could explore universal concerns; "the world of this novel," wrote Keneally of *Bring Larks and Heroes*, "is a world of its own."[43] Astley created out of his research a fictional world (whether for him it was "essentially" historical does not matter) in which he could also publicize an insular political philosophy. In this sense, at least, his fiction is simply an extension of his political journalism.

The conclusion reached by Seymour, that Astley's "studies" were "bits of each, and enjoyably, if exasperatingly, so," is not unfair. Some of the stories do have merit as literature, some indeed are rattling good yarns, others exasperate because with a little more care they could so easily have been better. But they also can be read as exercises in penology, and, more important, as history and myth; and on these grounds their place in Australian writing seems secure enough. For the historian, Astley's fiction is important evidence of how some Australians saw their past at a significant stage of the nation's development: he helped to perpetuate and publicize the legend about the convicts which is only now being brought into perspective. The convict legend was an integral part of the group myth about Australians and their destiny promoted by the *Bulletin*.[44] And because the *Bulletin* is commonly regarded as the most significant literary journal in this country, Astley's position in the history of Australian literature seems assured.

Yet Astley is surely one of the writers who have "an historical interest quite disproportionate to their literary merits," as our only Professor of Australian Literature has written.[45] The achievement of the convict stories, the effectiveness of Astley's indictment, is limited, most of all by an avenging spirit which betrayed Astley as well as Archibald. The effects of this betrayal are obvious enough in the serious stories, most of which are curate's eggs. They detain us because of their interest as autobiography and polemics and because of the promise they show as reconstructions of what could have happened. But they are flawed in the execution, and it is only the individual scenes which survive critical scrutiny—the ceremonies in the Ring stories, the procession and scaffold scenes in "Absalom Day's Promotion," the torture scenes in "Lieutenant Darrell's Predicament" and "The Pegging-out of Overseer Franke," the opening of "The Ross Gang 'Yarner'-ship," the closing of "A Day with Governor Arthur" and "The Liberation of the Other Three," the exposure of Hendy in "The Whale-boat Plot." The best narratives, however, the best stories, are the comic ones—the four Pounce tales, "The Felicitous Reminiscences of Scourger James," "The Pure Merinoes' Ball," "Marie Antoinette's Fandango," "Parson Ford's Confessional," "Mr. Slyde's Auction." To this list can be added "Dictionary Ned" and "The Incineration of Dictionary Ned." In these dozen or so stories (ironically, they are among Astley's most "fictitious") his particular qualities as a writer are most happily combined; for only when he was—or seemed to be—less serious about the convicts and their descendants did he manage to sustain his control so that his style strengthened rather than weakened the indictment about which he felt so strongly. And that is the central irony of his life and work.

Notes and References

Because the publishing history of Astley's stories is detailed in the bibliography that follows, quotations from the stories have been documented only where there is doubt as to the origin of the quotation. Within the text a series title with inverted commas refers to a newspaper series, an italicized title to a book series: thus "Tales of the Early Days" for the *Bulletin* series, *Tales of the Early Days* for the selection republished in book form. Where a story has been republished in book form, that source has been preferred in quotations. *Bulletin*, *Truth*, and other newspapers have been used only for stories which were not republished, and *Convict Days* only for stories which were not republished in earlier books. To keep the documentation necessary to this introductory study within bounds, the following abbreviations have been adopted in footnotes:

ADB	*Australian Dictionary of Biography*, Vols. 1–5, gen. ed. Douglas Pike (Melbourne, 1966–1974)
ALS	*Australian Literary Studies*
AL	William Astley Papers, A72, Mitchell Library
AP	Astley Papers, Uncataloged MSS, set 250, Mitchell Library
A&R	Angus and Robertson Pty. Ltd., Sydney
AW	*Australian Workman*, Sydney
B	*Bulletin*
BFP	*Bathurst Free Press and Mining Journal*
BP	G. B. Barton Papers, MS 829–833, Mitchell Library
CD	*Convict Days*
CON	Convict Records, Tasmanian State Archives
DL	Dixson Library, Sydney
DP	Astley Papers, Add 669, Dixson Library
HS	*Historical Studies*
JRAHS	*Journal of the Royal Australian Historical Society*
LaTL	La Trobe Library, Melbourne
MAP	Miscellaneous Astley Papers, Aa 9, Mitchell Library
ML	Mitchell Library, Sydney
NL	National Library, Canberra

NSWA	State Archives of New South Wales, Sydney
PP (HC)	*Parliamentary Papers,* House of Commons, Great Britain.
PP (HL)	*Parliamentary Papers,* House of Lords, Great Britain
RR	*Review of Reviews* (Australasian edition)
SMH	*Sydney Morning Herald*
TCS	*Tales of the Convict System*
"TED", TED	"Tales of the Early Days," *Tales of the Early Days*
"TID", TID	"Tales of the Isle of Death," *Tales of the Isle of Death* (*Norfolk Island*)
"TOR", TOR	"Tales of the Old Regime," *Tales of the Old Regime and The Bullet of the Fated Ten*
"TOS"	"Tales of Old Sydney"
"TR", TR	"Tales of the Riverine," *Half-Crown Bob and Tales of the Riverine*
"TS"	"Tales of the System"
WS	*Warrnambool Standard*

Preface

1. Vance Palmer, *The Legend of the Nineties* (Melbourne, 1954), p. 97.

2. *The Writer in Australia: A Collection of Literary Documents 1856–1964,* ed. John Barnes (Melbourne, 1969), p. xiii.

Chapter One

1. The fullest biographical accounts are in Vance Palmer, *The Legend of the Nineties,* pp. 96–100, in F. T. Macartney, "Sidelights on Price Warung," *Australian Literary Essays* (Sydney, 1957), pp. 105–111, and in E. Morris Miller, *Australian Literature from its Beginnings to 1935,* 2 vols. (Melbourne, 1940), I, 454–456. The last two depend heavily on [F. J. Broomfield], "William Astley ('Price Warung')–1892," unpublished galley in Sir John Quick Papers, MS 53, NL. The difficulties in discovering information about Astley are discussed in Nettie Palmer, *Fourteen Years: Extracts from a Private Journal 1925–1939* (Melbourne, 1948), p. 98.

2. *Naught to Thirty-Three* (Sydney, [1944]), p. 137.

3. Fox to Astley [January 1893], AP.

4. The most useful sources of information are the letters to Nettie Palmer from F. J. Broomfield (March 30, 1932), Sir Robert Garran (March 7, 1932), N. G. Rankin (November 12, 1931) and Ethel Newcombe (August 1, 1952), now in Palmer Papers, MS 1174, NL. Subsequent quotations from these letters are documented only where there is doubt as to the origin of the quotations.

5. *Much Besides Music* (Melbourne, 1951), p. 29.

6. See Ethel Newcombe to Nettie Palmer, Palmer Papers; *The Legend of the Nineties*, pp. 99–100; and "William Astley ('Price Warung')–1892."

7. Other pen names which Astley used or planned to use are "W", "P.W.," "The Workman," "Will Wilga," "Will Western," "Lucilius," "A Hireling Scribe," and "Aristides Blubb."

8. *B*, November 7, 1891.

9. See Teachers Time Book, 1872–1874, now part of the Parish Records, St. Stephen's Anglican Church, Richmond, Victoria.

10. Macartney, "Sidelights on Price Warung," p. 108.

11. *Ibid.*, p. 108; John Holroyd, *George Robertson of Melbourne 1825–1898: Pioneer Bookseller & Publisher* (Melbourne, 1968), pp. 19, 37.

12. *Richmond Australian*, March 7, 21, 28, August 28, September 4, 1874, March 27, 1875.

13. See *ibid.*, June 27, 1874.

14. Rankin to Nettie Palmer, Palmer Papers.

15. *B*, December 5, 1891.

16. See Ethel Newcombe to Nettie Palmer, Palmer Papers.

17. L. L. Robson, *The Convict Settlers of Australia* (Melbourne, 1965), and A. G. L. Shaw, *Convicts and Colonies* (London, 1966), are indispensable to an understanding of the convict system. The following are also useful background reading: F. K. Crowley, "The Foundation Years, 1788–1821," in *Australia: A Social and Political History*, ed. Gordon Greenwood (Sydney, 1955), pp. 1–45; Manning Clark, *A Short History of Australia* (New York, 1963); Ian Turner, "The Social Setting," in *The Literature of Australia*, ed. Geoffrey Dutton (Harmondsworth, 1964), pp. 13–54; J. V. Barry, *Alexander Maconochie of Norfolk Island: A Study of a Pioneer in Penal Reform* (Melbourne, 1958); and the same author's *The Life and Death of John Price: A Study in the Exercise of Naked Power* (Melbourne, 1964).

18. F. B. Waters to J. F. Archibald, undated, AP.

19. *Sydney Gazette*, May 21, June 8, August 8, 29, 1827; Rev. Thomas Sharpe, Papers, A1502, ML, pp. 35–36.

20. Astley to W. H. Fitchett, July 28, 1892, MAP.

21. Astley to G. B. Barton, March 25, 1898, BP.

22. Now in ML. Astley's flyleaf note is dated February 3, 1899.

23. "The Commandant's Picnic Party"; cf. Astley to Barton, BP.

24. Henry Graham, MRCS London, was registered as a medical practitioner in New South Wales on April 27, 1835. He served as a medical officer at Port Macquarie (1839–1841), Norfolk Island (1841–1846), Port Arthur (1847–1848), Tasman's Peninsula (1849), Ross (1850), and later in Launceston and Sydney.

25. Astley's note in presentation copy of *TID*, ML.

26. Astley to Barton, BP. "Scragge" has been wrongly identified as John Price by J. V. Barry in *The Life and Death of John Price*, p. 136.

27. J. F. Mortlock, *Experiences of a Convict*, ed. G. A. Wilkes and A. G.

Mitchell (Sydney, 1965 [London, 1864–5]), p. 73. See also Graham to Maconochie, July 26, 1843, MS 102, DL, and report of Graham and T. B. Naylor, August 12, 1845, Norfolk Island Papers, 220, DL.

28. Astley to Fitchett, MAP.

29. Astley to R. W. Gilder, May 20, 1891, to Alfred Bennett, February 9, 1892, both AP, to Fitchett, MAP.

30. Astley to Colonial Treasurer, October 31, 1892, AP.

31. For a description of the four main collections of Astley's papers, which all cover the period 1890–1893, see the author's "Price Warung: A Biographical and Critical Study," MA thesis, University of NSW, 1969, pp. 337–356.

32. Brian Elliott, *Marcus Clarke* (Oxford, 1958), pp. 140–145; L. L. Robson, "The Historical Basis of *For the Term of His Natural Life*," *ALS*, I (1963), 104–121; Decie Denholm, "Port Arthur: The Men and the Myth," *HS*, XV (1970), 406–423; I. D. Muecke, "William Hay and History: A Comment on Aims, Sources and Methods," *ALS*, II (1965), 117–137.

33. Cf. the bibliographies in *The Convict Settlers of Australia* and *Convicts and Colonies* with *Catalogue of Free Public Library* (Sydney, 1872).

34. On the provision of special accommodation, see Ida Leeson to F. T. Macartney, July 10, 1941, MSS 8229, LaTL (hereafter Macartney Correspondence), and E. A. Armstrong to Astley, July 21, 1892, AL.

35. Note in *TID*, ML.

36. *B*, October 12, 1911.

37. "Conversational Note, Blackheath, Mr. Gerard Phillips, Redlands St Leonards: 24/4/91", typescript, AP.

38. Astley to G. B. Barton August 24, 1891, Barton Papers, MSQ 102, DL.

39. Astley to A&R, [*c.* 1894], in D. S. Mitchell, Correspondence etc. 1844–1907, A1461, ML (hereafter Mitchell Correspondence).

40. Astley to Mitchell, August 29, 1894, Mitchell Correspondence. Cf. J. A. Ferguson, *A Bibliography of Australia* Vol. III 1839–1845 (Sydney, 1951), entries 3665, 3891.

41. E.g., *Bathurst Times*, BFP.

42. Astley to Fitchett, MAP.

43. *The Legend of the Nineties*, p. 91. See P. C. Naughtin, "The Literary Importance of the Sydney *Bulletin*," MA thesis, University of Adelaide, 1955, quoting comments by Louis Becke, Barcroft Boake, F. J. Broomfield, and Rod Quinn which support Palmer.

44. If the following item from the correspondence column is a reply to Astley, it is likely that he sent a contribution without prompting: " 'W. A': Not yet read", *B*, March 15, 1890.

45. On the *B* and its staff, see the reminiscences of Archibald and W. H.

Traill published as "The Genesis of *The Bulletin*," *Lone Hand*, I-II, May–November 1907; Agnes Macleod, *Macleod of the "Bulletin"* (Sydney, 1931); Sylvia Lawson, "Jules Francois Archibald," *ADB*, III, 43–48; S. E. Lee, "The *Bulletin*—J. F. Archibald and A. G. Stephens," in *The Literature of Australia*, pp. 273–287; Ailsa G. Thomson, "The Early History of the *Bulletin*," *HS*, VI (1954), 121–134; and the *Bulletin* Jubilee Number, January 29, 1930. On literary life in Sydney at the turn of the century, see also Bedford, pp. 89–91, 136–141; Norman Lindsay, *Bohemians of the Bulletin* (Sydney, 1965); A. W. Jose, *The Romantic Nineties* (Sydney, 1933); and G. A. Taylor, *Those Were the Days!* (Sydney, 1918).

46. E.g., August 8, 1891.

47. *B*, May 5, 1894.

48. *Ibid.*, February 29, 1896, in an article entitled "Over the Coals." See also G. A. Wilkes, "The Eighteen Nineties," in *Australian Literary Criticism*, ed. Grahame Johnston (Melbourne, 1962), pp. 30–40, and John Barnes (who quotes Greene), "Australian Fiction to 1920," in *The Literature of Australia*, pp. 159–163.

49. From "Australian Literature," *Hits! Skits! and Jingles!* (Sydney, 1972 [1899]), pp. 143–144.

50. See A. G. Serle, *From Deserts The Prophets Come: The Creative Spirit in Australia 1788–1972* (Melbourne, 1973), p. 60, Taylor, p. 116, and Lawson, p. 46.

51. Astley to H. P. Steel (his solicitor), June 15, 1891, David Gilbert to Astley, [June 1891], both in AP. In 1882 Archibald and John Haynes were imprisoned for failing to pay legal costs arising from a libel action instituted after an editorial by W. H. Traill.

52. Macleod to Astley, July 24, 1891, Astley to Macleod, February 9, 1892, AP. The agreement did not include "TED," a later *B* series.

53. I.e., three years after the publication of *TED*.

54. Ryan to Astley, January 15, 1892, DP.

55. Macleod to Astley, April 13, 1892, AP.

56. George Robertson and Company to Astley, November 14, 1892, AP.

57. Archibald to Astley, October 21, 1892, AP.

58. D. J. Hopkins, *Hop of the "Bulletin"* (Sydney, 1929), p. 89; cf. Palmer, *The Legend of the Nineties*, p. 99, and W. W. Stone, "Price Warung's Convict Days," *Biblionews*, XIII (1960), 30–31.

59. Macleod to Astley, March 25, 1892, AP.

60. Smyth to Astley November 10, 1892, G. E. Russell Jones to Astley, December 16, 1892, AP.

61. G. B. Barton, Diary, April 14, 1893, MS 86, DL. On Astley's dispute with Barton, see "Price Warung: A Biographical and Critical Study," pp. 54–57.

62. Nettie Palmer, *Fourteen Years*, p. 98; *The Legend of the Nineties*, p. 99.

63. *B*, October 12, 1911.

64. "The Strike of '95" was not published until 1893, but was written in 1891: see Macleod to Astley, November 19, 1891, AP.

65. Quoted in *Fourteen Years*, p. 98.

66. *Truth*, February 7, 14, 28, 1897; cf. *SMH*, February 25, 1897.

67. *Truth*, July 4, 1897.

68. *Daily Telegraph*, August 15, 1896.

69. Charles White to George Robertson, January 11, 1899, A & R Correspondence, item 15.

70. R. H. Holt to G. A. Taylor, October 19, 1918, quoted in Henry Lawson, *Letters 1890–1922*, ed. C. Roderick. (Sydney, 1970), p. 502. See also *The Legend of the Nineties*, p. 100.

71. See, for example, *National Advocate* (Bathurst), December 7, 19, 22, 1896, *Truth*, February 14, 28, 1897, and Astley to Edmund Barton, October 29, 1896, Bathurst People's Federal Convention, Papers, Uncat. MSS set 269, ML, item I, pp. 413–414 ("hampered as I am, with more than a touch of my old enemy insomnia").

72. *Truth*, February 14, 28, 1897.

73. *Ibid.*, February 28, 1897.

74. For a description of *tabes*, a form of tertiary syphilis, see *The British Encyclopedia of Medical Practice* 10 vols., gen. ed. Lord Horder (London, 1952), IX, 252–256. The pain caused by the disease would explain Astley's initial use of drugs; the progress of the disease is undoubtedly the cause of his disappearance from public life after 1903.

75. *Westralian Worker*, May 24, 31, 1901.

76. See Stone, "Price Warung's *Convict Days*," p. 31.

77. Meetings of Central Committee, Commonwealth Literary Fund, March 6, 1907, July 7, 1908, February 9, September 15, 1910, March 28, 29, 1912, in Commonwealth Literary Fund, Minutes of Meetings 1907–1920, in possession of Prime Minister's Department, Canberra.

78. Rookwood Benevolent Asylum, Register of Admissions, 1911, now in Lidcombe State Hospital Archives.

79. *SMH*, October 7, 9, 1911, *Daily Telegraph*, October 7, 1911, *Bathurst Times*, October 9, 1911, *B*, October 12, 19, 1911.

80. B. Nesbitt and S. Hadfield, *Australian Literary Pseudonyms: An Index* (Adelaide, 1972), p.v.

Chapter Two

1. *B*, October 12, 1911.

2. E.g., no files of the *Richmond Guardian*, the *Storekeeper*, and the *Tumut Independent* for the years in which Astley was associated with those newspapers.

3. See "A Visit to Bryan O'Lynn," "Jottings at the Junketings," *WS*, October 1, 3, 20, 21, 1884.

4. The best historical survey of the period remains Robin Gollan's "Nationalism, the Labour Movement and the Commonwealth 1850–1900," in *Australia: A Social and Political History*, pp. 145–195. Clark, Jose, Palmer, Taylor, and Wilkes are useful, as are the following: H. M. Green, *A History of Australian Literature* 2 vols. (Sydney, 1961), I, pp. 347–359; Bruce Mansfield, *Australian Democrat: The Career of Edward William O'Sullivan 1846–1910* (Sydney, 1965); Bede Nairn, *Civilising Capitalism: The Labor Movement in New South Wales, 1870–1900* (Canberra, 1973); Cyril Pearl, *Wild Men of Sydney* (London, 1958); and Russel Ward, *The Australian Legend* 2nd ed. (Melbourne, 1966).

5. See Molly Robarts to Nettie Palmer, July 29, 1952, Palmer Papers.

6. None of the editorials which are quoted in this chapter was signed by Astley. My attribution is based partly on stylistic parallels (e.g. repetition of characteristic phrases and images) but also on factual evidence which survives to confirm his authorship. For example, Astley's authorship of almost all the *BFP* editorials quoted or cited in this chapter is confirmed in letters from Charles White, the editor, which are now in the AL, AP, and DP. All references to the *BFP* in this chapter are to editorials appearing on p. 2.

7. *Bathurst Times*, January 14, 1888.

8. See C. S. Blackton, "Australian Nationality and Nationalism: The Imperial Federation Interlude," *HS*, VII (1955), 1–16.

9. *Bathurst Times*, January 14, 1888.

10. On the question of race, see Astley's "Undesirable Immigrants" and "Federation and Servile Labour," *BFP*, June 2, 1891, May 20, 1892, and his "What 'The Workman' Says," *AW*, September 9, 1893.

11. *Bathurst Times*, January 26, 1888; see also *ibid.*, January 28, 1888.

12. *Ibid.*, January 28, 1888. See also *ibid.*, December 29, 1887, and "An Open Letter," *B*, April 11, 1891.

13. *BFP*, March 3, May 21, June 1, 6, 9, October 23, 1891.

14. *Ibid.*, October 23, December 12, 1891, January 15, March 3, June 11, August 20, 1892, August 4, 1894.

15. *B*, May 9, 1896; cf. "Parkesiana," May 16, 1896.

16. E.g., *BFP*, October 29, 30, November 2, 1891, January 11, 18, February 20, August 13, 1892.

17. Subsequent quotations from *ibid.*, January 24, 25, 27, 28, February 3, 8, 10, March 10, 25, April 19, 22, 29.

18. *Ibid.*, November 2, 1891.

19. *B*, February 9, 1893, MS in DP. Cf. Barton to Astley, January 8, 1893, DP.

20. *The Legend of the Nineties*, p. 99.

21. For an account of one brawl see Pearl, *Wild Men of Sydney*, pp. 76–81.

22. *SMH*, March 5, July 10, 1895.

23. For a fuller discussion of this point see the author's " 'Dynamite, Barricades, Brimstone': Price Warung's Political Themes," *Labour History*, No. 22 (1972), pp. 1–12.

24. *AW*, March 4, 1893.

25. *BFP*, July 2, 1892.

26. "John Norton, Reformer and Pioneer, Tribune and Publicist: A Character Sketch," *Truth*, December 12, 1897.

27. "The Australian Democracy and Literature," typescript, AP.

28. *BFP*, December 17, 1891, June 11, 1892.

29. White to Astley, January 24, March 2, 1893, AP. Cf. *BFP*, March 1, 1893.

30. See "An M.P. Convict," *BFP*, November 3, 1891.

31. *Ibid.*, June 2, 1891, June 11, 1892; see also "'Distrust the Politicians'. A Letter to the Wage-Earners of New South Wales," typescript, AP.

32. *BFP*, June 11, 1892.

33. See Robin Gollan, "The Australian Impact," in Sylvia Bowman *et al.*, *Edward Bellamy Abroad: An American Prophet's Influence*, (New York, 1962), pp. 119–136.

34. See also the draft copy, prepared by Astley and now in the DP, of an advertisement of the novel which appeared in the *AW*, February 4, 1893.

35. Installments of "The Strike of '95" were published in the *AW*, February [18, 25], March 4, [11], 18, [25], April [1, 8], 15, 29, 1893. Subsequent quotations are from the four extant installments, three of which began with a summary of installments now missing.

36. Cf. Astley's plot summary of "The Explosion" with his editorials, *BFP*, May 14, 1891, *AW*, May 20, July 15, 1893.

37. See the series of sixteen editorials under the general title of "The Federal Constitution," *BFP*, May 12–June 9, 1891.

38. *Australian Federalist*, March 23, 1898.

39. *BFP*, May 12, 1891.

40. *Nhill Free Press*, January 30, 1891.

41. Reprinted *Bathurst Daily Argus*, April 2, 1904.

42. See Mansfield, *Australian Democrat*, pp. 258–264.

43. S. A. Rosa to *AW*, *AW*, February 18, 1893.

44. *CD*, p. 96, *TOR*, p. 30. A note by Astley indicates that at the time referred to, No. 14 Downing Street was the residence of the Secretary of State for the Colonies.

45. Chatto and Windus to Astley, May 31, 1892, AL.

46. F. T. Macartney, *Proof Against Failure* (Sydney, 1967), p. 147. The unpublished selection, with an introduction by Macartney, is now in the NL.

Chapter Three

1. Clarence Kendall and Stuart Mitchell to Astley, June 15, 1892, AL.

2. *B*, February 9, 1893.

3. See "Jottings at the Junketings," "Marcus Clarke," and "Chippings and Chatterings," *WS*, October 20, November 24, 1884, January 19, 1885. All subsequent references to *WS* are to these articles.

4. *B*, January 3, April 11, 1891.

5. K. A. McKenzie, "Joseph Furphy, Jacobean," *ALS*, II (1966), 268; Henry Lawson, "A Fragment of Autobiography," in *The Stories of Henry Lawson*, ed. Cecil Mann (Sydney, 1964), First Series, p. 25; Alan Brissenden, *Rolf Boldrewood* (Melbourne, 1972), p. 14; Joan E. Poole and Michael Wilding, "Marcus Clarke's Contributions to *Notes and Queries*," *ALS*, VI (1973), 186–189; Wilding, "Marcus Clarke's *Old Tales of a Young Country*" and "Marcus Clarke in the Colonial City," *Southerly*, XXXIII (1973), 398, 443–448.

6. Wilding, "Marcus Clarke in the Colonial City," p. 441.

7. *National Portraits*, 3rd ed. (Melbourne, 1954), p. 163.

8. " 'For the Price of Two Drinks!' A Book Study," *Worker*, March 23, 1901.

9. "The Local Celebration of the Centenary," *BFP*, January 26, 1888.

10. "Literature. Freshly-Cut Pages. Notes on Books and Bookmen," *Spencer's Weekly*, July 13, 20, 27, August 3, 1895; see also "A Love Episode: A Wholesome Novel by Zola," *ibid.*, August 17, 1895. Subsequent quotations in this section are from these columns and reviews, unless otherwise indicated.

11. N. L. Dowden to Astley, July 27, 1892, AP.

12. Parkes to Astley, September 27, November 4, 1892, AL, Astley to Parkes, November 2, 1892, AP.

13. Wilding, "Marcus Clarke in the Colonial City," p. 445.

14. *Worker*, March 23, 1901.

15. *WS*, November 24, 1884, *Spencer's Weekly*, August 3, 17, 1895.

16. *WS*, October 20, 1884.

17. "Australian Fiction to 1920," p. 165.

18. *The Receding Wave: Henry Lawson's Prose* (Melbourne, 1972). Matthews's argument is summarized in his introduction to *Henry Lawson: Selected Stories* (Adelaide, 1971).

19. *Spencer's Weekly*, August 10, 1895.

20. *Worker*, March 23, 1901.

21. *Spencer's Weekly*, July 27, 1895.

22. *BFP*, August 31, 1896. The review was first published on August 29, but an irate Astley had it republished after several paragraphs had been

transposed. The August 29 date was cited when the August 31 text (minus the first paragraph) was reprinted in *Henry Lawson Criticism 1894–1971*, ed. Colin Roderick (Sydney, 1972), pp. 48–50.

23. E.g., J.A. Barry, *A Son of the Sea* (London, 1899), C.E.W. Bean, *The Dreadnought of the Darling* (London, 1911), E.J. Brady, *River Rovers* (Melbourne, 1911).

24. Archibald (referring to " 'Brothers Twain' ") to Astley, October 17, 1892, AL.

25. Matthews, *The Receding Wave*, p. 12. Cf. H.J. Oliver, "Lawson and Furphy," in *The Literature of Australia*, pp. 291–293.

26. See the checklist of published and projected stories annotated by Astley, DP.

27. *TR*, p. 71.

28. *Ibid.*, p. 76.

29. When TR was published Astley acknowledged his gratitude to the proprietors of the *SMH* and the *Sydney Mail* for permission to reissue " 'Half-Crown Bob'," and "The Idyl of Melool Wood-pile," the two stories not previously published in the *B*. I have not been able to locate their publication before *TR*, although several years before Astley discussed with the editor of the *SMH* the possibility of literary contributions to the *Echo*, a *Herald* subsidiary.

30. Joseph Furphy, *Rigby's Romance* (Adelaide, 1971 [Sydney, 1946]) p. 225; Barry, *A Son of the Sea*, p. 116.

31. Ian Mudie, *Riverboats* (Melbourne, 1961), p. 29.

Chapter Four

1. This tally includes "The Ship of the Black Death," unpublished MS in DP.

2. The published exceptions are four short *B* pieces, " 'From the Documents,' " "An Episode of Early Exploration," "In Substitution," and "The Dead–Bearers," two convict stories first published in other newspapers, "Race-Day at the Cascades" and "An Endorsement in Red," and two stories first published in George Robertson volumes, "The Bullet of the Fated Ten" (*TOR*) and "The Finding of Benson, Baronet" (*TID*).

3. Scragge makes an appearance in all eight Norfolk Island "TS" but is not as dominant as in "TID"; in "TS" there are stories set in eight different penal settlements. In the sense that "Secret Society of the Ring" dominates "TED" Maconochie is the main character in that series, but he appears in only five installments.

4. In all five series there are at least three sequences of two or more stories.

5. The only significant differences between "TID" and any of the *B* series is that six of the *Truth* stories have alliterative titles, in keeping with John Norton's colorful editorial policy (e.g. "Foreign, Foul and Filthy/

Alleged Awful Offence/Abominable Allegations Concerning/Disgusting Doings by a Dago," *Truth,* October 10, 1897).

6. Quoted in R. G. Howarth's introduction to *The Escape of the Notorious Sir William Heans (and the Mystery of Mr. Daunt): A Romance of Tasmania* (Melbourne, 1955 [London, 1919]), p.x.

7. "Oline Keese" [Carolyn Leakey], *The Broad Arrow: Being Passages from the History of Maida Gwynnham, a Lifer* 2 vols. (London, 1859); "Giacomo Di Rosenberg" [James Tucker, 1808–1888], *Ralph Rashleigh, or The Life of an Exile* (Sydney, 1952, ed. Colin Roderick); Marcus Clarke, *For the Term of his Natural Life* (originally titled *His Natural Life* and serialized *Australian Journal,* 1870–1872; revised and published under same title Melbourne, 1874; long title used when published London, 1885); J.B. O'Reilly, *Moondyne: A Story of the Underworld* (Boston, 1879); Hal Porter, *The Tilted Cross* (London, 1961); Thomas Keneally, *Bring Larks and Heroes* (Melbourne, 1967). Other works of fiction about the convict system include: [Henry Savery], *Quintus Servinton* (Hobart, 1832); John Lang, *The Forger's Wife, or Emily Orford* (London, 1855); and the same author's *Botany Bay, or True Stories of the Early Days of Australia* (London, 1859).

8. The exception is Halloran in *Bring Larks and Heroes.*

9. Pounce is the only Astley convict to appear in several stories not part of a sequence.

10. There has been a suggestion that Astley helped Clarke to write the serial version of *His Natural Life* (see Molly Robarts to Nettie Palmer, Palmer Papers). Astley's comments in his review article on Clarke in the WS suggest otherwise.

11. E.g., the episode of convict cannibalism in *For the Term of his Natural Life* (Book III, Ch. 27) is based on a famous case of two Macquarie Harbour convicts, Pierce and Cox (see Report of the Select Committee on Transportation, August 3, 1838, *PP*(HC), 1837–1838, Vol. 22, Paper 669, hereafter *Molesworth Report* (1838), 313–316). Astley's "In Shoes of Death: The Tanning of the Hide" and "The Wearing of 'the Shoes of Death' " are based on the same incident.

12. L. T. Hergenhan, "The Redemptive Theme in *His Natural Life,*" ALS, II (1965), 32–49; cf. the same author's "The Corruption of Rufus Dawes," *Southerly,* XXIX (1969), 211–221, and L. H. Allen's introduction to the World's Classics edition of *For the Term of his Natural Life* (London, 1952). Subsequent references to the novel are from this edition.

13. Ropewell is one of several Astley characters to have allegorical names; cf. the warder Tuff and the scourger Cracknecke. The name "Stoneman," however, is a cryptic reference to the original for that character, one Thomas Mason.

14. *CD*, p. 1, *TR.* p. 315.

15. *Ralph Rashleigh* (Sydney, 1962), pp. 170–173.

16. *B*, November 11, 1890.

17. Cf. *For the Term of his Natural Life*, pp. 310–321.

18. *TED*, p. 216.

19. Ward, *The Australian Legend*, pp. 30–31; Barry, *Alexander Maconochie of Norfolk Island*, pp. 97–98, 155–156.

20. See "T. Inglis Moore, "The Meaning of Mateship," *Meanjin Quarterly*, XXIV (1965), 45–54, H. McQueen, *A New Britannia* (Harmondsworth, 1970), pp. 130–132.

21. *TOR*, p. 183.

22. *CD*, p. 4, *TOR*, pp. 183–184. Astley's judgment of Price is vindicated in *The Life and Death of John Price*, ch. 7.

23. See Adrian Mitchell's introduction to *The Tilted Cross* (Adelaide, 1971).

24. *CD*, p. 91, *TOR*, pp. 5–7, *B*, September 13, 1890.

25. See especially "The Convict's Sacrament," "Miss Latchford's Overseer," "Vesper," and "In the Granary."

26. E.g., " 'Special Commission Sunday,' " " 'In Floggers' Corner,' " "Marooned on the Grummet," "A Day with Governor Arthur," and "The Felicitous Reminiscences of Scourger James."

27. E.g., "The Commandant's Picnic Party," "The Skeleton Banquet," " 'The Hanging of the Eight,' " and " 'The Ripple of Dene's Laughter.' "

28. Astley to Fitchett, MAP, Astley to Parkes, November 2, 1892, AP.

29. See Astley to the executors of the estate of Mrs. J. D. Lang, October 16, 1891, P. G. King to Astley, January 7, 1892, Astley to Parkes, November 2, 1892, all in AP; Astley to Parkes, April 17, 1895, Parkes Correspondence, A872, ML, II, 14; Astley to Angus and Robertson, January 8, 1901, A&R Correspondence, item 15; and the checklist of projected work in DP.

30. Astley to Colonial Treasurer, AP.

Chapter Five

1. *TID*, p. 210.

2. *Ibid.*, p. 224.

3. See especially L. L. Robson, *The Convict Settlers of Australia*, *passim.*, and the same author's "The Historical Basis of *For the Term of His Natural Life*," p. 121.

4. "The Immersion of Captain Bankes," "The Drowning of Captain Bankes," and "The Torture of Jane Applegarth."

5. Robson, "The Historical Basis of *For the Term of His Natural Life*," p. 121. On the horrors of transportation see *The Government and Mr. W. H. Barber* (London, 1866), W. B. Ullathorne, *The Catholic Mission in Australasia* (Liverpool, 1837) and *The Horrors of Transportation, Briefly Unfolded* (Dublin, 1838), Report of the Select Committee on Transportation, July 14, 1837, *PP*(HC), 1837, Vol. 19, Paper 518 (hereafter *Molesworth Report* (1837)), 16–17, 86–87, 139, 309 etc., and [T. B. Naylor], *A Tale of Norfolk Island* (London, 1845). Astley used all these sources and

claimed to have corresponded with Ullathorne; see Astley to G. B. Barton, March 25, 1898, BP.

6. Quoted in R. W. Rigby, "William Astley: The Present and the Past," B. A. thesis, Australian National University, 1971, p. 34.

7. J. A. Ryan, "Ned Kelly: The Flight of the Legend," *ALS*, III (1967), 109.

8. George Farwell, "New light on the convict image," *SMH*, May 26, 1973.

9. Astley to Fitchett, MAP.

10. See also " 'Benefit o'Clargy Bill,' " " 'The Hanging of the Eight,' " "Convict Arden's Yellow-Heart," "The Bullet of the Fated Ten," "The Pardon that never came," " 'The Sins of the Fathers,' " and "The Procession of the Buttercup."

11. Quoted in *A Marcus Clarke Reader*, ed. W. Wannan (Melbourne, 1963), p. 147. See also J. W. Beattie, *Port Arthur* (Hobart, n.d.) p. 4, V.M. Coppleson, *Shark Attack* (Sydney, 1958), pp. 104–106.

12. B. Coultman Smith, *Shadow Over Tasmania*, 13th ed. (Hobart, 1961), p. 48.

13. The precise number is difficult to calculate but it includes some, at least, of "The Skeleton Banquet" and "The Rationing of the Sentinels" groups, the tales for which Henry Graham was probably Astley's main source, and the tales in which Astley appears as a character.

14. White to Astley, June 7, 1892, AP.

15. No survey of transportation literature (i.e. writings about transportation) has been published, but the following surveys of early historical writing are useful: J. M. Ward, "Historiography," in *The Pattern of Australian Culture*, ed. A. L. McLeod (Melbourne, 1963), pp. 195–251; R. M. Crawford, "History," in *The Humanities in Australia*, ed. A. Grenfell Price (Sydney, 1959) pp. 148–162; and H. M. Green's chapter, "Prose of Controversy," in *A History of Australian Literature*, I, 45–64.

16. J. Mudie, *The Felonry of New South Wales* (London, 1837), p. 13. For an account of James Mudie's harshness towards convicts, see Bernard T. Dowd and Averil Fink, "James Mudie," ABD, II, 264–266.

17. Quoted in J. Syme, *Nine Years in Van Dieman's Land* (Dundee, 1848), pp. 200–201.

18. See Ullathorne, *The Horrors of Transportation*, and his *Memoir of Bishop Willson* (London, 1887), J. West, *The History of Tasmania* 2 vols. (Launceston, 1852), and E. Morris Miller, *Pressmen and Governors* (Sydney, 1952).

19. See Barry, *Alexander Maconochie of Norfolk Island*, *passim.*, and James Backhouse, *A Narrative of a Visit to the Australian Colonies* (London, 1843), a work referred to in Astley's papers.

20. Anne Conlon, " 'Mine is a Sad yet True Story': Convict Narratives

1818–1850," *JRAHS*, LV (1969), 43–82, is an excellent survey of the convict memoirs.

21. Green, *A History of Australian Literature*, I, p. 20.

22. Quoted in *Old Bush Songs and Rhymes of Colonial Times*, ed. Douglas Stewart and Nancy Keesing (Sydney, 1957), pp. 24–25. The origin and transmission of the song are discussed in J. S. Manifold, *Who Wrote the Ballads? Notes on Australian Folksong* (Sydney, 1964), pp. 30–33. On transportation songs generally, see also Hugh Anderson, *Farewell to Old England* (Adelaide, 1964), and Edgar Waters, "Ballads and Popular Verse," in *The Literature of Australia*, 1964, pp. 259–272.

23. See J. M. Ward, pp. 202–207.

24. *Argus*, September 27, 1877.

25. *The History of Australasia* (Glasgow, 1879), p. 91.

26. "Convict Tales," *SMH*, October 8, 1960, p. 16.

27. See Brian Elliott, *Marcus Clarke* (Oxford, 1958), p. 142, J. W. Beattie to George Robertson, January 10, 1899, Mitchell Correspondence, p. 173, and NSWA, Colonial Secretary's In Letters, 63/3329, Secretary of State Despatches M6604/B.

28. *Marcus Clarke*, p. xi.

29. Legislative Assembly, New South Wales, *Votes and Proceedings*, 1901, Vol. 6, p. 946.

30. "The Plot Thickens," *B*, January 7, 1888.

31. This and subsequent quotations from *B*, January 21, 1888.

32. Macleod to Astley, November 19, 1891, AP.

33. See Ken Levis, "The Role of the *Bulletin* in Indigenous Short Story Writing during the Eighties and Nineties," *Southerly*, XI (1950), 220–228.

Chapter Six

1. Astley to Steel, AP, *Truth*, September 19, 1897, *TCS*, p. v; *TID*, pp. vii-viii.

2. Astley to Bennett, AP.

3. E.g., in "A Bathurst Field Day," "Convict Rudde's Proposal of Marriage," and "Beneath the Summer Sun."

4. E.g., *TED*, pp. 10–11, 13, 46, 81, 103, 125, 137, 141, 162, 189, 248.

5. Introduction to "The History of Bushranging in Australasia," unpublished *B* galley in AP.

6. *B*, May 16, 1891.

7. See J. S. Laurie to *B*, December 27, 1890, J. L. Dickson to B, undated, both annotated by Archibald, AL.

8. See "Answers to Correspondents," *B*, May 23, August 1, October 31, November 28, 1891, September 3, 10, 24, October 1, November 19, 1892.

9. *Ibid.*, August 27, September 3, 1892.

10. See *ibid.*, May 23, August 1, October 31, November 28, 1891,

September 10, October 29, 1892. Several letters from *B* readers passing on historical information or requesting further details survive in Astley's papers.

11. "New Books," *Australian Star*, June 25, 1892, p. 9, "Tales of the Convict System," *Daily Telegraph*, June 27, 1892, p. 2; cf. "Literature," *ibid.*, May 29, 1897, p. 3, "Literary Notes for Australasian Readers," *RR*, XI (1897), 69.

12. G. A. Wood, "Convicts," *JRAHS*, VIII (1922), 177–208.

13. Ward, *The Australian Legend*, pp. 30–31, Barry, *Alexander Maconochie of Norfolk Island*, pp. 155–156, *The Life and Death of John Price*, p. 136, Turner, "The Social Setting," pp. 16, 53.

14. Eric Partridge, *A Dictionary of the Underworld.* (London 1950), pp. 2, 18, 59, 156, 246, 396, 456, 470, 500, 610, 708, 721, 779 etc.

15. *Marcus Clarke*, p. 150.

16. Morris Miller, *Australian Literature from its Beginnings to 1935*, I, 455.

17. John F. Bayliss, "Slave and Convict Narratives: A Discussion of Australian and American Writing," *Journal of Commonwealth Literature*, No. 8 (1969), p. 148.

18. Green, *A History of Australian Literature*, I, 565.

19. Nettie Palmer, "What is a Diary? The Recent Vogue?", *Brisbane Courier*, October 5, 1929, p. 26, "Letting the Cat Out of the Bag," *Stead's Review*, LXVII (1930), 13–14, "Price Warung," *Illustrated Tasmanian Mail*, July 3, 1929, p. 4.

20. Morris Miller, I, 455.

21. "Price Warung," p. 4, "Convict System Studies: Work of William Astley," *Age*, July 26, 1952, p. 14.

22. E. Morris Miller and F. T. Macartney, *Australian Literature: A Bibliography to . . . 1950* (Sydney, 1956), p. 483. Cf. Barry, *The Life and Death of John Price*, p. 136.

23. A. F. Pike, "Thomas Mason," *ADB*, II, 214–215.

24. *Ibid.*, p. 214, *The History of Tasmania*, II, 250.

25. Joan E. Poole, "A Source for 'John Price's Bar of Steel,' " *Southerly*, XXVII (1967), 300–301.

26. *B*, August 1, 1891.

27. One of the several texts prepared by Whitley and now in the ML is dated April 22, 1891. The two typed fragments of the poem now in the AP are almost exact copies of this text, and further evidence in the AP reveals Astley to have visited Whitley in Blackheath on April 21.

28. See also "Lieutenant Darrell's Predicament," "Janet Guilfoyle's Delusion," and the stories listed n. 10, ch. 5.

29. The "Manuscript of the Rev. Mr. Schofield," which Astley cited in reply to his *B* correspondent as the "main authority" for one of the Jane

Applegarth stories, is obviously Schofield's Journal 1827–1863, A1428, ML (n.b. pp. 19 *et seq.*). This MS was part of the original Mitchell bequest, which included items sold by Astley to Mitchell in the mid-1890's.

30. *Memoir of Bishop Willson*, pp. 63–64.

31. *Ibid.*, pp. 18–19.

32. *TOR*, pp. 133, 206.

33. Astley's note in ML *TID*.

34. *c.* April–July, 1891.

35. AL, II, 221–223, John Cape to Louisa Astley, May 9, 1891, AP, *Hobart Mercury*, August 10, 12, 1891.

36. *Correspondence between the Secretary of State for the Colonial Department and the Governors of the Australian Provinces, on the Subject of Secondary Punishment* (London, 1834). The material used by Astley is on pp. 39–56.

37. See Whitley to Astley, August 4, 1891, AP. A fragment of Astley's typescript copy of the original letter survives in the AP.

38. *Chronicles of Newgate*, 2 vols (London, 1884), II, 412; cf. *Life and Recollections of Calcraft* (London, 1880).

39. Green, *A History of Australian Literature*, I, 530.

40. Whitley to Astley, August 4, 1891, White to Astley, June 1, 1891, AP; *B*, December 6, 1890.

41. Cracknecke ("TID") is on Norfolk Island for "The Flogging of Fergie" at the same time as he is enjoying "A Bathurst Field Day." Lieutenant Darrell's Predicament" presumably ends with his death in Tasmania in the 1820's, but he reappears as Superintendent Darrell on Norfolk Island in the 1840's in "Under the Whip, or the Parson's Lost Soul." Cf. "William Bedford," and "Joseph Childs," *ADB*, I, 77–78, 220–221.

42. In Astley's source, thirty-five of the one hundred applications of tickets of leave were approved. On the other anachronisms and inaccuracies, cf. P. Eldershaw, *Guide to the Public Records of Tasmania 3: Convict Department Record Group* (Hobart, 1965), pp. 53, 57.

43. For most of the Astley phrases included in *A Dictionary of the Underworld, TED* is the only source cited by Partridge.

44. For detailed examples see "Price Warung: A Biographical and Critical Study," pp. 185–192, which includes a discussion of "The Evolution of Convict Hendy."

45. *Royal Sovereign, Pyramus*, and *Tory*: Eldershaw, *op. cit.*, pp. 55–56.

46. After 1840 convicts were numbered consecutively as they arrived; before then the most common method was to number them both alphabetically and chronologically. Thus for convicts arriving during the period of Astley's story there is a series of numbers for each letter of the alphabet, and none of Astley's six highest numbers had been assigned to any convict.

47. See CON 31, *passim.*
48. CON 33/36; cf. CON 33/39, 33/34, 33/59, 33/69, 33/62.

Chapter Seven

1. See Avrom Fleishman, *The English Historical Novel: Walter Scott to Virginia Woolf* (Baltimore, 1971), pp. 31–36, and James C. Simmons, "The Novelist as Historian: An Unexplored Tract of Victorian Historiography," *Victorian Studies*, XV (1971), 293–305.

2. Norman Sherry, *Conrad's Western World* (Cambridge, 1971), pp. 9–124, 339–350.

3. Fleishman, *op. cit.*, p. 3.

4. "Rewriting Australian History," in *Australian Signpost*, ed. T.A.G. Hungerford (Melbourne, 1956), p. 143. Cf. A. M. Schlesinger, "The Historian as Artist," *Atlantic Monthly*, CCXII (July 1963), 35–41.

5. See Edward Wagenknecht's introduction to *A Tale of Two Cities* (New York, 1950), p. xiii. Fleishman, *op. cit.*, pp. 3–4, argues that the "historical novel is distinguished among novels by the presence of a specific link to history; not merely a real building or a real event but a real person among the fictitious ones. When life is seen in the context of history, we have a novel; when the novel's characters live in the same world with historical persons, we have a historical novel." If this argument is accepted Astley is the *only* writer of convict fiction to be writing historical fiction, for there are no historical characters in the novels of Hay, Clarke, Porter, Keneally, and so on. Porter, in his preface to *The Tilted Cross*, states that when he "deliberately smudged" only one fact he crossed the line from history to fiction.

6. Quoted by Clarke, p. 143.

7. *The English Historical Novel*, p. 10.

8. Cf. C. L. R. James, *Beyond a Boundary* (London, 1963), p. 70, Joseph Conrad, *Notes on Life and Letters* (London, 1905), pp. 13–17.

9. *The English Historical Novel*, pp. 6–7.

10. "Price Warung," *B*, September 7, 1960, pp. 2, 58.

11. "Notes on *The King Must Die*," *Afterwords: Novelists on their Novels*, ed. T. McCormack (New York, 1969), pp. 84–86.

12. Astley "quotes" Robert Howe's report of the Chester ball, but no such report appeared in Howe's *Sydney Gazette* between 1827, when Charles Darling arrived in the colony, and 1831, when his uncle left it. Howe himself was drowned in 1829, but another reason why no report appeared was because Darling steered a middle course between sectional interests in the colony and attended no public entertainments save those he gave himself; see *Sydney Gazette*, November 16, 1827, May 9, 1828.

13. The only written account of the Ring is the famous report by Robert Pringle Stewart, quoted in Robson, "The Historical Basis of *For the Term of*

His Natural Life," p. 118. Astley knew of this report, and also had the personal recollections of people like Henry Graham to assist him. But in a footnote to "The Convening of 'The Ring,' " *B*, April 9, 1892, he made for him the uncharacteristic admission that the Ring had caused him greater trouble than any other part of his research.

14. *For the Term of his Natural Life*, Book IV, Chapter 3.

15. "Convicts," *Observer*, September 3, 1960, p. 29.

16. Ford is wrongly identified as Samuel Marsden by Colin Roderick, *An Introduction to Australian Fiction*, (Sydney, 1950), p. 29.

17. J. B. Cooper, *The History of Tasmania* (Melbourne, 1915), p. 124; Kathleen Fitzpatrick, *Sir John Franklin in Tasmania 1837–1843* (Melbourne, 1949), pp. 80–81. Fitzpatrick's source was stated as Robert Crooke's unpublished MS "The Convict, a Tale Founded on Fact." What seems to have been a version of this MS was published in Hobart in 1958 as *The Convict, a Fragment of History*, in which it is implied that Bedford was involved in two separate incidents at the Factory.

18. When Frank, a highwayman, arrives in Hell he is refused entrance. Satan detests the poor and reserves admission for the penal officials and their associates.

19. "William Bedford," p. 78.

20. Turner, however, accepts the probability of there being storytellers in probation gangs; "The Social Setting," p. 16.

21. Dispatch from Alexander Maconochie to Sir George Gipps, March 20, 1841, *PP*(HC), 1846, Vol. 7. Subsequent quotations are from 14–27.

22. This incident is now part of Maconochie family legend; see J. V. Barry to Macartney, October 30, 1959, Macartney Correspondence.

23. Astley's use of history in these and other stories is discussed in the appendix to the author's selection of Astley's work, *Tales of the Convict System* (Brisbane, 1975) pp. 277–294.

24. "Australian Fiction to 1920," p. 148.

25. See W. D. Forsyth, *Governor Arthur's Convict System* (London, 1935), A. G. L. Shaw, "Sir George Arthur," *ADB*, I, 32–38.

26. George Lukacs, *The Historical Novel*, trans. Hannah and Stanley Mitchell (London, 1962), p. 50.

27. See especially M. Barnard Eldershaw, *The Life and Times of Captain John Piper*, (Sydney, 1939).

Chapter Eight

1. *B* Red Page, July 3, 1897.

2. "Price Warung," p. 58.

3. Frank R. Stockton, "The Lady, or the Tiger," *Century Magazine*, XXV (1882), 83–86.

4. E.g., in "TS" there are mass hangings in three stories, five of the first

eight are about the degradation of the lash, and three more about excessive use of the lash.

5. ML.

6. *B*, October 25, 1890.

7. *Ibid.*, September 6, 1890.

8. See especially "The Pardon that never came," "The Commandant's Picnic Party," "The Convict's Sacrament," and "John Price's Bar of Steel."

9. See especially "'The Hanging of the Eighteen' (Spinning the Hemp)," "A Port Arthur Episode," and "Mr. Slyde's Auction."

10. *B*, January 2, 1892, October 11, 1890, *TED*, p. 293.

11. "Convict Tales," p. 16.

12. *TED*, p. 13, *TOR*, p. 11.

13. *The Legend of the Nineties*, pp. 98–99.

14. The Men of the Regime and the humanitarians are cataloged in "Miss Latchford's Overseer," "Convict Smith the Second," and "The Drowning of Captain Bankes."

15. *B*, October 11, 1890.

16. *Ibid.*, May 16, 1891.

17. F. M. Todd, "The Poetry of Bernard O'Dowd," *Meanjin*, XIV (1955), 97.

18. "Books Relating to Australia," *RR*, I (1892), 7.

19. Quoted in Naughton, "The Literary Importance of the Sydney *Bulletin.*"

20. Seymour, "Convicts," p. 29, Cecil Hadgraft, *Australian Literature: A Critical Account to 1955* (London, 1960), p. 94, P. Abotomey, "Convict Days," *Westerly*, (No. 3 for 1961), pp. 44–45.

21. See J. H. Plumb, "The Historian's Dilemma," in *Crisis in the Humanities* (Harmondsworth, 1964), pp. 33–34.

22. "Price Warung," p. 4.

23. *Worker*, April 29, 1893.

24. *Australian Literature from its Beginnings to 1935*, I, 455.

25. Green, *A History of Australian Literature*, I, 530, 565.

26. *TID*, p. 228.

27. *B*, February 21, 1891, October 11, 1890.

28. *Ibid.*, April 25, 1891.

29. The other former penal settlement to which access was difficult was Macquarie Harbour, on the desolate western coast of Tasmania. However, a resident of the area who confirmed the accuracy of Astley's description of the Harbour and wondered at the fact, was informed that Astley had made a special trip there to study the topography and soak up the atmosphere; John Johnson to *B*, May 14, 1891, AP, *B* "Answers to Correspondents," August 1, 1891.

30. *B*, April 11, 1891, January 2, 1892.

31. *TCS*, p. 81.

32. Macartney, "Sidelights on Price Warung," p. 106, seems to miss the point here when he suggests that Astley's vilification of officialdom is carried to the point of ascribing to the horses bred by "a military captain the viciousness attributed to their master."

33. "Price Warung," p. 4.

34. *Henry Lawson: Poet and Short Story Writer* (Sydney, 1966), p. 57; cf. the same author's *Suckled by a Wolf or, The Nature of Australian Literature* (Sydney, 1968), p. 17.

35. *B*, February 21, 1891, November 8, 1890.

36. *For the Term of his Natural Life*, p. 365.

37. In the AP and AL there are MSS of several stories, *Bulletin* galleys and letters from Archibald.

38. "Forty nine years a *Bulletin* printer," Jubilee *B*, January 29, 1930.

39. See Macleod to Astley, April 13, June 22, 1892, East to Astley, October 16, 1892, AP.

40. "Australian Fiction to 1920," pp. 160–163.

41. "Convicts," p. 29.

42. See *For the Term of his Natural Life*, p. xxv.

43. *Bring Larks and Heroes*, preface.

44. Serle, *From Deserts The Prophets Come*, pp. 60–61.

45. Leonie Kramer, in a review of two Adam Lindsay Gordon volumes, *ALS*, V (1971), 104.

Selected Bibliography

PRIMARY SOURCES

1. Manuscript and Bibliographical Material
There are four main collections of Astley papers, three in the Mitchell
  Library, Sydney, and one in the Dixson Library, Sydney. The most
  extensive and most valuable of these is the set of Astley Papers, Un-
  catalogued MSS set 250, ML, which comprises letters to and from
  Astley (including most of his extant correspondence with various
  publishers); the original MS of seven *Bulletin* stories; *Bulletin* proofs;
  and historical notes and jottings. Letters by Astley and material about
  him form part of a number of other collections in Australian libraries
  and institutions. See the appendices and bibliography to the author's
  "Price Warung: A Biographical and Critical Study, with particular
  reference to the Later Years, 1890–1911," unpubl. M. A. thesis, University of New South Wales, 1969, pp. 319–361.

2. Stories by Astley
The following is a list of the main collections. For details of the publishing
  history of all of Astley's stories, see the author's "Price Warung: Some
  Bibliographical Details and a Checklist of the Stories," *ALS*, III (1968),
  290–304, Bruce Nesbitt, "Price Warung's Fiction," *ALS*, V (1972), 322,
  and the author's "Price Warung: Some Corrections and Additions,"
  ALS, VII (1975), 95–98.

"Tales of the System": Twenty-five installments, *Bulletin*, May 24, 1890–Jan-
  uary 10 1891, in the following sequence: May 24, June 14, July 19,
  weekly August 9–December 13 and December 27, 1890–January 10,
  1891. The series comprised "How Muster-Master Stoneman Earned
  His Breakfast," "How 'Lifer' Dale attended the Guest–Dinner,"
  " 'Egerton of Ours,' " "Absalom Day's Promotion," "The Convict's
  Sacrament," "Under the Whip, or the Parson's Lost Soul," "Miss
  Latchford's Overseer," "The Commandant's Picnic Party," "The Little
  Joke of No. 6006," " 'Special Commission Sunday,' " " 'The Hanging of

181

the Eighteen' (Spinning the Hemp)," " 'The Hanging of the Eighteen' (Knotting the Rope)," "The Wooing of Convict Denham," "Janet Guilfoyle's Delusion," " 'The Sins of the Fathers,' " "A Bathurst Field Day," " 'In Floggers' Corner,' " "Mr. Slyde's Auction," "The Procession of the Buttercup," "Lieutenant Darrell's Predicament," "Convict Rudde's Proposal of Marriage," "A Port Arthur Episode," "The Platooning of Private Trench," "On Dead Man's Isle," "Marooned on the Grummet."

Tales of the Convict System. Sydney: The *Bulletin* Newspaper Company, 1892. A reprinting of eleven "Tales of the System," ten of the first dozen and the last. Prepared from *Bulletin* sheets extensively revised by Astley with minor changes in title. Reviewed in *Australian Star*, June 25, 1892 ("New Books," p. 9); *Daily Telegraph*, June 27, 1892, ("Tales of the Convict System," p. 2); *Review of Reviews* (Australasian edn.), I (1892), ("Books Relating to Australia," 7).

"Tales of the Old Regime." Sixteen installments (no No. XI, Nos. XII–XVII wrongly numbered), *Bulletin*, February 21–December 5, 1891, in the following sequence: fortnightly February 21–March 21, April 11–25, May 2–30, July 4–August 1, and August 8–22; September 12, October 24, November 7, December 5. The series comprised "Convict Jerrick's Death-Mask," "The Rationing of the Sentinels," "Convict Arden's Yellow-Heart," "Convict Smith the Second," "The Immersion of Captain Bankes," "The Drowning of Captain Bankes," "The Torture of Jane Applegarth," "The Burial at Govett's Leap," "The Liberation of the First Three," "The Liberation of the Other Three," "A Day with Governor Arthur," "The *Henry Porcher* Bolter," "John Price's Bar of Steel," "The Ross Gang 'Yarner'-ship," "Flash Whelan's Curse," "The Felicitous Reminiscences of Scourger James."

"Tales of Old Sydney." Fourteen installments (no No. VII, Nos. VIII–XV wrongly numbered), *Bulletin*, February 28–December 12, 1891, in the following sequence: fortnightly February 28–March 28, April 18, fortnightly May 9–23, June 13, fortnightly July 11–August 8 and October 3–17, November 21, December 12. The series comprised "The Pure Merinoes' Ball," Marie Antoinette's Fandango," " 'Mr. Pounce, Writer and Forger,' " "Mr. Pounce's Reprieve," "Mr. Pounce's 'Busy Day,' " "Mr. Pounce's Obnoxious Client," "Bob Warphy's Kindly Deed," "The Skeleton Banquet," " 'The Ripple of Dene's Laughter,' " " 'Benefit o'Clargy Bill,' " "The Hanging of the Eight," "Andy Webster's Last Will and Testament," "For His Child's Pleasure," "The Preliminaries of Overseer Franke's Pegging-Out."

Tales of the Old Regime and The Bullet of the Fated Ten. Melbourne: George Robertson and Company, 1897. First publication of "The Bullet of the Fated Ten," which appeared with the following stories reprinted from the *Bulletin:* " 'Mr. Pounce, Writer and Forger' " and

"Bob Warphy's Kindly Deed" ("Tales of Old Sydney"), "The Burial of Govett's Leap," "The Liberation of the First Three," "The Liberation of the Other Three," "A Day with Governor Arthur," "The *Henry Porcher* Bolter," "John Price's Bar of Steel." Copy texts uncertain, but only minor revisions and changes in title. Reviewed *Daily Telegraph*, May 29, 1897, ("Literature," p. 3); *Bulletin* Red Page, July 3, 1897; *Review of Reviews*, XI (1897), ("Literary Notes for Australasian Readers," 69).

"Tales of the Early Days." Seventeen installments, *Bulletin*, February 13–December 24, 1892, in the following sequence: fortnightly February 13–27, March 26–July 16, October 1–15, November 12, 26, December 10–24. The series comprised "Overseer Franke's Pegging-Out," "Captain Maconochie's 'Bounty for Crime,' " "The Heart-Breaking of Anstey's Bess," "The Convening of 'The Ring,' " "The Session of Denunciation," "The Conclave of Doom," "The Falling of the Doom," "In Shoes of Death; The Tanning of the Hide," "The Wearing of the 'Shoes of Death,' " "In the Granary," "Parson Ford's Confessional," "Beneath the Summer Sun," "At Burford's Panorama," "The Paying-Out of Constable Crake," "Bill Eastwood's Scarred Back," "The One Chance of Lifer Harley," "The Pardon that never came."

Tales of the Early Days. London: George Robertson and Company, 1894. Reissued in London the same year by Swann Sonnenschein and Routledge and Kegan Paul under the title *Tales of Australian Early Days*. A reprinting of the last "Tales of Old Sydney" and eleven "Tales of the Early Days": "The Preliminaries of Overseer Franke's Pegging-Out" (combined with "Overseer Franke's Pegging-Out" as "The Pegging-out of Overseer Franke"), "Captain Maconochie's 'Bounty for Crime,' " "The Heart-breaking of Anstey's Bess," "The Convening of the Ring" (combined with the next three "Tales of the Early Days" as "Secret Society of the Ring"), "In the Granary," "Parson Ford's Confessional," "At Burford's Panorama," "The Amour of Constable Crake," Prepared by Astley from *Bulletin* sheets with minor revisions, reordering and changes of title.

"Tales of the Riverine," ten installments (series title not always used), *Bulletin*, December 20, 1890–October 27, 1894, in following sequence: "The Last of the Wombat, Barge" (December 20, 1890), " 'Brothers Twain' " (December 19, 1891), "In Pugga Milly Reach" (July 30, 1892), "Dictionary Ned" (September 3, 1892), " 'Bess o' the Rivers' " (December 17, 1892), "Jim the Rebater" (January 7, 1893), "The Incineration of Dictionary Ned" (January 21, 1893), "The Doom of Walmsley's *Ruby*" (March 18, 1893), "Brocknell's Prodigal" (September 8, 1894), "The Snagging of the Saucy Nell" (October 27, 1894).

Half-Crown Bob and Tales of the Riverine. Melbourne: George Robertson and Company, 1898, part of series Robertson's Colonial Library.

Reissued in London in 1898 by Swann Sonnenschein, part of series
Robertson's Library of Australian Authors. A reprinting of the first
eight "Tales of the Riverine" listed above, together with: "Beneath the
Summer Sun" ("Tales of the Early Days"), "Vesper" (*Bulletin*, February 6, 1892), "His Father" (see later entry), and "Half-Crown Bob' "
and "The Idyl of Melool Wood-pile," two stories probably reprinted
from *Sydney Mail* or *Echo* but original publication undiscovered. Copy
texts uncertain, but only minor revisions by Astley.

"The Strike of '95: A Story of the Passing Time," ten installments, *Australian Workman, February* [18, 25], March 4 [11], 18 [25], April [1, 8]
15, 29, 1893. Unfinished.

"Tales of the Isle of Death." Thirteen installments, *Truth*, weekly with two
installments spread over two issues, June 20–September 19, 1897. The
series comprised "The Fluctuations of Fergie," "The Revolt of Com-
pany B-I," "The Revolt of Company B-II," "The Flogging of Fergie,"
"Toulmin of Toulmin," "The Annihilation of Austin," "The Spread-
Eagling of Convict Cunliffe," "The Consequences of Cunliffe's Crime,"
"The Initiation of 'Pine-tree Jack,' " Mrs. Taylor's 'Letter-Day,' " "The
Evolution of Convict Hendy," "The Whale-boat Plot," "His Father."

Tales of the Isle of Death (Norfolk Island). Melbourne: George Robertson
and Company, 1898, part of series Robertson's Colonial Library. A
reprinting of all but the last of the *Truth* series, together with the new
story "The Finding of Benson, Baronet." The deleted story, "His
Father," was published in *Half-Crown Bob and Tales of the Riverine.*
Copy texts uncertain, but extensive revision, with changes of title, by
Astley of the *Truth* series, which were originally dictated in a fortnight
and were very badly printed.

Convict Days. Sydney: Australasian Book Society, 1960. A reprinting of
thirteen stories: "Lieutenant Darrell's Predicament," "The Bullet of
the Fated Ten," " 'Mr. Pounce, Writer and Forger,' " "John Price's
Bar of Steel," "The Liberation of the First Three," "The Liberation of
the Other Three," "Mr. Pounce's Reprieve," "The Evolution of Convict Hendy," "The Whale-boat Plot," "Secret Society of the Ring,"
"How Muster-Master Stoneman Earned His Breakfast," "The Crime of
Convict Cunliffe," "The Consequence of Cunliffe's Crime." Reviewed
in *Age*, August 27, 1960 (Ian Mair, "The Convict Stories of 'Price
Warung,' " p. 19); *Biblionews*, XIII, 1960 (W. W. Stone, "Price
Warung's *Convict Days*", *30–32*); *Bulletin*, September 7, 1960 (Doug-
las Stewart, "Price Warung," pp. 2, 58); *Meanjin Quarterly*, XX, 1961
(J. V. Barry, "An Unacceptable Foreword," 96–101); *Observer*,
September 3, 1960 (Alan Seymour, "Convicts," p. 29); *Overland*, No.
18, 1960 (S. Murray-Smith, "Convict Days," pp. 56–57); *Sydney
Morning Herald*, October 8, 1960 (Russel Ward, "Convict Tales," p.

16); *Westerly*, No. 3 for 1961 (P. Abotomey, "Convict Days," pp. 44–45).

Tales of the Convict System. Brisbane: University of Queensland Press, 1975. An edition of seventeen stories, with introduction and notes by B. G. Andrews. Contains "The *Henry Porcher* Bolter," "How Muster-Master Stoneman Earned His Breakfast," "The Felicitous Reminiscences of Scourger James," "Absalom Day's Promotion," "A Day with Governor Arthur," "Parson Ford's Confessional," "The Liberation of the First Three," "Mr. Slyde's Auction," "The Liberation of the Other Three," "Secret Society of the Ring," "The Pure Merinoes' Ball," "The Evolution of Convict Hendy," "The Whale-boat Plot," "Marie Antoinette's Fandango," "The Bullet of the Fated Ten," "The Ross Gang 'Yarner'-ship," "Mr. Pounce's Obnoxious Client."

3. Selected Journalism.

The following lists Astley's literary journalism and a selection of his political and historical writings. It does not include the political leaders written for the *Warrnambool Standard* (October 1884–February 1885), the *Bathurst Times* (December 1887–January 1888), the *Bathurst Free Press and Mining Journal* (1889, 1891–1894, *passim.*), the *Nhill Free Press* (November 1890–February 1891), and the *Australian Workman* (February–September 1893).

Unless otherwise stated, all contributions are signed "Price Warung" or "P.W."

"A Visit to Bryan O'Lynn." *Warrnambool Standard*, October 1, 3, 1884. Unsigned. Report of a visit to a local property, and a good example of Astley's occasional journalism.

"Jottings at the Junketings." *Warrnambool Standard*, October 20, 21, 1884. Signed "From Our Reporter's Pencil." A report of the visit to Warrnambool of the Victorian Governor, but gives some clues about Astley's early journalism and literary interests.

"Marcus Clarke." *Warrnambool Standard*, November 24, 1884. Unsigned review of the *Marcus Clarke Memorial Volume*, ed. H. Mackinnon (Melbourne, 1884). Mainly biographical, but discusses Clarke's achievement.

"Chipping and Chatterings." *Warrnambool Standard*, January 19, 26, February 2, 9, 1885. Signed "Will Western." A column of local gossip, but useful for the many literary allusions.

"The Great Pro-Consul: Sketches from a Life of Action." *Bulletin*, January 31, February 7, 14, 28, March 14, 1891. Last installment signed "W", the others unsigned. A series of articles on Sir George Grey, Governor of New Zealand.

"Bushranging & Outlawing in Australasia." *Bulletin*, August 13, 20, Sep-

186

PRICE WARUNG

tember 17, 1892. Astley's unfinished history of Australian bushranging. Similar in historiography and style to the convict stories.

" 'Close Up Your Ranks!' To the Members of the New South Wales Labor Party in Parliament." *Bulletin,* October 24, 1891. A strong appeal for solidarity on the part of parliamentary members of the Labor Party.

"Sir Henry Parkes's New Book." *Daily Telegraph,* December 3, 1892. Unsigned review of *Fifty Years in the Making of Australian History.*

"The Greatest of Australia's Dead." *Bulletin,* January 7, 1893. Eulogistic obituary of the Victorian statesman, George Higinbotham. Quoted in biographies of Higinbotham.

"An Open Letter to the Fat Lord Justice of the Federation." *Bulletin,* February 11, 1893. A virulent attack on Edmund Barton, MS in Dixson Library, Sydney.

"What 'The Workman' Says." *Australian Workman,* April 15, May 20, June 24, September 9, 1893. Signed "The Workman." A political column conducted by Astley while editor of the newspaper.

Labor in Politics. The Conference of November, 1893. A Criticism and an Appeal. Sydney: Australian Workman Newspaper Company, 1893. A reprinting of Astley's report in the *Australian Workman,* November 25, December 2, [9] 1893, of the Labor Party conference. Astley's copy of the pamphlet is now in the Mitchell Library.

"An Australasian Character Sketch. A New Australian Writer: Mr. Louis Becke." *Review of Reviews,* VI (March 1895), 283–287. Mainly biographical. Unsigned, but Astley's authorship advertised in previous issues.

"The Rev. W. B. Clarke, M.A., F.R.S. 'The Nestor of Australian Philosophers.' " *Cosmos,* I (July, 1895), 534–539. Eulogistic tribute to Clarke, an Australian geologist.

"Literature. Freshly-Cut Pages. Notes on Books and Bookmen." *Spencer's Weekly,* July 13, 20, 27, August 3, 1895. Contains literary notes and brief reviews of Australian and European books.

"A Love Episode: A Wholesome Novel by Zola." *Spencer's Weekly,* August 17, 1895. A favorable review of *Une Page D'Amour,* useful for what it reveals about Astley's attitude to European authors; unsigned.

" 'Within an Ace of Greatness.' " *Bulletin,* May 9, 1896. Signed "P.W." Obituary of Sir Henry Parkes.

"Parkesiana." *Bulletin,* May 16, 1896. Unsigned collection of gossip and reminiscences about Parkes.

Review of *While the Billy Boils. Bathurst Free Press and Mining Journal,* August 31, 1896.

"Sydney Public Library. Wanted: A Royal Commission." *Truth,* June 20, 27, 1896. A strong attack on the Library trustees. Unsigned.

"John Norton, Reformer and Pioneer, Tribune and Publicist: A Character

Sketch." *Truth*, December 12, 1897. Extravagant tribute to Norton, editor of *Truth*.

" 'For the Price of Two Drinks!' A Book Study." *Worker*, March 23, 1901. Largely a strong attack on A. G. Stephens.

Bathurst: The Ideal Federal Capital. Bathurst: Glyndwr Whalan, 1901. A glossy, illustrated booklet prepared in support of the claims of Bathurst to be the site for the federal capital.

The Federal Capital: An Argument for the Western Sites. Bathurst: Glyndwr Whalan, 1903. When Bathurst dropped out of the running to be the federal capital, Astley transferred his claims to the district at large.

"Death of Mr. John Farrell: A Great Journalist Gone." *Bathurst Free Press and Mining Journal*, January 9, 1904. Eulogistic tribute to Farrell, a Sydney contemporary.

The Federal Capital: A Ratio of Values. An Argument and an Exposition. Bathurst: Glyndwr Whalan, 1904.

SECONDARY SOURCES

(Reviews and bibliographical material are not listed.)

ANDREWS, BARRY. " 'Dynamites, Barricades, Brimstone': Price Warung's Political Themes," *Labour History*, No. 22 (May, 1972), pp. 1–12.

———. "Price Warung: A Biographical and Critical Study, with particular reference to the Later Years, 1890–1911," unpublished M.A. thesis, University of New South Wales, 1969.

———. "William Astley," *Australian Dictionary of Biography Vol 3. 1851–1890 A-C*, gen. editor Douglas Pike (Melbourne: Melbourne University Press, 1969), 56–57.

BARRY, J. V. *Alexander Maconochie of Norfolk Island: A Study of a Pioneer in Penal Reform.* Melbourne: Melbourne University Press, 1958. Discusses Astley's Ring stories.

———. *The Life and Death of John Price: A Study in the Exercise of Naked Power.* Melbourne: Melbourne University Press, 1964. Discusses Astley's characterization of John Price.

GREEN, H. M. *A History of Australian Literature.* 2 vols. Sydney: Angus and Robertson, 1961, I, 530, 564–566. Offers traditional view of Astley.

HADGRAFT, CECIL. *Australian Literature: A Critical Account to 1955.* London: Heinemann, 1960. Contains a brief but sound assessment of Astley's work.

INGLIS MOORE, T. *Social Patterns in Australian Literature.* Sydney: Angus and Robertson, 1971. Discusses the abuse of mateship in "The Liberation of the First Three" and "The Liberation of the Other Three."

LANSBURY, CORAL. *Arcady in Australia: The Evocation of Australia in Nineteenth Century English Literature.* Melbourne: Melbourne

University Press, 1970. Chapter 10, "The Convict Redeemed," mentions Astley's contribution to the development of a romantic convict legend.

MACARTNEY, FREDERICK, T. *Australian Literary Essays*. Sydney: Angus and Robertson, 1957. Has a chapter on Astley, "Sidelights on Price Warung," which is inaccurate on some biographical details but sound on Astley's techniques of construction.

———. *Proof Against Failure*. Sydney: Angus and Robertson, 1967. Details Macartney's preparation, and the subsequent suppression, of a selection of Astley's convict stories.

———. and MORRIS MILLER, E. *Australian Literature: A Bibliography to 1938 . . . extended to 1950*. Sydney: Angus and Robertson, 1956. Contains a bibliographical and critical entry on Astley under "Warung" prepared by Macartney.

MORRIS MILLER, E. *Australian Literature from its Beginnings to 1935: A Descriptive and Bibliographical Survey . . . with subsidiary entries to 1938*. 2 vols. Melbourne: Melbourne University Press, 1940. Contains an entry on Astley which is quite misleading on his style and use of sources but useful on his early biography.

POOLE, JOAN E. "A Source for 'John Price's Bar of Steel'," *Southerly*, XXVII (1967), 300–301.

PALMER, NETTIE. "Australian Author's Week," *Illustrated Tasmanian Mail*, September 14, 1927, p. 4. Nettie Palmer did most to keep Astley's name known by her periodic articles in newspapers and journals, listed here in chronological order of publication. In most of them she laments the difficulty in getting his books and in finding information about him. Also useful for criticism.

———. "Price Warung," *Illustrated Tasmanian Mail*, July 3, 1929, p. 4.

———. "What is a Diary? The Recent Vogue," *Brisbane Courier*, October 5, 1929, p. 26.

———. "Letting the Cat out of the Bag," *Stead's Review*, LXVII (November, 1930), 13–14.

———. "Convict System Studies. Work of William Astley," *Age*, July 26, 1952, p. 14.

———. *Fourteen Years: Extracts from a Private Journal 1925–1939*. Melbourne: Meanjin Press, 1948. The entry for July 10, 1932, p. 98, records the recollections of George Beeby about Astley's work for the labor press.

PALMER, VANCE. *The Legend of the Nineties*. Melbourne: Melbourne University Press, 1954. An impressionistic but very sound account of Astley's life and work, using material collected by his wife Nettie.

RIGBY, RICHARD W. "William Astley, The Present and The Past," unpublished BA thesis, Australian National University, 1971. Looks at Astley in the context of the 1890's.

RODERICK, COLIN. *Henry Lawson: Poet and Short Story Writer.* Sydney: Angus and Robertson, 1966. Sees the "sardonic mood" as characteristic of the Australian short story and argues that Lawson inherited it from Astley.

———. *An Introduction to Australian Fiction.* Sydney: Angus and Robertson, 1950. Assesses Astley as the "best exponent of the short story of incidents connected with the penal system."

WARD, RUSSEL. *The Australian Legend.* 2nd. ed. Melbourne: Oxford University Press, 1966. Discusses Astley's convict oath and its historical basis.

Index

(Only lengthy Notes and References have been indexed; creative works are indexed under the names of their authors.)